P9-APF-939

Caring for Your Plants

Staff for Successful Gardening (U.S.A.)
Editor: Fiona Gilsenan
Senior Associate Editor: Carolyn Chubet
Art Associate: Martha Grossman
Editorial Assistant: Joanne M. Wosahla

Contributors
Editor: Thomas Christopher
Consulting Editor: Lizzie Boyd (U.K.)
Consultant: Dora Galitzki
Copy Editor: Sue Heinemann
Art Assistant: Antonio Mora

READER'S DIGEST GENERAL BOOKS
Editor in Chief: John A. Pope, Jr.
Managing Editor: Jane Polley
Executive Editor: Susan J. Wernert
Art Director: David Trooper
Group Editors: Will Bradbury, Sally French,
Norman B. Mack, Kaari Ward
Group Art Editors: Evelyn Bauer, Robert M. Grant, Joel Musler
Chief of Research: Laurel A. Gilbride
Copy Chief: Edward W. Atkinson
Picture Editor: Richard Pasqual
Head Librarian: Jo Manning

The credits and acknowledgments that appear on page 176
are hereby made a part of this copyright page.

Originally published in partwork form.
Copyright © 1990 Eaglemoss Publications Ltd.

Based on the edition copyright © 1993
The Reader's Digest Association Limited.

Copyright © 1994 The Reader's Digest Association, Inc.
Copyright © 1994 The Reader's Digest Association (Canada) Ltd.
Copyright © 1994 Reader's Digest Association Far East Ltd.
Philippine Copyright 1994 Reader's Digest Association Far East Ltd.

All rights reserved.
Unauthorized reproduction, in any manner, is prohibited.

Library of Congress Cataloging in Publication Data

Caring for your plants.
       p.   cm.
    Includes index.
    ISBN 0-89577-603-0 — ISBN 0-7621-0045-1(pbk.)
    1. Gardening.   2. Greenhouse gardening.   3. Garden pests.
I. Reader's Digest Association.
SB453.C317   1994
635'.0973—dc20   93-46853

READER'S DIGEST and the Pegasus logo are registered trademarks of
The Reader's Digest Association, Inc.

Printed in the United States of America

Opposite: Good garden management
shows in weed-free flower beds, correct pruning,
and well-trimmed lawns.

Overleaf: Greenhouse gardening protects
a wealth of exotic plants, half-hardy annuals,
and tender food crops.

THE READER'S DIGEST ASSOCIATION, INC.
Pleasantville, New York / Montreal

Caring for Your Plants

CONTENTS

Garden management

Gardening indoors

Pest & weed control

Problems in the flower garden

Problems in the kitchen garden

Fall colors The crimson and scarlet leaves of *Euonymus alata* herald the end of the gardening year.

GARDEN MANAGEMENT

When gardeners seek guidance, they want specific instructions; they need to know what to do and when to do it. After all, successful gardening is largely a matter of organization. To transplant annual flowers into the garden in late spring, for example, you must sow each species indoors at the correct point in early spring. If the broad-leaved weed killer you are spreading on your lawn is to be effective, then you must apply it when weeds are growing actively in midspring. The following pages present this kind of specific advice in the form of a year-round calendar of gardening tasks.

But in the United States the climates vary widely — making a traditional written calendar very different from nature's calendar. On a written calendar, spring arrives with the equinox in every region. Yet Houston, Texas, sees the arrival of spring weather in February; while in Helena, Montana, the garden isn't safe from a cold snap until late May. Gardeners in different areas must adjust their schedules accordingly.

The following pages walk you through the gardening year— but you must adapt this information to your own local climate and geographical conditions. Much of the advice given is aimed at the average climate. In the U. S. that climate is located in USDA (United States Department of Agriculture) zone 7 — a band of territory beginning in the mid-Atlantic states and sweeping

Spring display Flowers such as these may arrive after the date of the last frost.

westward across the country through the upper South, the central West, and the Southwest, then continuing up the coastal mountain ranges of the Pacific to Washington State. Zone 7 is the transition point between North and South; in this temperate zone winter's average coldest temperatures fall into a range of 0° to 10°F (-18° to -1°C), and average summer temperatures rise to 75° to 85°F (24° to 30°C). The techniques and timing that work in this region will, with minor adjustments, suit the colder areas above it and the warmer areas immediately below.

However, if you are located outside of zone 7, you must adapt the calendar to suit your local conditions. To do this, first determine the timing of your seasons. You can calculate the spring season by referring to the Final Spring Frosts map on page 10. Generally, early spring begins 6 weeks before this date, and late spring ends 6 weeks later.

Once you've set your spring calendar, determine when fall arrives. The First Fall Frost dates on page 43 will tell you when to expect the first severe frost of the year. If you take that as fall's midpoint, this season generally begins some 6 weeks earlier and ends about 6 weeks later.

When adjusting the calendar, always remember that it must reflect your local climate if it is to suit your garden's needs. In zone 7 — as in the written calendar — the seasons are of 12 weeks'

duration. However, in northern regions, especially in the center of the country, you will find that spring doesn't last as long as 12 weeks; this season begins later but still turns into summer in June. In Des Moines, Iowa, the spring season is compressed to approximately 6 weeks. By contrast, in the mild coastal climate of the Pacific Northwest, spring lasts several weeks longer than in Iowa. But even where the length of the seasons varies from the norm, you can still use these maps to determine the midpoints of spring and fall and plan your gardening tasks accordingly.

One final word for gardeners in the extreme South (USDA zones 9-11): in referring to the calendar, you will sometimes find it helpful to actually reverse the instructions for spring and fall. For instance, classic spring flowers such as pansies flourish during cold, moist weather and are cut short by arrival of southern summers, which begin early and bring fierce heat. So these cool-loving "spring" flowers bloom much longer if planted in midfall in the South to bloom through the winter. In addition, summers are so hot in the Deep South that they can prove fatal to annual plants and force perennials into dormancy. In these regions of the country, consider summer rather than winter to be your garden's season of dormancy.

EARLY SPRING

As the days lengthen and the warm sun dries out the soil, the gardener's year gets under way with spring planting.

Longer days and stronger sunlight make early spring a time of warming — yet this can also be a volatile season.

In the North, temperatures often rise above freezing, but may also fall in hours to set the stage for a last blizzard. In the South, too, early spring brings dramatic temperature swings. Watch for periods when drizzle gives way to clear, still weather; this signals the arrival of a cold front, and often a rapid, severe drop in temperature. In both the North and South, such fluctuations generate wind and rain. April showers are frequent, and except for South Florida (where early spring is a warmer postscript to the winter dry season), early spring is rainy.

Take advantage of dry spells to prepare planting beds. But remember that in most areas more frosts will come, and planting too early can be disastrous.

Borders

Fairly trouble free and long-lived, hardy herbaceous perennials

▼ **Early spring in zone 7** The yellow-green flower clusters of *Helleborus argutifolius* set off to perfection the clear pink blooms of double-flowered camellias.

LAWN MAINTENANCE

Set your lawn mower blade to the lowest height recommended for your type of grass. By cutting the grass very short at this time of year, you will help clean out the dead grass blades that have accumulated over winter.

In the North, this is the time to repair the damage that winter has wrought. Level any depressions in your lawn by filling them with soil. Rake the soil to a fine tilth, and then sprinkle with new grass seed.

Rake the lawn vigorously several times, first in one direction and then at right angles. This raking will remove dead grass, debris, and moss, and allow air and water to enter the surface of the turf.

As soon as temperatures have risen to 65°F (18°C) for at least 5 days in a row, it is time to apply a preemergent herbicide. This will help to control annual lawn weeds such as crabgrass. Choose a windless day and follow the safety instructions provided by the herbicide manufacturer.

Attend to the edges of your lawn, cutting off overgrown margins with a half-moon edging tool. Use a plank laid on the grass as a straight-edge guide. Stand on the plank and cut the turf down and away from you slightly to prevent the lawn edge from crumbling.

Where a lawn edge has crumbled or become worn, cut out the damaged area as a square or rectangle and turn it around so that there is sound turf at the edge. This creates a bare area inside the patch; level it with sifted soil, sow grass seed, and cover the seeds with another light sifting of soil.

Early spring is also a good time to lay sod for new lawns.

In the South, the arrival of warm weather will bring beetle grubs to the surface of the lawn. Control them now by applying insecticides or beneficial nematodes. Warm-season grasses, such as Bermuda grass and St. Augustine grass, will also return to active growth and should be fertilized with a complete fertilizer rich in slow-release organic nitrates or water-insoluble nitrogen (listed as W.I.N. on the product label).

In the West, especially in areas that suffer from extreme summer heat or drought, this is the best season to plant grass seed or lay new sod. If started now, the new lawns or reseeded patches will have time to develop well-established protective roots before the arrival of the summer heat or drought. This is also the time to apply preemergent herbicides.

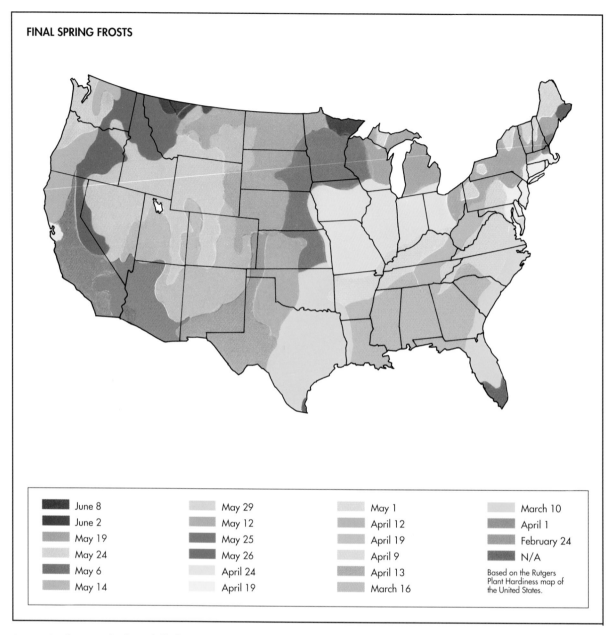

FINAL SPRING FROSTS

June 8	
June 2	
May 19	
May 24	
May 6	
May 14	

May 29	
May 12	
May 25	
May 26	
April 24	
April 19	

May 1	
April 12	
April 19	
April 9	
April 13	
March 16	

March 10	
April 1	
February 24	
N/A	

Based on the Rutgers Plant Hardiness map of the United States.

Last spring frosts At the first whiff of spring, most gardeners are eager to sow seeds and transplant seedlings into outdoor beds and borders. But planting prematurely may well expose tender transplants to a late frost or plunge seeds into chilly soil that can cause them to rot.

The map above will help you avoid such disasters. It divides the U.S. into zones, based on climatological data. First identify the zone in which you are located. Then consult the chart for the last expected frost date for your zone. Planting only after this date will keep your seeds and seedlings safe.

reward a little work with satisfying results. Early spring to midspring is time to start their routine care.

Clear away debris that has accumulated around shrubs and the crowns of dormant perennials. Avoid stepping on naturally heavy, wet soil or soil that is sticky from rain or thawing frost, as your weight will compress it. Prune trees and large shrubs that overhang herbaceous borders.

In southern areas, watch for slugs. They usually retreat during the day, leaving visible slime

trails. Pick and destroy these pests, or set out beer-filled traps or poisoned pellets.

Remove any protective leaves or straw you placed over tender plants to protect them from winter cold as you find green shoots emerging from the plant's crowns or any other new growth.

Existing perennials Most perennials benefit from routine division every few years. Lift and divide overgrown clumps of perennials when they show signs of renewed growth. The plants most likely to show early signs of

regrowth are those that flower in early summer, including delphiniums and lupines. Postpone dividing them, though, if the soil is still wet or the weather cold.

New perennials Stock just purchased from the nursery may be planted in early spring, if the soil is warm and dry enough to be worked. Garden centers stock a wide variety of container-grown plants and balled-and-burlapped trees and shrubs at this time of year; this is also the season when mail-order nurseries ship bare-root plants — dormant plants that have been packed without soil around their roots. These are typically less expensive than container-grown plants.

Annuals If weather and soil conditions are favorable, sow the hardiest annuals outdoors in their flowering sites. Suitable plants include candytuft *(Iberis)*, clarkia, gypsophila, cornflower *(Centaurea)*, godetia, and in zone 8 and south, poppy *(Papaver)* and pot marigold *(Calendula)*.

To make subsequent weeding and thinning easier, sow the seeds in rows. A straight line of seedlings is easily distinguished as the work of the gardener, whereas a random sprinkling may be hard to tell from weeds.

Bulbs, corms, and tubers This is the season of the delicate, mostly dwarf, species narcissi: *Narcissus bulbocodium, N. cyclamineus, N. juncifolius, N. pseudonarcissus, N. rupicola,* and *N. triandrus.* Remove flower heads from narcissi and daffodils as they fade. Cut just below the dead head, leaving the stalk intact. The remaining green tissue strengthens the bulb for the next year.

The last of the bulbs forced in pots or bowls indoors have finished flowering now. Many, including narcissus, hyacinth, crocus, and some smaller iris

PRUNING SHRUBS IN EARLY SPRING

1 Trim winter jasmine *(Jasminum nudiflorum)* after flowering. Remove dead or weak stems, and prune flowering stems back to two or three buds from the main branches.

2 To reduce *Buddleia davidii* to a low framework of branches — from which new shoots will grow and flower in summer — cut back the previous year's stems to two or three buds from the base.

species, can be planted out to flower again within the next year or two and each spring thereafter. Tulips are less likely to recover from forcing, but may flower again for a year or two. When you plant these bulbs outdoors, keep them in the potting mix in which they were grown. This encourages continued growth, which will replenish the bulbs for future flowering, and you will not disturb the roots. Choose a planting site between shrubs, perennials, or rock plants, depending on their flowering height.

At this time finish planting any lily bulbs that were not planted in fall. In addition, lift, divide, and replant overgrown clumps of snowdrops *(Galanthus)*. They are easier to establish at this time of year, while they are still in leaf, than in the fall.

Roses
Plant roses in early spring. If you have not prepared beds the previous fall, dig them now to a spade's depth, mixing in plenty of compost or well-rotted manure. Add a dressing of bonemeal. Before planting, prune bush and standard roses to make them easier to handle. Cut back damaged roots and those over 1 ft (30 cm) long.

In milder regions (zone 7 and south), start pruning established rosebushes of the everblooming types (hybrid teas, floribundas, and grandifloras) in early spring during frost-free weather. In areas prone to late, hard frosts, delay pruning until midspring.

Shrubs and trees
Plant deciduous shrubs and trees at any time during early spring, provided that the soil is not frozen or waterlogged and the

◄ **Pruning roses** Hybrid tea and floribunda roses should be pruned when their buds swell. Cut out dead, diseased, and crossing stems, and prune the remaining stems back by one-third to one-half, making a sloping cut to an outward-facing bud. Prune old garden roses and species roses only after they have flowered.

TAKING DAHLIA CUTTINGS

1 Early spring is the ideal time to propagate overwintered dahlias. Spray the tubers daily with tepid water to encourage new shoots. When the shoots are 3-4 in (7.5-10 cm) long, cut them off close to the base.

2 Remove the lower pair of leaves, and make a clean cut across the stem just below the joint from which they were growing. Dip the cutting in fresh hormone rooting powder. Buy fresh powder each year.

3 Insert each dahlia cutting about 1 in (2.5 cm) deep in a small pot filled with well-drained, organically enriched potting soil. Alternatively, insert several cuttings together in a box of potting soil. Water the cutting thoroughly.

4 To conserve moisture and warmth, place clear-plastic bags over the pots or boxes, or place the containers in large boxes covered with glass. Keep the cuttings shaded until they have begun to root — indicated by renewed growth.

weather is fair. Bare-root and balled-and-burlapped trees and shrubs are best planted in early spring; container-grown specimens that are planted without disturbance to the root ball can be put in at any time.

Propagating shrubs Layering is a simple method of propagation at this time of year for flexible-stemmed shrubs, such as shadblow (*Amelanchier canadensis*), bittersweet (*Celastrus*), wintersweet (*Chimonanthus*), lilac (*Syringa*), and all species of ornamental sumac (*Rhus*), except for staghorn sumac (*Rhus typhina*). Peg down selected branches into sandy loam, either in the ground around the parent plant or in pots sunk in the soil. Rooting usually takes a year or more, after which the layers can be cut away and replanted.

Some shrubs, including shadblow, produce offsets — branches that arise at ground level and root naturally. These may be severed in early spring and replanted immediately in a suitable spot, or if poorly rooted, potted up and grown on until fall and then transplanted. Other shrubs, such as kerrias (*Kerria japonica*), send up suckers, which may be handled in the same way.

Divide the roots of St.-John's-wort (*Hypericum calycinum*) and perennial sweet peas (*Lathyrus*), replanting the separated pieces in their flowering sites.

Some other shrubs can be raised from seed sown in early spring. Sow clematis, cotoneaster, genista, laburnum, and wisteria seeds in flats or pots of seed-starting mix, just covering the seeds. Place them in a closed cold frame or on a cool windowsill. Sow seeds of Chilean gloryflower (*Eccremocarpus scaber*) and shrub mallow (*Lavatera olbia* 'Rosea') in the same manner, but place the seeds in a propagation box or on a horticultural heating pad or tape and keep at a temperature of 55°-64°F (13°-18°C).

Camellias can be propagated by taking leaf cuttings that are 1 in (2.5 cm) long in early spring. Insert them in potting soil, and cover the pots with clear-plastic bags, maintaining them at a temperature of 55°-61°F (13°-16°C) until well rooted. Transplant rooted cuttings to individual pots, and keep them in a shaded cold frame or other protected spot until the following spring.

For *Campsis radicans, Rhus typhina,* and Californian tree poppy (*Romneya coulteri*), take root cuttings 2-3 in (5-7.5 cm) long. Insert them singly in pots of soil, and keep at a temperature of about 55°F (13°C). When the cuttings root, repot the new plants and leave them in an open cold frame or other protected spot where they can grow on.

Pruning shrubs After a severe winter, some tender deciduous shrubs, such as cistus, hebe, *Hydrangea macrophylla*, laburnum, and potentilla, will need light pruning to remove dead, damaged, or weak stems. Other shrubs, such as barberry (*Berberis*), ivy (*Hedera*), and *Hypericum patulum*, will produce more vigorous growth after a light thinning out of old wood to maintain shape.

Caryopteris × clandonensis, deciduous *Ceanothus* species, and *Hypericum calycinum* should have the previous year's shoots removed almost to the ground. Cut winter-killed hardy fuchsias, *Buddleia davidii,* and shrub mallow (*Lavatera*) back to live wood at the base.

As soon as early-flowering shrub honeysuckle (*Lonicera fragrantissima*) and winter jasmine (*Jasminum nudiflorum*) have finished flowering, cut back the flowered stems. For dogwoods (*Cornus*) and willows (*Salix*) grown for their colored bark in winter, cut stems back hard.

Hedges With the exception of broad-leaved evergreens, early spring is the time to plant hedges grown from bare-rooted plants. If planted later, young growth may wilt and die while the roots try to become established.

It is very important to clear weeds from the bases of all hedges by hand or with a scuffle hoe. Pull up large, deep-rooted perennial weeds by hand. If you use a contact herbicide, keep the liquid off the hedging plants.

Complete hard pruning of any large, old hedges not finished in late winter.

The fruit garden

In regions with harsh winters, this is the best season for planting fruit trees and bushes. Also finish pruning established and fall-planted fruits as soon as possible, before the bud-burst stage (when the branch tips just begin to show green).

Feed established trees and bushes growing in cultivated soil. All berries, except strawberries, benefit from a dressing of well-rotted manure. Do not feed trees growing in grass until late spring, and feed then only if the fruit set is good. If properly planted, new trees and shrubs should not need any feeding in their first season.

With apple trees at bud-burst stage, control apple scab by spraying with a recommended fungicide such as Bordeaux mix. Applying a horticultural oil — a light, highly refined petroleum oil — at the same time will kill overwintering eggs of such pests as scale insects and aphids.

Watch both apples and pears for a sudden blackening of leaves on new shoots — a symptom of fire blight. Treat by pruning off affected branches, disinfecting your tools with bleach or alcohol between cuts. Dispose of infected

FRUIT BUD STAGES

1 The stages of fruit tree bud development provide a key to the timing of spray applications for controlling pests and diseases. At the bud-burst stage the tips of the small bud scales begin to separate, as shown above.

2 At the green cluster stage there are small green flower buds in the center of the opening foliage. The growth rate varies from year to year — which is why it is impracticable to determine spraying dates by the calendar.

3 At the pink or white bud stage the plant's flowers are not yet open but the petals are showing pink or white. Don't spray when the flowers are fully open, because the chemicals can kill pollinating insects such as bees.

4 The petal-fall stage is when nearly all the blossoms have fallen off the tree. After this comes another stage, when the fruitlets start to swell. Learn to recognize each stage, because spraying at the wrong time can be ineffective.

prunings. If pear trees have previously shown signs of scab — small, drab olive spots on leaves and fruit — spray trees at the green cluster or white bud stage with recommended fungicide.

Inspect plum trees for hard black galls on the branch tips, swellings up to 1½ in (4 cm) in diameter and 1 ft (30 cm) long. These are caused by black knot. Prune off the affected branches at least 4 in (10 cm) below the gall.

Feed apple, pear, and plum trees in open ground with an organic slow-release fertilizer for fruit trees or ammonium sulfate.

◄ **Early potato planting** Provided the soil is not too wet, plant early-bearing potato cultivars such as 'Irish Cobbler' as soon as the ground thaws and can be worked. Plant in trenches 12 in (30 cm) wide and 9 in (23 cm) deep, spacing the tubers 12-14 in (30-35 cm) apart. Cover them with soil to form a ridge over each row.

PLANT OF THE MONTH

Dutch crocuses *(Crocus vernus* hybrids) are ideal for naturalizing in grass, perhaps in an informal swath at the edge of a lawn, or in rougher grass in a meadow garden or on a bank. Flower color ranges from intense purple, through shades of mauve and lilac, to vivid yellow or pure white. Cultivars are available singly or in packages of mixed-color corms.

To ensure that the corms build up strength for the following year's flowers, do not mow the lawn for the first time until the crocus leaves have died down. If left undisturbed, naturalized crocuses will eventually multiply to form dense clumps.

Other early-spring flowers A wide selection of bulbs are available for early-spring color. These include Dutch hyacinths *(Hyacinthus orientalis* hybrids), grape hyacinths *(Muscari),* narcissi and daffodils, early tulips, and many of the dwarf irises, such as *Iris danfordiae.*

These bulbs provide vivid color in all shades, so there is plenty of scope for planting calculated arrangements of colors or multihued blends. Biennial polyanthus primulas *(Primula* x *polyantha)* make ideal bedding partners for many bulbs, as do common English daisies *(Bellis perennis* 'Monstrosa Hybrids').

For taller early-spring color, there are several attractive shrubs to choose from, such as pink, red, or white camellias; sweet-scented daphnes; flowering currant *(Ribes sanguineum);* Japanese quince *(Chaenomeles);* and yellow forsythia. The white-flowered *Magnolia stellata* blooms while quite young as a small shrub; with age it develops into a small tree with many trunks.

Cherry trees should be fertilized in early spring until they begin to bear fruit.

Also fertilize bush and cane fruits. Grapes should not be fertilized unless the foliage shows signs of nutrient deficiency.

The vegetable garden

In areas with hot summers, start spring crops such as lettuce, spinach, radishes, peas, and arugula as soon as the soil can be worked. Where spring soils are wet, raised beds will help protect seeds from decay.

Plant asparagus, unless the ground is saturated. If you receive asparagus plants by mail and you cannot plant them immediately, make a shallow trench and bury the roots under 4-6 in (10-15 cm) of soil, marking them with stakes.

Plant onion sets any time from early spring to midspring.

Sow mustard greens and collards about 3 to 5 weeks before the last spring frost; set out hardened-off transplants of broccoli and kohlrabi at the same time.

Begin planting beets 30 days before your last spring frost date, first soaking the seeds overnight in tepid water. For a prolonged harvest, make repeated sowings at intervals of 3 to 4 weeks.

Sow carrots at least 3 to 4 weeks before the last frost date. Make successive sowings at 3-week intervals; plant a few feet of each row at a time.

Sow eggplant seeds indoors 60 days before the last spring frost date; start tomatoes 50 days before the last spring frost. Set pots or flats in a warm spot to germinate, then move them to a sunny windowsill.

Begin sowing early-maturing potatoes as soon as the soil can be worked. After tilling the bed, prepare a trench 6 in (15 cm) × 8 in (20 cm) in diameter, digging in a light dressing of superphosphate (a handful per 1 ft/30 cm) at the bottom. Drop in the seed potato pieces, spacing them according to the grower's instructions, then fill the trench with soil, tamping it down lightly.

Plant Jerusalem artichokes at the end of early spring or the beginning of midspring. These plants are invasive and need plenty of space.

MIDSPRING

As spring weather reaches across the country, the garden bursts into life and cries out for attention.

In the extreme South (zones 9 to 11), midspring is marked by a change in precipitation. In southern Florida, the humidity and rainfall increase; in southern California and at lower elevations of the desert Southwest, the winter rains end as summer's prolonged drought draws near.

Elsewhere, however, midspring is the season that brings safety from frost. It may start with sleet or even a late snowfall, but these unseasonable events disappear with mild temperatures. Yet from the gardener's point of view the most important changes occur below ground. The soil dries and warms, stimulating seeds to germinate, and roots awaken, forcing the buds above into growth.

Midspring is a busy time in the garden, but wet spells can cause delays — especially if you garden only on weekends. Dry spells, however, bring a need for watering, as new seedlings cannot tolerate dehydration.

LAWN MAINTENANCE

Wherever spring weather is moist and cool, fungal diseases such as leaf spot and cottony blight are likely to appear. Control them with applications of recommended fungicides or by spreading homemade compost at a rate of 10 lb (5 kg) per 1,000 sq ft (90 sq m).

Some 7 to 10 days after the spring fertilization, and at least 3 days before or after mowing, apply a selective weed killer. Dig out persistent perennial weeds and coarse grasses by hand.
In the North, use a complete fertilizer rich in slow-release organic nitrates or in water-insoluble nitrogen (listed on the product label as W.I.N.). Before feeding, however, have your soil tested by your local Cooperative Extension or the state agricultural university. The results will include a prescription for the amount and type of fertilizer you need. Such a test should also provide information about pH — soil acidity — which will tell you if your lawn will benefit from an application of lime. Excessive acidity is a common problem throughout the eastern half of the country.
In the South, warm-season grasses (Bermuda, St. Augustine, Bahia, zoysia, and centipede grass) should all be growing actively, even in cooler regions. Fertilize them now if you have not already done so. It is a good time to lay sod in this region.
In the West, aerate the lawn with a coring machine to relieve soil compaction and enhance penetration of water. In the cooler northern part of this region there is still time to sow new seed.

Beds and borders

Plant late-flowering herbaceous perennials and those which are slow to make new growth — New York asters (*Aster novi-belgii*) and red-hot pokers (*Kniphofia*).

Complete the routine division and replanting of border perennials. New York asters deteriorate fairly quickly, and finer flowers and healthier growth come from young plants. Lift and divide these plants every few years, keeping only the healthiest

◄ **Flowering cherry** The bare branches of this weeping oriental cherry (*Prunus serrulata* 'Kiku-shidare-sakura') are clothed with glorious clusters of deep pink flowers in midspring. Beneath are other true harbingers of spring — bright blue grape hyacinths, red tulips, and multicolored primulas.

15

shoots from the outside of each clump. The taller rudbeckias, helianthuses, monardas, and heleniums need similar treatment.

Toward the end of midspring, stake delphiniums before their heavy flower spikes reach half their ultimate height. Insert a sturdy bamboo cane or a wooden stake with a 1 in (2.5 cm) diameter behind each plant. Tie string around the stake once with a single knot, and then make a knotted loop around the spike, allowing room for the stems to grow. As the spikes lengthen, tie them at intervals of about 1½ ft (45 cm). The shorter Belladonna delphiniums can be supported with pea sticks, brushy branches whose tops can be interlaced.

Also insert pea sticks or wire-hoop supports around other shorter weak-stemmed plants, such as pyrethrums *(Tanacetum)*. Stake pinks *(Dianthus)*, if necessary, by pushing small branched twigs into the ground so that the flower stems can grow up through them.

By the end of midspring, most herbaceous plants have emerged from winter dormancy, so winter losses can be assessed. But some tuberous-rooted plants don't emerge for another few weeks. Fill any gaps with annuals and other bedding plants.

When all danger of frost is past, it is also a good time to plant out healthy overwintered dahlia tubers in warm, sheltered areas.

Discard any tubers that are shriveled or have rotted at the crown.

Continue to deadhead early bulbs, leaving the flower stalks and all leaves intact.

As the ground warms, mulch beds and borders. If a late frost freezes tender plants, cover them with newspaper or burlap, or spray cold water on them before sunrise; these measures allow them to thaw out more gradually.

Rebait beer traps or renew slug pellets around susceptible plants, and look out for early attacks of aphids and other pests.

Annuals You can sow many near-hardy annuals outdoors in midspring if the weather and soil are favorable. These include cosmos, gaillardia, lavatera, stock *(Matthiola)*, sunflower *(Helianthus)*, scabious, and annual phlox. Before sowing, fork in a dressing of general flower fertilizer.

Complete the indoor sowing of half-hardy annuals. Begin hardening off any half-hardy annual seedlings you have started indoors: Move the plants to a cold frame or set them outside during the warmer hours, gradually increasing the exposure as the weather warms. Take special care with more tender plants. In the case of French and African marigolds, bedding dahlias, and ageratums, cover the cold frame with an old blanket or move them indoors if a hard frost is forecast. (There is more frost protection near the center of a cold frame than around the edges.)

Yellowing leaves indicate slight starvation of seedlings; apply a liquid flower fertilizer weekly.

Plant out pots of early spring-sown sweet peas as soon as they are growing strongly. Loosely tie the leader to a cane, leaving ample room for the stem to thicken. From now on, carefully remove all the tendrils while they are still small. Also remove all side shoots that form in the leaf axis. Dwarf sweet peas, of course, need no staking or pruning.

Roses
Complete the pruning of ever-blooming roses (hybrid teas, floribundas, and grandifloras) as soon as possible. Feed established roses with a fertilizer specially formulated for roses, taking care to apply it at the recommended rate. Rake in the fertilizer, breaking up the surface of the soil.

TASKS IN THE FLOWER GARDEN

1 Support pinks *(Dianthus)* by inserting twiggy sticks close to the clump so that the stems can grow up through and around the supports. Staking in this way is most likely to be needed with tall-growing cultivars, especially in rich soil and in gardens subject to heavy rainfall or strong winds.

2 Divide large, tough clumps of herbaceous perennials that have been lifted from the ground by thrusting in two garden forks, back to back, and levering them apart. Use a strong, sharp knife to divide plants that have thick fleshy root growths. Pull smaller clumps apart by hand.

3 Hoe the ground around perennials and shrubs to keep them free from weeds, which appear soon after the ground begins to warm up. If necessary, use a contact weed killer. When the soil is reasonably moist, apply an attractive organic mulch such as shredded leaves or bark, cocoa, or peanut shells.

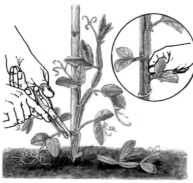

4 For the finest flowers, restrict the growth of climbing sweet peas. When they are 9-12 in (23-30 cm) tall, select the strongest shoot on each plant and cut off the remainder of the growths. Tie the leader shoot to a cane or stake. Remove all tendrils and side shoots as soon as they are big enough to handle.

Mulch established rose beds with at least a 1 in (2.5 cm) thick layer of well-rotted compost or manure. Alternatively, apply ½ in (12 mm) of grass clippings, but don't use mowings from a lawn that has been treated with weed killer. Only apply a mulch of shredded bark for newly planted roses — compost and manure are too strong at this stage.

Pull up weeds by hand, rather than hoeing, as roses have shallow, easily damaged roots. A thorough mulching should stop new weed seeds from germinating.

During prolonged dry weather, give newly planted roses 1 gal (4 lit) of water per plant twice a week. Although the bare-root planting season is past, you can buy container-grown roses from a garden center to fill any gaps that winter has left in the beds.

Shrubs and trees

Plant evergreen shrubs during overcast or drizzly weather. Continue to plant deciduous shrubs such as clematis, honeysuckle, jasmine, ornamental vines, and wisteria.

Water newly planted trees and shrubs during dry spells. Mulch around these plants with black plastic or grass clippings to reduce water loss from the soil.

Propagate *Hydrangea paniculata* and magnolias by layering. The layerings can be cut and replanted after 1 or 2 years.

Lightly prune trees and shrubs that have finished flowering: Shorten branches and cut off dead flower spikes and old, weak shoots of *Chaenomeles japonica* and spring-flowering clematis. Cut back forsythia to within one or two buds of the old wood. The arching stems of *Forsythia suspensa* often root on their own where they come in contact with the ground. Sever the rooted pieces and replant elsewhere.

Hedges Plant broad-leaved evergreen hedging plants, such as holly *(Ilex),* laurel *(Prunus laurocerasus),* and escallonia. Keep the plants well watered.

The fruit garden

Apple, pear, plum, and cherry trees generally flower in midspring to late spring. Watch for pests that damage the developing fruit. An application of phosmet at petal-fall may be needed to control green fruitworms and

TASKS IN THE KITCHEN GARDEN

1 Transplant cabbage sets, or seedlings, to rows in the garden bed 2 to 3 weeks before the last frost. Apply lime if soil pH is below 7.2 to protect plants against clubroot disease. Set the seedlings so that their bottom leaves are at soil level, firming them in well and watering them immediately afterward.

2 Harvest forced rhubarb stalks: First, lift off the upturned bucket or barrel. Pull the pink-red stems from the plant, grasping them close to the base and pulling away from the crown with a slight twisting motion. Do not cut rhubarb sticks with a knife — the base that remains after the cut will rot.

3 At the northern edge of their range, peach flowers may open before pollinating insects are really active. To ensure a good crop, hand-pollinate peach blossoms with a camel-hair artist's brush at about midday every day during flowering. Gently dab yellow pollen from one flower to another on the same tree.

4 Protect the flowers of peaches, nectarines, and other early-flowering wall shrubs from frost damage by draping the plants with small-mesh netting or old bedsheets at night. Insert tall stakes at an angle in front of the plants to form a support for the screen. Roll up the screen during the day.

plum curculios. Reduce your need for chemical sprays by setting out pheromone (sex-attractant) traps for codling moths. Because the adults are attracted to the traps before they lay eggs on the fruit, these devices allow you to time sprays accurately and achieve control with one dose of ryania, an organic insecticide. Bright yellow boards coated with mineral oil or a special horticultural adhesive serve as traps for fruit flies, while similarly coated nonreflective white boards will trap tarnished plant bugs. These traps will alert you to the presence of pests so that you can time insecticide treatments effectively.

Do not spray fruit trees with insecticides while the flowers are open, because you may kill the pollinating insects that ensure a good crop of fruit.

Late frosts may nip flowers and so reduce fruit crops. Protect espaliered trees and berry bushes by covering them with old bed sheets on cold nights.

If cold weather has delayed the growth of apple trees so that bud burst takes place in midspring, apply a spray as recommended for early spring. At the pink bud stage, spray against apple scab with an approved fungicide, especially if the weather alternates between periods of rain and relatively high temperatures. At the early white bud stage, spray pear trees with fungicide to protect them against pear scab.

This season's warm days and cool nights promote the spread of powdery mildew, which coats leaves of many kinds of fruit trees and bushes with a gray-white powder, sapping the plant's vitality. Treat powdery mildew with sprays of an approved fungicide, repeating at intervals of 10 to 14 days until after the petals drop.

With espaliered plums, cherries, damsons, peaches, and nectarines, cut out shoots growing directly toward or away from the wall as new growth starts. If necessary to control aphids, spray with insecticidal soap.

If you find spider mites on peaches or nectarines, spray with an approved pesticide after the petals have fallen from the tree.

Make sure that pollinating insects can reach strawberry flowers by opening up plastic tunnels or any other form of protection you may have applied to promote early growth and protect against frost. Remove the flowers from new plants or runners and from fall-fruiting varieties. Watch for aphids, and spray with insecticidal soap if you see any of these soft-bodied insects. Top-dress strawberries with a general fertilizer, such as 5–10–5 (2½ lb/ 1 kg per 100 ft/30 m row), or a manure "tea" made by soaking a bucketful of fresh manure in a barrel of water. Be sure not to overfeed, or foliage will flourish at the expense of fruit.

The vegetable garden

Continue planting onion sets and salad crops; plant parsley and other herbs when the soil is sufficiently dry to work to a fine tilth. In colder areas, plant early potatoes (this is done in early spring in milder areas).

As soil warms to 60°F (16°C), generally about a week before the last spring frost, begin sowing beans. For strongest growth, coat the seeds with a legume inoculant, a powdered form of bacteria that help beans and pea roots absorb atmospheric nitrogen. This is also the time to begin sowing corn. To ensure good pollination and large, well-developed ears, sow seed corn in blocks of four to six rows set 2-4 ft (60-120 cm) apart; each row should be at least 10 ft (3 m) long.

Set out transplants of cabbages, cauliflower, and broccoli 3 weeks before the last spring frost. All of these members of the cabbage family are prone to club-root disease. To protect seedlings, test the soil in this bed with a soil-test kit, available at most garden centers. If the soil proves acidic, apply lime to raise the pH to at least 7.2. With a good loam soil, 4-6 lb (2-2.5 kg) of lime per 100 sq ft (9 sq m) will raise the pH one full point (e.g., from 6.0 to 7.0). Sandy soils require less — 1½-4½ lb (.7-2 kg) — while soil that contains a lot of clay requires more — 8-10 lb (3.5-4.5 kg).

Cut asparagus spears from beds that are at least 2 years old when the growths are 4-6 in (10-15 cm) above the soil. Using a sharp knife, cut about 2-3 in (5-7.5 cm) below ground. Repeat this task several times each week.

Continue sowing beets and carrots at intervals of 3 to 4 weeks. Mulch carrots 6 weeks after sowing to protect root tops from sunlight; this ensures that their flavor will be sweet.

Protect emerging potato shoots from frost damage as they grow higher by hilling up earth around them with a draw hoe. When the ridges can be made no higher, cover the shoots with straw if frost threatens. Remove the straw cover the next morning when the frost has thawed.

PLANT OF THE MONTH

Pasqueflower (*Anemone pulsatilla*) produces a tufted clump of soft ferny leaves from which slightly nodding goblet-shaped flowers appear in midspring, standing 8-12 in (20-30 cm) high. The typical petal color is rich mauve-purple, but cultivars are available with pale mauve, pink, red, or white flowers. They always have a prominent grouping of golden yellow stamens in the center. When the flowers fade, pretty silken seed heads develop, resembling those of clematis.

Other midspring flowers Bulbs continue to dominate the scene when it comes to midspring color — choose from the hundreds of varieties of narcissi, tulips, hyacinths, fritillaries, and grape hyacinths (*Muscari*). For a powerful sweet scent, lily of the valley (*Convallaria*) cannot be beaten.

Blue gentians; gold doronicums; pink, red, or white mossy saxifrages; and white arabis all bring color to the rock garden. For shrubs, there are red or white Japanese quinces (*Chaenomeles*), yellow forsythia, creamy fothergilla, pure white *Magnolia stellata*, and orange *Berberis darwinii*.

LATE SPRING

Warmer nights mark the end of spring, but a cool spell can still stunt the growth of vegetable seedlings or tender annuals.

Late spring brings some of the year's most pleasant weather to much of the United States and typically provides ideal growth conditions for plants. Temperatures in the upper Midwest, for example, often rise to an average daytime high of around 70°F (24°C), dropping at night to 40° or 50°F (4.5°-10°C). Even along the Gulf Coast, the temperatures are moderate, rarely rising over 89°F (32°C) and falling to the upper 60's F (high teens C) at night.

Rainfall continues to be abundant or at least adequate for plant needs, except in the desert Southwest and southern California, where irrigation will keep the garden from going dormant. In some of the drier regions of the Mountain West — Salt Lake City, Utah, or Cheyenne, Wyoming, for example — this is the wettest season of a semiarid climate. Along the northwestern Pacific Coast, precipitation decreases as summer sets in, but there is usually enough rainfall to satisfy plants in well-cultivated soils.

Beds and borders
Continue hoeing between perennials and shrubs to kill growing weeds. Also continue to stake and support tall plants, such as delphiniums, which are liable to be damaged by winds or rain close to flowering time.

Pinching back To check the growth of perennials that are inclined to grow too tall, and to make the plants branch out, pinch back the tips. Plants that respond well to this treatment are those that form a leafy clump opening into heads of flowers — such as phlox, goldenrods (*Solidago*), heleniums, New York asters, and rudbeckias.

When a plant has reached about a quarter of its expected height, and at least a month before flowering time, pinch back the leading shoots. This may reduce the ultimate height by a quarter, but will

LAWN MAINTENANCE

Mow weekly with sharp mower blades. Cut grass at the highest recommended height to improve rooting and drought resistance. Water the lawn thoroughly in dry weather. Treat for weeds, and apply fungicides if needed.

In the North, insects will become active — brown patches of turf may be symptoms of billbug, sod webworm, or grub infestation.

In the South, sow seeds of warm-season grasses. Fertilize established turf again.

In the West, give lawns 1 in (2.5 cm) of water, wetting the soil to a depth of 6-12 in (15-30 cm). Irrigate lawns in arid regions.

not shorten the typical flowering period — although it may retard flowering by a week or two.

However, if plants are more than 3 years old and are producing many shoots with inferior blooms, or if you are in a cold district where later blooming may be caught by fall's first frost, thin

▼ **Late-spring symphony** Golden laburnum is draped with long chains of flowers in late spring and early summer; these will be followed by poisonous seedpods. Mature trees such as this provide splendid support for the rambling, pale pink *Clematis montana*.

TASKS IN THE FLOWER GARDEN

1 Plant out half-hardy annuals as soon as danger of frost has passed. Lay the plants in position until you feel that your design is well balanced, then dig holes deep enough for all the roots. Firm in the plants, and water them well.

2 Use a sharp knife to remove surplus shoots from the center of clumps of older perennials, selecting the weakest growths and cutting them as close to the ground as possible. Do not remove more than half the total number of shoots.

3 Water young but established plants during dry spells by using the puddling method: First scrape soil away to form a low bank around the plant. Add water until a puddle forms, then level the soil once the water has drained away.

4 To encourage bushier, branching growth from herbaceous perennials that tend to grow tall, pinch back the leading shoot tips. Do this at least a month before flowering. The plant's ultimate height may be reduced by a quarter.

out some of these shoots. The remaining shoots will be more vigorous. Do the thinning at the same time as you pinch back shoot tips, or even earlier. Remove the weakest shoots, concentrating on those at the center of the crown. Take out up to half the total, severing them close to the ground.

Watering Young plants — even the drought-resistant species — may require watering during dry spells. Where only a few new kinds have been planted among established plants, use the puddling method: Scrape away 1 in (2.5 cm) of the dry topsoil to make a low bank all around the plant or group. Fill the basin

once or twice with water. When the water has soaked in, push back the soil with a rake or hoe.

If an entire newly planted bed is too dry, use a sprinkler or a sprinkler head on a watering can or hose. Make sure that the water comes out as a fine spray and not in large drops, which tend to crust the soil surface.

As soon as the surface begins to dry a little, scratch over it with a rake to restore the tilth necessary for aeration.

Chrysanthemums Plant out garden varieties when all danger of frost is past, using pot-grown plants raised from cuttings or bought from a garden center. Insert a stake at each planting

hole, and tie the stem loosely in place; water the plants well.

Bulbs and tubers Deadhead daffodils, tulips, hyacinths, and irises as they finish flowering. If it is necessary to make way for summer beds, lift daffodils and tulips now, but otherwise wait until their foliage yellows — typically in early summer.

Heel in lifted bulbs in a temporary bed in a spare corner of the garden, so that they can die back gradually: First dig a trench about 1 ft (30 cm) deep. Put a length of fine wire or fiberglass screening on the bottom, and lay in the bulbs. Cover the lower half of the stems with soil. By early summer the foliage will have shriveled and the bulbs can be lifted for storage. A sharp pull on the screening should lift all the bulbs at once.

Plant crinum bulbs 6-8 in (15-20 cm) deep in a south-facing border. In cold regions, also plant them in tubs that can be moved under cover in fall.

Plant out young dahlias (your own rooted cuttings or store-bought plants) when danger of frost is over. In colder areas, plant out dormant tubers now.

Tall dahlias need staking, as their stems are generally too weak to support the heavy flower heads. For each dahlia, drive a stout stake into the ground at the back of the planting hole before inserting the tuber. As the stems grow, tie them loosely to the stakes with soft garden string or twine. If a late frost is forecast, cover the young plants with sheets of newspaper at night.

Annuals Continue to pinch off the side shoots and tendrils of climbing sweet peas. Peas grown in this fashion will produce bigger, finer blossoms but will not be self-supporting, so they must be tied to their stakes or trellis as the shoots continue to lengthen. Pinch back the first few flowers when they are tiny, but leave the little stems, bearing more buds, which will soon appear.

There is still time to sow hardy and half-hardy annuals outdoors, including alyssum, calendula, candytuft, cosmos, gaillardia, nasturtium, phlox, and marigolds. Hardy biennials can also be sown now in nursery beds.

In mild areas, you can begin planting out half-hardy annuals as soon as the risk of frost has

passed. Don't be rushed into planting earlier by the flood of bedding plants appearing in garden centers; these centers often bring out stock before outdoor planting conditions are suitable. If in doubt, it is safer to wait until the first week of early summer.

Before setting out half-hardy annuals, water borders and beds cleared of spring bedding plants. Your annuals should be hardened off and given a good watering before planting. Remove them from

their containers with as much root as possible. Most garden centers sell annuals in plastic packs or flats. If the plants have been grown in cell packs, one plant to each molded plastic compartment, you can push at the bottom of the pack to remove each plant. Those grown together in packs or flats must be removed as a group so that the root balls can be cut apart with a sharp knife; if given a feeding with a weak liquid fertilizer at planting time, the

▲ **Bedding displays** Mark your plan for bedding annuals with trails of sand to define the divisions between different plants. Roughly estimate the number of each plant available, and make sure that, with the correct spacing, the layout will fill in evenly as the plants grow.

Taller-growing varieties should be placed near the back or at the center of the bed, with shorter ones at the front and edges. Plant the taller-growing types first, stepping on the soil as little as possible; you can lay a plank across the soil to get to the back and center of the bed.

TENDING PLANTS IN THE ROCK GARDEN

1 Destroy weed seedlings between rock plants and alpines by hoeing carefully during dry weather. An onion hoe *(above)* or Cape Cod weeder is the ideal size and shape for this purpose. Pull up larger perennial weeds by hand.

2 After flowering, trim aubrietas, saxifrages, and other vigorous rock plants to encourage fresh, compact growth. Doing this may also promote a second flush of flowers later in the season and will prevent self-seeding.

3 Sedums, saxifrages, and other cushion-forming rock plants benefit from a sprinkling of fine soil mixed with sand and organic fertilizer. Work this in among the plant rosettes with your fingers, firming it in lightly.

◄ **Acid-loving rhododendrons** Through-out the eastern United States and in the Pacific Northwest, late spring brings to mind rhododendrons and azaleas. These plants thrive in the shade and burst into glorious colors, from very pale pastels to fiery reds and blues. After blooming, carefully twist off the faded flower heads by hand, without damaging the new growth buds at the base.

Roses

Unfortunately, protecting garden roses from pests and diseases involves regular spraying in most regions. Aphids, caterpillars, black spot, and mildew are the major rose pests and diseases this season brings. Insecticides should be applied only after an infestation has been observed, but fungicides are most effective when applied regularly as a preventive. For best results, use a fine-mist sprayer and cover both sides of the leaves and the stems. Insecticidal soap may be sufficient to discourage many insect pests; use stronger insecticides and fungicides with caution, applying only those designed for roses and for the pest specified.

Shrubs and trees

Complete the planting of evergreens. Keep roots moist after planting, and spray the foliage with water in the evenings during dry or windy weather.

plants will quickly recover.

Whatever container your annuals have been raised in, make sure that after planting each batch you water them well with a sprinkler or a watering can fitted with a sprinkler head. Light watering of young annuals merely results in attracting their roots to the surface.

Rock gardens

Late spring is the peak period for color in the rock garden, but weeds are also growing strongly. Use a Cape Cod weeder or an onion hoe to loosen small annual weeds. Pull the weeds up by hand and also destroy any larger perennial weeds.

Also remove any unwanted self-sown seedlings of aubrietas, saxifrages, and other rock garden plants — these will almost certainly not bloom as well as the parent plants, if the parents are select cultivars. After flowering, trim the stalks and surplus growth of fast-growing species. This will promote new compact growth and encourage more flowers — especially with aubrietas.

If your sedums and saxifrages appear ragged, sprinkle a mixture of fine soil, sand, and a mild, organic fertilizer among the green rosettes. Trickle the mixture onto the plants through your fingers, then work it in below the leaves and stems and underneath trailing stems. Alternatively, if the weather is damp, lift the plants, then dig and fertilize the soil. Reset the plants a half-inch or so deeper than their previous positions, placing them close together in bunches.

PROPAGATING HERBS

Propagate thyme, marjoram, rosemary, and sage by taking cuttings 3-4 in (7.5-10 cm) long from branches produced during the previous year; cut just below a node. Remove the lower leaves *(above, left)*, then insert several cuttings each into pots of equal parts sharp builder's sand and screened sphagnum peat. Stand the containers in a cool, protected spot out of direct light, and mist the cuttings daily with water.

Herbs that make runners, such as mint *(above, right)*, are best propagated by cutting the runners into sections, each with a shoot and roots.

When the cuttings are rooted, transplant them to the garden.

For shrubs that have finished flowering — such as kerria, pieris, flowering currant, and spring-blooming spirea — deadhead, shorten long stems, and thin out or completely remove weak shoots. Also deadhead rhododendrons and azaleas by snapping off the stalks with your fingers, taking care that the new growth buds at the base of the old flower cluster are not damaged in the process.

Hedges Clip hedges of *Lonicera nitida* monthly from now until the end of early fall to keep them neatly shaped and prevent them from breaking open as they grow. Some other hedges, such as common privet, also need regular clipping to look their best.

Clip hedges of forsythia and flowering currant after the flowers have died. Do not prune them again until the following year, otherwise you will remove the new flower buds and thus lose the spring display.

The fruit garden

There is a risk of damage from an unseasonably late frost, but trees are now producing leaves and shoots, which will help to protect the flowers. Soil temperatures are also rising, so low-growing fruits are unlikely to freeze.

Most fruits contain a lot of water and need irrigation in dry spells. To avoid the formation of soft, flavorless growth, water mainly after flowering, during the fruit-swelling stage.

If the fruit set appears good on trees such as apple, pear, or plum, fertilize now with a com-

TRAINING RUNNER BEANS

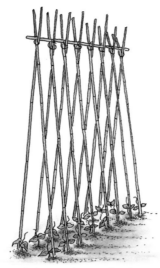 

1 Provide bean poles or tall stakes alongside the plants, setting them at an angle. Tie opposing poles together near their tops. For added strength and rigidity, lay a horizontal strut across the top and secure it to the uprights.

2 A tent shape of poles or canes provides an alternative means of supporting runner beans where space cannot be spared for a row. This system is also more attractive in a small garden, but the yield may be reduced slightly.

plete fertilizer formulated for fruiting plants. This will help to swell the fruit and form buds for next year. Do not feed if the trees are not fruiting — the extra nutrients will only encourage excessive leaf and sucker growth.

Continue to spray against apple and pear scab disease every 10 to 14 days, especially in a wet spring. Also continue to watch for plum curculio and codling moths, spraying with a recommended pesticide if necessary.

Hang traps — bright yellow boards coated with a specially formulated adhesive — in cherry trees, and watch for the appearance of cherry fruit flies. As soon as these pests appear, spray them with a recommended pesticide.

New raspberry canes should now be growing up strongly. Pull out unwanted shoots that are causing overcrowding in a row or growing in the space between rows. If the fruit set appears good, apply a mulch to conserve moisture. Also fertilize at this time, preferably with a balanced, slow-release organic fertilizer. If cane tips should suddenly wilt, examine for the tunneling of the raspberry cane borer. Prune infested tips, cutting off below the pest's entry wounds. Bag and dispose of damaged prunings.

Blackberries, loganberries, and hybrid berries should be producing new shoots from the ground, which will bear next year's crop. To check the spread of disease from old canes to new, keep them apart as much as possible by training them along separate wires or in opposite directions. Fertilize these plants in the same way as raspberries.

Except in very poor soils, gooseberries and currants will not benefit from strong chemical fertilizers. Instead, mulch bushes with 1 in (2.5 cm) of well-rotted manure.

Control weeds among cane and

THINNING PEACHES

1 Left unthinned, peaches may bear numerous small fruits of poor quality. Start thinning fruit in late spring, removing any small or misshapen fruits. Those that remain will grow larger and become more succulent.

2 Once thinned out, the small peach fruits on espaliered trees should be spaced 3-4 in (7.5-10 cm) apart on the branches. Further fruit thinning, to a spacing of about 9 in (23 cm), will be needed in early summer.

bush fruits by hoeing carefully.

Fertilize strawberries again with a general fertilizer such as 5–10–5 (2½ lb/1 kg per 100 ft/30 m row) or a manure "tea," which you can make by soaking a bucketful of fresh manure in a barrel of water. Protect developing strawberries by spreading a mulch of straw or black plastic under them, or by surrounding the plants with tar-paper collars.

The vegetable garden

Sow carrots, if you did not do so in midspring. Continue to cut asparagus spears. In the North, sow late-maturing potato cultivars. Continue planting corn, setting out a new block every 2 weeks to ensure a regular supply later. Keep different types (popcorn, hybrid sweet corn, and the new supersweet cultivars) at least 250 ft (75 m) apart as cross-pollination will ruin the flavor of the harvest.

Transplant seedlings of peppers, tomatoes, and eggplants into the garden after all danger of frost is past and the nights are warm — at least 55°F (13°C). A week before planting, prepare beds by fertilizing soil with 1 lb (450 g) of general fertilizer such as 5–10–5 per 100 sq ft (9 sq m). Protect newly transplanted seedlings from cutworms by wrapping the bottom of the stem with a 6 in (15 cm) collar of cardboard pushed down to root level in the soil.

During the last 2 weeks of late spring, sow runner beans, preferably on a site that you prepared earlier. Insert bean poles or support stakes before sowing.

Plant squash, cucumber, and melon seeds once all danger of frost has passed and the soil has warmed. Sow in "hills" — circles of four to six seeds — and cover emerging seedlings with "floating" row covers of fine netting or some light and translucent horticultural fabric of polypropylene. If kept in place for the first month of growth, these covers will ward off cucumber beetles and the plant diseases they carry.

Late spring is time to make a last sowing of salad greens; switch to heat-resistant "summer" strains such as 'Buttercrunch' or 'Oakleaf.' Plant New Zealand or Malabar "spinaches." These plants come from different families from true spinach but are far more heat tolerant and produce a similar, very tasty leaf.

PLANT OF THE MONTH

Common lilac (*Syringa vulgaris*) is unparalleled among garden shrubs for its beauty, elegance, and rich color in late spring. Cultivars and hybrids, sometimes listed under *Syringa* x *hyacinthiflora*, come in a range of colors in addition to the typical lilac-mauve: mauve-purples, pinkish mauves, wine-reds, creamy whites, and pure whites.

Growing up to 12 ft (3.5 m) in height, with a spread of up to 10 ft (3 m), lilac is best suited to a large shrub bed, or it can be grown on its own as a specimen plant. The distinctively and strongly scented flowers are borne in pyramid-shaped clusters up to 9 in (23 cm) long.

Other late-spring plants Azaleas and rhododendrons are among the most popular late-spring shrubs, but they are generally successful only in acid, humus-rich soil and do not flourish as a rule in the harsh climates of the upper Midwest and Rocky Mountain states. There are hundreds of species and cultivars from which to choose, in a vast range of colors and sizes. Make sure you verify the ultimate size of any plant before buying.

For a strong orange-blossom scent and starry white flowers, choose the evergreen Mexican orange (*Choisya ternata*). Hardy through zone 8, this compact shrub may be grown in a tub or against a sunny wall farther north.

Weigela florida and its hybrids burst into pink, red, or white blossoms in late spring, making an informal backdrop for the lower-growing mauve or pink cranesbill (*Geranium*), columbines (*Aquilegia*), blue forget-me-nots (*Myosotis*), honesty (*Lunaria annua*), and late tulips.

Rock gardens abound with flowering plants in late spring. The most stunning displays are given by *Aurinia saxatilis* (*Alyssum saxatile*), *Aubrieta deltoidea*, *Iberis semperflorens*, and *Phlox subulata*.

EARLY SUMMER

**The sun is at its strongest now
and plant growth is rapid, so try to maintain
soil moisture and keep weeds down.**

This season brings the longest days of the year, and in many areas it also brings clear weather. In parts of the Rocky Mountain states — Denver, Colorado, for example — this season brings the year's heaviest rainfall, and in southern Florida the June rainfall may total 9 in (23 cm). Throughout many other regions of the United States, this is a relatively dry time of year, but in most cases that is easily corrected by judicious watering. And temperatures, although warm, have not yet soared to their stifling midsummer highs.

Early summer weather promotes rapid, vigorous growth of weeds, as well as ornamentals and food crops. Pests and diseases also thrive, and they must be dealt with quickly.

Roses

Early summer is when the roses begin to bloom, generally starting with old garden roses and species types, followed by the modern bush and climbing roses.

Many hybrid tea (large-flowered) roses have flowering shoots that produce two or three side buds in addition to the main bud at the top. If you want large blooms with long stems for cutting and arranging indoors, disbud these — remove the small side buds as soon as it is possible to pick them off with your fingers.

Old garden roses, those shrubs which bloom only once each season, generally at the beginning of the summer, should be pruned as soon as their flowering ends. Remove all spindly or unhealthy canes and branches that cross back through the bush's center. Then shorten remaining canes by a third to keep shrubs compact.

Check rose beds for extra vigorous suckers emerging from the bushes' base or surrounding soil. These are shoots of the rootstock

LAWN MAINTENANCE

Mow regularly; during drought, raise the mower blades.
In the North, lawns may be allowed to go dormant during rainless spells. Healthy turf will quickly turn green again with the first rain or with irrigation.
In the South, warm-season grasses are at their best. If the weather turns hot and humid, watch for diseases such as brown spot and gray leaf spot on St. Augustine grass.
In the West, high temperatures may make applications of herbicides harmful to turf; remove weeds by hand. In arid regions, water regularly (native grasses such as buffalo grass and crested wheat grass are less thirsty). Brown patches of turf easily pulled away from soil may be evidence of cutworms or grubs; treat as necessary with beneficial nematodes or an approved insecticide.

▼ **Herbaceous borders** Early summer is the peak season for herbaceous borders, with fresh green foliage to offset vibrant flower colors. The hardy cranesbills (*Geranium* spp.) are covered in a profusion of blooms that range in color from white and pale pink through crimson and purple to shades of blue. Their dense growth habit helps to suppress weed growth in the border.

CARING FOR ROSES

1 Pinch the side buds from the flowering shoots of hybrid tea roses to get the best-quality, largest blooms from the terminal buds. This step is essential if you want long-stemmed blooms for exhibition or arranging indoors. Keep an eye out for aphids on the buds, and spray with a rose insecticide when necessary.

2 Suckers growing from rosebush rootstocks bear poor-quality flowers and are often distinguished by leaves and thorns markedly different from those on the rest of the top growth. Cut suckers flush where they sprout from the rootstock. If necessary, scrape away the soil to expose the point of origin.

onto which the garden roses were grafted; they will not bear attractive blooms, and should be cut off with a sharp knife or shears.

Use a scuffle hoe around roses to improve soil aeration and remove weeds. Don't slice deeper than ½ in (12 mm) or so, as rose roots grow close to the surface.

Mulch roses with garden compost, well-rotted manure, shredded bark, or lawn clippings. Don't use lawn clippings if the grass has been treated with herbicide.

Spray roses with insecticidal soap if aphids appear, and with rose fungicide at regular intervals as a precaution against mildew, rust, and black spot. The timing of the spray depends on the product, and you should follow the instructions on the package label.

Beds and borders
Where early-flowering herbaceous perennials are fading, cut them down to within 3 in (7.5 cm) of the ground and clear away any unsightly stakes. This encourages a fresh crop of foliage, which will provide attractive ground cover for the rest of the summer. In some cases, a second flush of flowers may develop.

Lay down a 1 in (2.5 cm) thick mulch of leaf mold or shredded bark between moisture-loving and shade-loving plants.

Chrysanthemums Pinch back the plants' growing tips as soon as buds show in the leaf axils on the main stem; this encourages

the growth of side shoots and earlier flowering. Water regularly.

Bulbs Early summer is the season when the foliage of spring bulbs yellows and withers. Tulips may be lifted from the soil and stored now. Most other bulbs — including daffodils — should be divided and replanted in fresh soil only if you want show-quality flowers or if the plants have become so crowded that they produce masses of leaves.

When dahlia tubers have begun to push new growth up above the soil surface — 2 to 3 weeks after planting — pinch the tip of each leading shoot. This will encourage the production of side shoots and make bushy plants that will give a long succession of flowers. When the shoots have reached a height of about 1½ ft (45 cm), tie them to the stakes with soft string or twine. Lay a thick mulch around dahlias, and water the plants well.

Annuals Finish planting half-hardy bedding annuals, waiting until all risk of late frosts has passed in cold regions or low-lying "frost pockets." Water both the prepared soil and the hardened-off plants before setting these out in their flowering sites.

In periods of dry weather, thoroughly water all recently planted half-hardy annuals and hardy annuals sown earlier. Wet the soil down to a depth of 6 in (15 cm) a couple of times a week.

Support taller-growing annuals

when they reach a height of 6-9 in (15-23 cm), particularly in exposed sites. Use pea sticks just shorter than the eventual height of the plants. Push the sticks in among individual clumps, so that they are concealed by the plants.

To control aphids and other sap-sucking insects, spray as necessary with insecticidal soap or an approved insecticide. Control weeds by hoeing.

Biennials Sow hardy biennials, such as wallflowers, if you did not in late spring. They can be raised outdoors, in a greenhouse, or in a cold frame. In the South, this task is best put off until early fall.

As soon as biennial seedlings reach manageable size, transplant them from the seed flats or outdoor seedbeds to well-dug nursery beds. Plant them 6-9 in (15-23 cm) apart. Set them in their final sites in early fall (spring, in the South).

Alternatively, biennials such as wallflowers and sweet Williams may be sown directly in their flowering sites, and the resulting seedlings thinned to a spacing of 6-9 in (15-23 cm) apart.

Rock gardens
Continue to weed and hoe the rock garden, placing weeds straight into a bucket or box to prevent their seeds from being scattered back into the garden.

Trim dead flowers from aubrietas and saxifrages to prevent self-seeding. Clipping with floral shears also keeps these plants compact and tidy. At the same time, trim back excessive growth on trailing plants. In the case of species whose branches root at the tips or send out runners below ground, trim back the plant by plunging a knife into the soil around the plant and then pulling up the severed shoots.

Shrubs and trees
Prune deciduous shrubs, such as deutzia, cutting out shoots that have just flowered. As soon as brooms (*Cytisus*) have finished

▶ **Blanching leeks** To produce the tender white stems for which leeks are known, the seedlings must be transplanted in midspring to late spring into the bottom of a 9 in (23 cm) deep, compost-enriched trench. Soak the soil weekly in dry weather, and in early summer begin pushing soil back into the trench, covering stems as they grow and readying them for a fall harvest.

flowering, cut back the shoots to prevent seedpod production. But do not cut into the old wood — it may refuse to send out new shoots and the plants will remain dormant or even die.

Deadhead lilacs *(Syringa),* and thin out weak shoots. If you grow senecios for their silvery foliage, remove the flower heads as soon as they appear. Propagate *Chaenomeles japonica* and clematis by layering sprawling shoots.

Many hedges need the first trim of the year in early summer; because the first flush of growth is ending at this time, a single treatment will ensure a neat appearance into fall. Continue to weed or hoe at the base of hedges.

The fruit garden
Control weeds around the base of fruit trees, and mow grass short. Slacken the ties on newly planted fruit trees to prevent strangulation. Where birds are pests, cover fruit trees with netting.

Watch out for aphids on apple, pear, peach, damson and other plum trees; these insects can be controlled with summer oil. In apple trees, hang red spheres covered with mineral oil or specially formulated horticultural adhesive to trap egg-laying apple maggot flies; for a dwarf tree, use one trap, for a semidwarf tree, use two to four traps, and hang six or more traps on a standard tree.

LIFTING AND STORING BULBS

1 If it is necessary to lift spring bulbs such as daffodils and tulips, do so after foliage yellows. Insert a garden fork well clear of the clump and deep enough to get right under the roots.

2 After lifting, spread the bulbs out to dry in shallow boxes, leaving the old leaves and roots in place for now. Stand them in a well-ventilated shed until all moisture has evaporated.

3 Once they are bone-dry, gently peel away the dead skins and cut or pull off the roots and shriveled leaves. Do not remove the inner skins to expose white flesh. Store the bulbs in a cool shed.

4 Some bulbs, such as narcissi and daffodils, multiply by offset bulblets. Gently break these away from the parent bulbs, and store them separately for planting later in a nursery bed.

Bronzing and early falling leaves are signs of red spider mites; control them with dimethoate.

Continue spraying regularly against apple and pear scab with a recommended fungicide. Continue to monitor pheromone traps in apples and pears to spot any new generations of codling moths, and spray with a recommended insecticide if necessary. Where fruit set is heavy, thin out the fruit for the first time, but remember that there can be a heavy natural drop quite soon, so do not be overzealous.

When the lateral branches of espaliered plums and cherries have about seven leaves, pinch the tips from those not required for extension of the existing framework or as replacements. Having deshooted espaliered peaches and nectarines in mid-spring, tie in the remainder of the developing shoots to the trellis. Train new shoots of blackberries, loganberries, and hybrid berries so that they are separate from the old fruiting stems.

Control weeds around all such cane fruits by shallow hoeing or by hand-pulling, taking care not to damage the crop's roots. Cover bush and cane fruits with netting to deter birds.

Watch raspberry and blackberry bushes for wilting canes, which may be a symptom of raspberry crown borers. Cut out affected canes below the soil line to kill borer larvae, and drench bushes with an approved fungicide the following spring. In dry weather, water cane fruits well, while the fruit is swelling.

If gooseberry bushes are carrying a heavy crop, thin the fruit to improve the size of the remaining fruit. You can use the fruit that you have thinned for cooking.

Don't let new strawberry plants set fruit the first year — pick off blossoms as they appear. Deter slugs and snails with a deep straw mulch, and use netting to protect the fruit from birds. Propagate strawberries by anchoring runners in the soil between rows.

The vegetable garden

In the North, sow brussels sprout seeds for harvesting in fall (when the first light frosts have sweetened the sprouts); in the South, do not sow them until fall. Early summer is also the time for northern gardeners to sow winter radish seeds.

With the arrival of longer, hotter days, tomato plants will begin sprouting new shoots from the bases of the leaves. If plants are being trained to stakes or a trellis, allow only two or three of these shoots to develop, by pinching off the rest as they appear. Tie the remaining shoots to the stakes or trellis with garden twine. Tomatoes planted in cages or allowed to run free over the ground may grow unpinched.

Side-dress tomato plants 3 weeks after setting out by sprinkling a handful of general purpose fertilizer such as 5–10–10 in a circle 6 in (15 cm) away from the stem. Repeat at 3-week intervals until midsummer. Side-dress peppers monthly, giving each plant 1 tbsp (15 ml) of 5–10–10; apply an identical dose to eggplants as soon as they set fruit.

Irrigate corn during dry weather, making sure that plants get at least 1 in (2.5 cm) of water (including rainfall) every week. When plants are 8-10 in (20-25 cm) high, side-dress with a nitrogen-rich fertilizer — 2 lb (900 g) of ammonium nitrate per 100 ft (30 m) is adequate. Yellowing leaves is a signal that this fertilizer-hungry crop needs an additional nitrogen side-dressing. Hoe out weeds until the corn is about knee high, then apply a layer 3 4 in (7.5 10 cm) thick of an organic mulch.

Mulch summer lettuces to keep soil cool and prolong the harvest. Gather leaves in early morning, when they are still crisp and moist. Make your last sowings of carrots and beans, using these warm-weather vegetables to fill vacant gaps left by spring crops.

PLANT OF THE MONTH

Peonies are among the most beautifully formed of all garden flowers; their satiny petals provide rich shades of red and pink, or soft creams and white, often with a prominent group of golden stamens in the center. Blooming from spring into early summer, these plants continue to be attractive long after the flowers fade, as the leaves remain very decorative until cut down by frost. Choose from the wide range of single, semidouble, and double hybrids of *Paeonia lactiflora*, or select crimson, white, or yellowish cultivars of that old-fashioned favorite *Paeonia officinalis*.

Other early-summer flowers are wide-ranging — herbaceous perennials and old-fashioned roses being the most prominent. Columbines, campanulas, delphiniums, and geraniums provide a wealth of blue and purple flowers and heights from just a few inches to 5 ft (1.5 m) or more. Dicentras, erigerons, and lupines add pink and white flowers to the early-summer scene, while hypericums and California poppies are valued for their hotter shades of orange and yellow.

MIDSUMMER

With perennials and annuals in full bloom and the sun at its hottest, watering is often the most important task.

During the midst of summer, midday temperatures may rise over 100°F (38°C) throughout much of the United States. The intense sunlight greatly increases plants' need for water. A week or two of rainless weather might pass unnoticed in the spring but can be serious now unless you are conscientious about irrigation.

This time of year regularly brings prolonged drought to California and much of the upper West. In the Southwest, midsummer brings monsoon rains that are intense but brief, and though moisture remains in the subsoil to nourish deep-rooted desert trees and shrubs, it soon evaporates out of the topsoil and thus is of little lasting benefit to shallow-rooted ornamental plantings. Throughout most of the West, in fact, the garden's survival depends on regular irrigation in this season, unless you have native species or plants from similarly dry regions. With these plants, you can simply allow the garden to go semidormant until the return of cooler weather.

In the eastern half of the country, midsummer tends to bring not only heat, but humidity as well. This combination is ideal for the spread of plant diseases,

LAWN MAINTENANCE

To keep the lawn green during prolonged dry weather, water it thoroughly once every 7 to 10 days in the early morning — more frequent shallow watering promotes turf diseases. Apply 1 in (2.5 cm) of water per irrigation, wetting the soil 6-12 in (15-30 cm) deep.

Cool-season grasses such as Kentucky bluegrass, perennial ryegrasses, and turf-type tall fescues may go semidormant in the heat of midsummer, so they require only infrequent mowing. But warm-season grasses thrive on heat if given adequate irrigation. Mow these lawns weekly to keep them in shape.

▼ **Midsummer glory** An annual kaleidoscope of vivid color includes red poppies, magenta-pink silene, golden rudbeckias, yellow chrysanthemums, blue echiums and cornflowers, and indigo larkspurs.

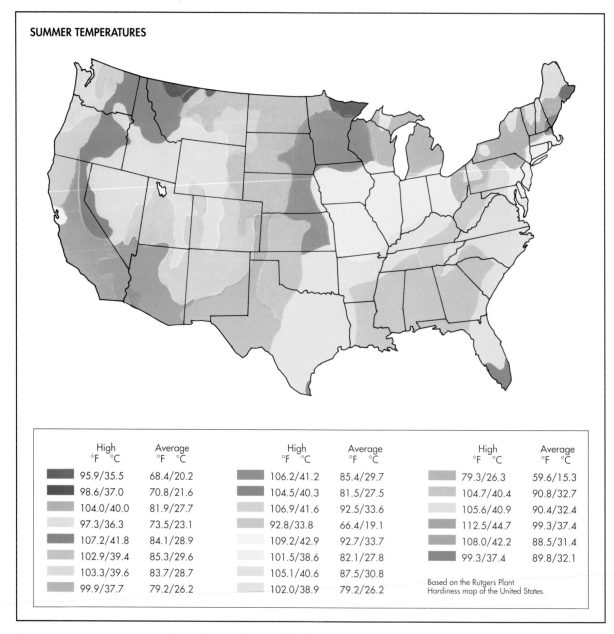

SUMMER TEMPERATURES

	High °F °C	Average °F °C		High °F °C	Average °F °C		High °F °C	Average °F °C
	95.9/35.5	68.4/20.2		106.2/41.2	85.4/29.7		79.3/26.3	59.6/15.3
	98.6/37.0	70.8/21.6		104.5/40.3	81.5/27.5		104.7/40.4	90.8/32.7
	104.0/40.0	81.9/27.7		106.9/41.6	92.5/33.6		105.6/40.9	90.4/32.4
	97.3/36.3	73.5/23.1		92.8/33.8	66.4/19.1		112.5/44.7	99.3/37.4
	107.2/41.8	84.1/28.9		109.2/42.9	92.7/33.7		108.0/42.2	88.5/31.4
	102.9/39.4	85.3/29.6		101.5/38.6	82.1/27.8		99.3/37.4	89.8/32.1
	103.3/39.6	83.7/28.7		105.1/40.6	87.5/30.8			
	99.9/37.7	79.2/26.2		102.0/38.9	79.2/26.2			

Based on the Rutgers Plant Hardiness map of the United States.

Summer temperatures Many gardeners choose plants based on the winter hardiness information provided by the USDA zone map. However, especially in warmer climates, summer heat may pose an equally serious challenge to plants, even those rated hardy in their USDA zone. This map gives both the average and maximum summer temperatures throughout the country. Identify the temperatures in your zone; then, before buying a new plant, consult your local Cooperative Extension service or a nurseryman to ensure that your purchase will be hardy in both winter and summer in your garden.

particularly fungal diseases. Indeed, in the central South and the Southeast, this season, not winter, is the true test of a plant's adaptation to the local climate.

Fungicides, applied as dusts or sprays, fight the spread of harmful fungi. Apply them at the first sign of infection; they are not effective if the disease has become well established in the plant.

You should always try preventive measures first. Speak with your local nursery or county Cooperative Extension agent to make sure a plant is adapted to your local climate before incorporating it into your landscape. And if your area is humid, make sure that your soil drains well, so that excess moisture doesn't collect around the plants. Also ensure good air circulation through your property. Don't surround the garden with high fences or hedges that create pockets of still air. Your plants will benefit from regular breezes, however slight.

Beds and borders
In very dry weather, water liberally to extend the flowering sea-son, but do not give so much water that leaf growth is encouraged at the expense of flowers. It is better to give a lot of water once or twice a week than a small amount every day. The latter method encourages the roots to grow toward the surface, where they dry out more quickly and find fewer nutrients.

Give support to taller-growing plants well before they show signs of flopping over. Continue to tie upright plants to their stakes or supports as they grow. Also check that the lower ties are not strangling the stems, which will have thickened by now.

Examine annuals and other border plants for infestations of aphids and other sap-sucking insects, and spray with a recommended insecticide if necessary. Hoe regularly to control weeds.

Biennials In the North, you may still sow wallflowers and sweet Williams in midsummer if you plant them directly in the spot where they are to flower the following year. In the South, this task is best delayed until fall.

The biennials that were previously started in seed flats or outdoor seedbeds should be planted out in a nursery bed now, as soon as they are large enough for you to handle them easily.

Annuals and perennials Deadhead all plants as soon as the flowers fade, unless you are saving the seed heads for their decorative value or you want to collect the seeds for sowing next year.

Continue cutting back early-flowering border perennials. Some kinds, such as the hybrid achilleas and *Salvia × superba*, will produce a second flush of flowers by late summer if they are cut back quite severely just before the main flowering is over. In temperate regions such as the Pacific Northwest, delphiniums and lupines may also flower again if cut down to ground level. However, don't cut back herbaceous peonies; just remove the dead flower heads.

Bulbs and corms Lift and store tulips if you have not already done so in early summer.

Plant your fall-flowering bulbs now. The best-known of these are autumn crocuses (*Colchicum* spp.), but winter daffodils *(Sternbergia lutea)* are a good choice up to zone 7, and fall-flowering crocuses such as *Crocus longiflorus* thrive as far north as zone 5.

Order spring-flowering bulbs as soon as possible — daffodils in particular benefit from early-fall planting. Order lily bulbs now, because they too are best planted in fall — in fact, as soon as you receive them in the mail.

If dahlias are growing too slowly (they should be about 2 ft/60 cm tall by the middle of summer), feed them every 2 weeks with liquid fertilizer.

At the beginning of midsummer, dig up and divide dwarf and intermediate bearded irises if they have been undisturbed for 3 years or they have formed a crowded clump of foliage.

When replanting bearded irises, cut the best single rhizomes from the old clumps. Place them in sunny sites in organically amended soil. Leave the tops of the rhizomes above ground level, and press the soil firmly on the roots; keeping rhizomes high and dry wards off bacterial and fungal diseases. After planting, cut off the upper leaves.

Roses
Cut blooms for display and deadhead spent flowers to encourage strong new shoots to grow in the directions you want and to help the next flush of blooms on repeat-flowering plants.

When cutting blooms from newly planted roses, remove only one-third of the flowering stem. Roses need all their leaves to produce enough food for subsequent flowers. Deadhead back to a compound leaf — a leaf stem that bears five or more leaflets — and one on the outside of the cane.

As soon as the first bloom is over, feed the plants with a specially formulated rose fertilizer. Spraying for fungal diseases is also especially important now.

Shrubs and trees
After flowering, prune deciduous shrubs such as *Philadelphus*.

Take cuttings of *Buddleia alternifolia, Callicarpa, Campsis,* cistus, clematis, cotoneaster, deutzia, euonymus, *Hydrangea paniculata, H. petiolaris,* mahonia, spirea, and viburnum. Root these cuttings in a cold frame.

Root cuttings of camellia, elaeagnus, honeysuckle *(Lonicera)*, hypericum, pyracantha, and rhus in pots under glass. Layer shoots of passionflower *(Passiflora)* and wisteria in pots of soil that you have sunk in the ground.

The fruit garden
Most of the soft fruits — berry-bearing plants — are in fruit now and will need attention after you harvest the fruit. Other fruit crops are nearing maturity.

Continue to watch for pest attacks and spray with a recommended pesticide if needed. However, if the fruit has been well protected until now against apple and pear scab, later attacks

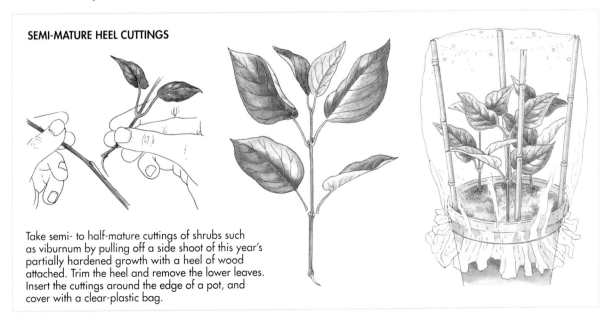

SEMI-MATURE HEEL CUTTINGS

Take semi- to half-mature cuttings of shrubs such as viburnum by pulling off a side shoot of this year's partially hardened growth with a heel of wood attached. Trim the heel and remove the lower leaves. Insert the cuttings around the edge of a pot, and cover with a clear-plastic bag.

will not harm it seriously and further spraying is unnecessary.

A low-toxicity treatment for a wide range of insect pests is provided by the new, super-refined horticultural oils, which are derived from petroleum distillates or vegetable oils. These kill on contact and have little residual toxicity. They provide excellent control of aphids, spider mites, scales, psyllas, mealybugs, and caterpillars. When using these pesticides, shake sprayers repeatedly during application to ensure that the oil does not separate from the water with which it is mixed for application. Apply when the weather is still and dry, and when the temperature is not higher than 90°F (32°C).

Complete the thinning of apple and pear fruit as soon as the fruit has stopped falling naturally, reducing the number of fruits to one from each cluster, with a final spacing of 4-6 in (10-15 cm). Support heavily laden branches of trained apples, pears, and other top fruit, either by staking each branch individually or by tying the branches to a center post.

Summer-prune espaliered apples and pears, beginning with pear trees because they are ready before the apples. Spread the task of pruning over the next 8 weeks. While working on trained trees, check that the ties are not cutting into stems and branches.

As soon as you have picked damsons and other plums, prune the trees. Continue to tie in new growths that you intend to keep as replacements on espaliered peaches and nectarines.

Fertilize cherry trees as soon as the harvest ends, using a balanced, slow-release organic fertilizer. Take care with high-nitrogen fertilizer (nitrogen content is indicated by the first of the three numbers on the fertilizer label: e.g., 20–10–10). Excessive doses of nitrogen promote the growth of new wood and leaves at the expense of the next year's fruit.

Pick raspberries as they ripen. Irrigation during periods of drought is crucial to the quality of the fruit — berry bushes need 1 in (2.5 cm) of water a week, and even more during hot, dry spells.

Once all the fruit has been harvested, cut off the old canes close to the ground. This procedure will leave room for the new growths, which will carry next

PLANT OF THE MONTH

Sweet peas (*Lathyrus odoratus* cultivars) come in a wide range of colors, including pastel and vivid shades, except yellows and oranges. The most familiar types climb to 5-10 ft (1.5-3 m). But for a small garden, the dwarf bushy types are ideal and need no support. 'Bijou Hybrids' are an early-flowering mixture, reaching 1½ ft (45 cm) high. **Other midsummer flowers** suitable for growing in association with dwarf sweet peas include cornflower (*Centaurea*), godetia, larkspur (*Consolida orientalis*), lavatera, petunia, and verbena.

year's crop. Tie new growths to supporting wires.

Train in the new shoots of blackberries and loganberries, keeping them separate from the fruiting shoots. Be sure to water these bushes well, especially during dry weather.

Pick black currants and gooseberries as they ripen. Prune the bushes after picking if necessary, leaving the more robust new shoots intact.

Tidy strawberry beds after you have harvested all the fruit. Don't leave remnants of berries on the plant, because they will encourage plant rot. Remove runners — unless you want them to produce more plants. Apply a side-dressing of manure tea: put a bucketful of fresh manure in a barrel of water and use 1 cup (250 ml) per plant. Or apply a 5–10–10 granular fertilizer at a rate of 2½ lb (1 kg) per 100 ft (30 m) of row.

The vegetable garden

In the North, sow the seeds of cabbages, brussels sprouts, and broccoli in a nursery bed or indoors in plastic seed flats; they can be planted out as fall crops in late summer. These plants are heat and drought sensitive, so be sure to keep the seedlings well watered, but not soaked.

Sow peas now for a fall crop. Setting the seed 2 in (5 cm) deep will protect it against dehydration. In warm-weather regions sow winter radishes now for a late-fall and winter harvest.

Pinch the side shoots that grow from the leaf axils of tomato plants that you are growing on stakes or a trellis. Do not pinch side shoots from unsupported bush tomatoes, but cover the ground beneath them with straw or black plastic to prevent the fruits from coming into direct contact with the ground.

Sweet corn is ready to harvest when the husks are dark green and the silks are brown but not brittle. If you wait to harvest until the husks turn yellow, you will end up with tough, starchy ears of corn.

LATE SUMMER

Watering, lawn mowing, and deadheading continue to be important tasks, and there are plenty of crops to harvest.

LAWN MAINTENANCE

Continue to mow regularly, trim edges, and water well once every 7 to 10 days during drought.
In the North and West, selective herbicides may be applied once the temperature drops below 80°F (27°C). Resume weed control. Sow cool-season grass seed.
In the South, warm-season grasses are still in active growth and should now be fertilized for the last time.

The weather in late summer usually follows the same trends as in midsummer. Late afternoon and evening thunderstorms keep precipitation relatively high in the desert Southwest, although heat and brilliant sunshine cause topsoil to dry quickly. Along the coast of southern California and in the central West there is little rainfall; this season brings the driest, clearest weather of the year.

In general, temperatures are moderating somewhat from their midsummer peaks. The nights lengthen considerably by late summer, and night temperatures drop. Dewfall can be heavy, and this aggravates plant disease problems. However, dry, cool, clear nights may also occur. In the northern regions of New England, the Midwest, and the Rocky Mountain states, night temperatures can occasionally approach freezing in sheltered valleys.

The last weeks of summer often bring high winds — on the Atlantic Coast this is the beginning of the hurricane season — so check that plants are securely attached to stakes or other supports. Repair gaps in hedges and fences, so that the garden is protected from wind damage.

Throughout most of the western half of the country (with the exception of the Pacific Northwest) rainfall during late summer rarely supplies all the water the garden needs, so regular watering is necessary — especially with shallow-rooted plants, such as bedding annuals and vegetables. Unshaded gardens with a south-facing aspect are most vulnerable to the effects of low rainfall.

Beds and borders

Continue deadheading annuals to keep them tidy and encourage more flowers. However, perennials flowering after midsummer are unlikely to flower a second time if cut back. Remember that the dead flowers may develop into attractive seed heads and that tufts of bare, cut stalks can look unsightly, so you might wish to leave the plants alone.

After tall plants have finished flowering, deadhead them, cut off any tall weak stems, and then remove the stakes or other supports if they are too obtrusive. The remaining stems should be strong enough to support themselves.

▼ **Late-summer borders** The huge straw-colored flower sprays of feather grass *(Stipa gigantea)* are the focal point in this herbaceous border, which is backed by dark green foliage. The sprays sway above orange Turk's cap lilies and border phlox, monarda, and liatris, whose range of pinks and contrasting flower forms are highlighted by white Shasta daisies *(Chrysanthemum x superba).*

Continue to guard perennials and annuals against fungal diseases such as mildew and insect pests such as aphids, spraying with recommended fungicides and pesticides if necessary. Asters, calendulas, dahlias, petunias, goldenrods, and sweet peas are particularly susceptible.

Mulch and, if necessary, fertilize and water sweet peas to extend flowering over a longer period. If you do not apply a new mulch, hoe between plants to eliminate competing weeds. Cut sweet pea blooms regularly — they last well in water indoors. Never allow blooms to fade and droop on the plants or to form seedpods; otherwise the flowering period will be drastically reduced.

Dig over any neglected beds and borders before the end of summer, hoeing off or turning over all annual weeds while the sun is still warm, so that they die rapidly. Pull up by hand or fork out any perennial weeds, trying to leave as few of their roots in the ground as possible — this is easier when the soil is moist. Cut back plants that have outgrown their space, even if this means sacrificing the remaining flowers.

Plant out well-grown perennial seedlings raised in cold frames or under lights indoors. They should be moved to a nursery bed where they will get good light and plenty of space — not to their final sites, which may be cramped at this time of year. The young plants will be ready for moving again, to their final positions, during fall or next spring.

Chrysanthemums Before the third week of late summer, complete the disbudding of those outdoor chrysanthemums that are grown for cut flowers and should have single-stemmed, extra-large blooms. Fertilize periodically with a liquid feed, but discontinue the application once the buds show color. Keep the plants well supported to allow for the increasing weight of the flowering stems.

Bulbs, corms, and tubers Plant Madonna lilies (*Lilium candidum*) as soon as possible, with not more than 1 in (2.5 cm) of soil above each bulb.

Feed dahlias with liquid fertilizer, and keep the plants carefully tied to avoid wind damage. Continue to spray dahlias as necessary against aphids, and watch for damage to buds, flower parts,

PROPAGATING LILIES FROM BULBLETS

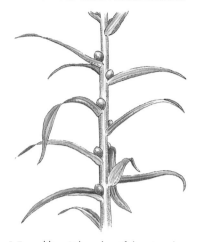

1 Tiger lilies (*Lilium lancifolium*) and some hybrid lilies produce bulblets (small bulbs) on their stems, nestling in the axils of the leaves. Gather the dark-colored bulblets when they fall easily at a touch.

2 Plant the bulblets about 2 in (5 cm) apart in a deep seed flat filled with a well-drained potting soil. Either cover the bulblets with ½ in (12 mm) of soil or just press them into the surface with your fingertips.

and leaves. Distorted growth and browning buds, flower parts, and leaves are symptoms of the European corn borer — a pest that if not controlled with such pesticides as rotenene, will bore into stems, killing plants.

Cut gladioli for indoor display when the first flower on the spike is just opening. Leave at least four leaves when cutting, otherwise the new corm developing from the old one for next year's flowers will be deprived of its source of nourishment.

Rock gardens
Take cuttings of rock garden plants that are becoming straggly with age or are producing too few flowers — such as helianthemums, alpine pinks (*Dianthus*), achilleas, alpine saxifrages, and most of the shrubby plants. All these should have finished blooming in late summer.

A shaded cold frame or even the top cut off a 2 qt (2 lit) plastic soft-drink bottle will provide enough winter protection. (Don't put rock plant cuttings in a greenhouse unless you have a mist propagation unit.) Dig the soil well, reducing it to a fine tilth, and lighten heavy soil by mixing in sand. Spread a surface layer of sharp builder's sand to help improve drainage.

There are four main types of alpine cuttings, as follows:
❏ Tip cuttings are made from the top section of nonflowering shoots, cut off cleanly just below a leaf node. The length of these cuttings will vary from 1½ in (4 cm) to 3 in (7.5 cm), depending on the plant's growth habit. Trim leaves from the lower half with a sharp knife.
❏ For heel cuttings, pull off short growths from a larger branch. Torn gently downward, they will come away with a little tailpiece or heel. Pare away any ragged wood and trim the leaves from the lower half of the shoot before putting it in soil.
❏ Basal cuttings are made by severing shoots at, or just below, ground level. These need little trimming and may already show traces of new roots.
❏ Root cuttings are pieces of fleshy root taken while the plant is dormant. Prepare them by cutting the roots into sections about 2 in (5 cm) long.

Roses
Continue to remove blooms as they fade. Do not apply rose fertilizers after the end of midsummer, because they encourage late, soft growth that will not harden before the first frost.

If aphids appear on the roses' shoots or flower buds, spray them with insecticidal soap or a horticultural oil; if the infestation persists, use a systemic insecticide. Also, if black spot, mildew, or rust appears in your garden, continue to spray regularly with a recommended rose fungicide.

TAKING ROCK PLANT CUTTINGS

2 Insert the lower halves of tip, heel, and basal cuttings in sandy soil in small holes made with a dibble *(above)* or pointed stick. Firm in the cuttings gently with your fingers. Level the surface of the bed, and water thoroughly.

1 The four types of material used for propagating rock plants are tip cuttings, heel cuttings, basal cuttings, and root cuttings. Root the cuttings in a cold frame, under soft-drink bottle tops, or in a miniature commercial "greenhouse."

3 Cuttings need protection from dehydration while rooting; spray them daily with water during hot weather. Remove the bottle tops or mini-greenhouse *(above)* when new growth indicates that the cuttings are rooting.

screened peat moss. Leave them until the following late spring.

In a greenhouse, porch, or cold frame root semi-mature cuttings, 4-6 in (10-15 cm) long, from the current year's growth of bay *(Laurus nobilis), Buddleia davidii,* caryopteris, fuchsia, hebe, holly *(Ilex),* ivy *(Hedera),* lilac *(Syringa),* pernettya, pieris, senecio, and skimmia. Take half-mature heel cuttings, 3-4 in (7.5-10 cm) long, of broom *(Cytisus),* ceanothus, and genista.

Propagate rhododendrons and azaleas in late summer by layering them *in situ*. The pinned-down shoots should be growing on their own roots after 2 to 3 years, when they can be severed from the parent and planted out.

Continue to trim all fast-growing hedges, such as privet and *Lonicera nitida*. Remove weeds growing at the base of a hedge.

The fruit garden

Early apple varieties are beginning to ripen in late summer, and most berries come to an end. Protect ripening fruit from birds by netting the trees, and lure wasps away from the trees with traps consisting of a spoonful of jam mixed with water in a glass jar. Protect late-fruiting raspberries from attack by birds by covering the canes with fine-mesh netting.

Watch early-maturing apples and pears carefully, and pick them while slightly underripe —

Shrubs and trees

Prune shrubs that have just finished flowering by shortening the flowering shoots and thinning out old and weak wood. Shrubs needing this treatment include evergreen ceanothus, escallonia, lavender *(Lavandula),* senecio, and deciduous species of honeysuckle *(Lonicera)*.

Well-established, vigorous wisteria may need cutting back. To contain growth, take out the tips of young shoots after they have made three or four leaves.

If not already carried out in midsummer, take cuttings of callicarpa, cistus, cotinus, escallonia, euonymus, honeysuckle, hypericum, *Jasminum officinale,* pyracantha, spirea, and viburnum. Root them in a cold frame or some other protected spot, such as a cool but frost-free glass-enclosed porch, in pots filled with a rooting mixture of sand and

RIPENING SQUASHES

To assist the ripening of winter squashes and other fruits for storage in fall, rest them on platforms of glass or wood, supported on bricks. This will raise the fruits above the leaves, where they will get more sun.

PLANT OF THE MONTH

Hardy fuchsias (*Fuchsia magellanica* cvs.) flower for a long period, beginning in midsummer and continuing right through until the first hard frost of fall, but they are especially showy in late summer. Growing up to 8 ft (2.5 m) tall with age, they can be used for informal hedging or as specimens in a mixed border or shrubbery. The cultivar 'Riccartoni' bears slender scarlet-and-purple flowers and, in a protected spot, can overwinter as far north as New York City.

Other late-summer flowers that make good partners for fuchsias include the shrubby blue, mauve, red, or white hibiscuses; pink, blue, or white hydrangeas; and cheery bright yellow hypericums.

Among the colorful range of herbaceous perennials and bedding annuals still in the garden are dahlias, white Shasta daisies (*Chrysanthemum* x *superba*), golden rudbeckias, orange or yellow African marigolds (*Tagetes erecta*), red or pink nicotianas, and pink, mauve, or purple petunias. Blue agapanthus and white summer hyacinth (*Galtonia*) are real gems.

they retain their best flavor for only a short period. Fruits are nearly ripe when you can easily part them from the spur.

Continue to prune espaliered apple and pear trees as in midsummer. Complete summer pruning of damsons and other plums.

Take care to remove windfall apples, as they may harbor apple maggot larvae, which will crawl from the fruit down into the soil and overwinter to emerge as adult flies the next spring.

When the fruit from wall-trained peaches, nectarines, and sour pie cherries has been picked, prune the shoots that have borne fruit, leaving the current season's growth to replace them. Retie new shoots where necessary to make the best use of space and to encourage the growth to ripen.

Pick blackberries, loganberries, and hybrid berries. Continue to train new shoots. When harvesting has finished, cut out all shoots that have fruited.

The leaves of black currant bushes continue to feed the present season's shoots. Control leaf spot and rust by spraying with mancozeb, benomyl, or carbendazim after fruit picking is over.

Plant rooted strawberry runners in late summer to ensure a good crop the following year. Runners rooted in pots in early summer are the most successful.

The vegetable garden
Sow seeds of spring cabbage, first checking soil pH and raising with lime as necessary as a precaution against clubroot (for a more complete discussion of this disease, see page 134). Make the seedbed in ground that has not been composted since the previous fall. Until the middle of late summer, sow 'All Year Round' lettuces for cutting in early winter.

Harvest self-blanching celery when there are sizable plants. Clear this crop before the first hard frost.

Herbs Every 4 years, chives should be divided in late summer. Lift the clumps and cut them into segments with a sharp knife, taking care that each segment retains a number of roots. Replant the clumps 1 ft (30 cm) apart.

Take cuttings of bay, hyssop, lavender, mint, rosemary, rue, and sage. Insert the cuttings in well-drained soil in open ground. For the first 2 weeks, until the roots have formed, protect the cuttings with a covering, and water them in the evenings. Alternatively, put the cuttings in pots filled with sand and place them in a cold frame.

Collect and dry the seeds of dill and fennel. Cut and prepare herbs grown for foliage that you will be drying. Store dried herbs quickly, before they reabsorb moisture from the air. Rub them between your hands, discarding stems and other chaff, and store the remaining leaves in tightly sealed containers.

EARLY FALL

As fruit is harvested and dahlias and chrysanthemums blaze with color, shortening days signal the onset of fall.

As the last days of summer draw to a close and the sun's rays weaken, temperatures fall, especially at night. In the Northeast and Northwest, where cooler temperatures may be accompanied by continued humidity, this brings increased problems with mildew. In the Southeast and central South, more moderate temperatures and the end of summer droughts start a whole new growing season and the best opportunity for cultivating traditional "spring crops." In the arid West, early fall brings relief from summer's torrid highs and begins the most temperate weather of the year. Early fall also brings opportunity in the desert Southwest — moisture from summer storms remains deep in the earth and can

be bolstered with irrigation to start the flowers and vegetables that will furnish the harvests of winter and early spring.

North of zone 7, inland gardeners must watch for early-morning frost. Because cold air flows downhill, this is especially common in the bottom of valleys and sheltered pockets, even when surrounding hillsides and higher slopes remain well above freezing. Keep old covers handy to drape over annual beds if a light overnight frost is forecast — this may prolong the flowers' display by several weeks.

In the eastern half of the country, fall can bring gales with strong winds as well as rain. To protect plants from wind damage, check that stakes and ties are secure.

LAWN MAINTENANCE

In the North, early fall is the best time to fertilize cool-season grasses. This promotes stronger growth through the rest of the fall and helps turf get off to a quick start in the spring. Use a turf fertilizer designed for fall application; excessive nitrogen now will encourage fungal diseases during the cold weather.

The warm days and cool nights also make this a good season for sowing seed or laying new sod. **In the South,** this is the best time to sow cool-season grasses. **In the West,** this is an excellent time to aerate the lawn; this treatment reduces water waste during irrigation and discourages fungal diseases. Fertilize cool-season grasses as in the North.

▼ **Early-fall blaze** A multitude of dahlias, in their numerous different shapes and colors, jostle for space with brown-eyed, golden orange rudbeckias and a cascade of mauve-cerise New York asters *(Aster novi-belgii)*. In the left foreground, snapdragons *(Antirrhinum)* add their bright red spires.

REPAIRING A LAWN

1 In early fall, repair damaged patches in the lawn by reseeding. Use a half-moon edging tool to cut round the damaged area, and lift out the turf carefully with a spade. Loosen the soil beneath with a garden fork.

2 Fill the hole with a thin layer of screened topsoil, and tamp gently. Repeat in layers until the surface of the soil in the patch is at the same level as the surrounding turf. Sow seed at the rate of 1½-2 oz (40-60 g) per sq yd/m.

3 Gently sift a mixture of soil and compost over the seed to a depth of ½ in (12 mm). To protect the bed from birds, stick short pegs in the grass around the patch and crisscross black thread between them.

Beds and borders

For the first 2 to 3 weeks, continue deadheading and cutting back. Hoe new beds prepared in midsummer or late summer, particularly if deep digging was followed soon afterward by rain.

Continue to harden off rooted cuttings of garden pinks *(Dianthus)*. Plant them out when they are growing strongly. At the end of early fall, pinch back pinks that start to run to flower without making good side shoots. Do this in early morning during damp weather, when the tops snap off most easily.

Continue frequent watering of plants in containers, and remove faded flowers. Discard plants that are past their best, and prepare the empty containers for spring bulbs. Replenish the potting soil, and plant spring bulbs slightly deeper than normal, so that you can place plants for winter color on top. Store indoors any empty wooden containers that will not be used during the winter.

Annuals Remove fading annuals to make room for spring bedding plants. In mild-winter regions such as zone 8, directly sow the hardiest of the annuals — such as calendula, cornflower *(Centaurea)*, and candytuft *(Iberis)* — to overwinter outdoors. Plants that are 2-3 in (5-7.5 cm) high by midwinter stand the best chance of coming through harsh weather. In zone 9 and southward, where summer heat may have killed annuals planted in spring, replant now to begin a second and even more glorious season of bloom. Most hardy and half-hardy annuals flourish best in the cooler weather of wintertime here.

Biennials Water hardy biennials growing in a nursery bed, then plant them out in their flowering sites the next day. Water the ground thoroughly beforehand. Dig planting holes with a trowel, set in the plants, and water them generously around their roots.

Chrysanthemums Outdoor types are now in full flower. Label the best for next year's stock. Cut fully open blooms for display.

Bulbs and tubers Plant bulbs, preferably in groups, amid shrubs or perennials, in rock gardens, and in lawns. A general rule of thumb is to bury a bulb twice as deep as its height. For instance, plant a 2 in (5 cm) tall daffodil bulb 4 in (10 cm) deep.

Pot up bulbs for indoor flowering during winter and spring.

ROSE CUTTINGS

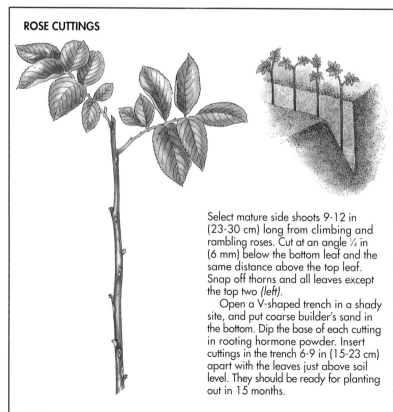

Select mature side shoots 9-12 in (23-30 cm) long from climbing and rambling roses. Cut at an angle ¼ in (6 mm) below the bottom leaf and the same distance above the top leaf. Snap off thorns and all leaves except the top two *(left)*.

Open a V-shaped trench in a shady site, and put coarse builder's sand in the bottom. Dip the base of each cutting in rooting hormone powder. Insert cuttings in the trench 6-9 in (15-23 cm) apart with the leaves just above soil level. They should be ready for planting out in 15 months.

BULB PLANTERS

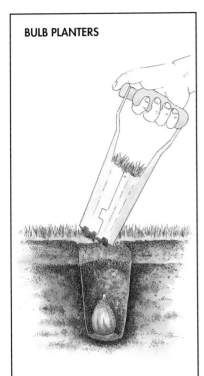

Planters save time and effort when you are setting out large numbers of bulbs. They are particularly useful for planting bulbs in grass and among other plants, where it is important to disturb the soil as little as possible.

Holding the planter by the handle, push the metal cylinder firmly into the soil. Withdraw the planter, which automatically brings the plug of soil with it. Place the bulb in the hole, and replace the plug of soil by pressing the release catch on the tool's handle.

Toward the end of early fall, use bulbs to replace unattractive summer beds. Plant the bulbs on their own, or between wallflowers, forget-me-nots, and polyanthuses.

With dahlias, check stakes and ties to prevent windstorm damage. Use a liquid fertilizer every second week to maintain good-quality blooms and build up strong tubers.

Roses

Continue to deadhead faded blooms. On weak plants, cut the stem above the first leaf; on vigorous plants cut off faded blooms with one or two leaves.

Disbud hybrid teas to maintain the blooms' quality. To harden new growth before the first frost, feed by scattering wood ashes over the beds at a rate of two handfuls per sq yd/m, leaving bare a 6 in (15 cm) circle around each bush. Scratch the ashes into the surface with a garden rake.

Bend and tie in shoots of climbers to form a fan shape. This will encourage the sprouting of new side shoots, which will bear flowers. Make sure the ties are tight enough to hold the stems in place, but loose enough to allow for thickening of the stems.

Prune climbing and rambling roses that have only one flush of blooms, as well as weeping standards, removing old growth that has flowered during the preceding summer. Also take cuttings from strong side shoots of mature wood. Floribundas and hybrid teas can sometimes be propagated successfully in the same way.

Spray regularly against mildew and black spot — the cool, moist conditions common in northern falls encourage the latter.

Shrubs and trees

At the beginning of early fall, dig the ground thoroughly in preparation for planting trees and shrubs later on. Incorporate plenty of garden compost or well-rotted manure into the soil rather than quick-acting fertilizers.

Plant evergreens, preferably during drizzly weather, at the end of early fall. Support upright shrubs with stakes until they are established. During dry spells, water freely and spray foliage with water to prevent leaf drop.

Propagate barberry, juniper, phlomis, potentilla, privet, and yew from hardwood and half-mature heel cuttings. Root in sandy soil in a shaded cold frame or in sheltered, shady, open ground. In cold weather, cover cuttings in open ground with tunnels of clear plastic or the tops that you cut from clear plastic soft-drink bottles. Hardy species should be ready to plant out the following spring; pot tender or semihardy species before winter and keep in the cold frame or on a cool windowsill before planting out in late spring.

Late-flowering shrubs, such as phlomis and stewartia, need light pruning after flowering.

Hedges Clip new growth for the

HARVESTING PEARS

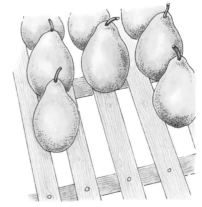

1 Harvest pears before they are fully ripe, when the color is changing from green to yellow. Fruits left on the tree too long become dry and floury. To harvest a piece of fruit, place one hand under it and twist it gently.

2 The stalk should part from the spur easily. If the stalk is left attached to the tree, the fruit will not store well. If the stalk brings some leaves with it, it is not mature enough and will fail to ripen in storage.

3 Arrange harvested pears on clean slatted racks in a dry, moderately warm atmosphere. Do not let the pears touch one another. Fruit that is to be stored for a long time should be blemish free and not too large.

PLANT OF THE MONTH

Sedums have dense, often flattened, heads of flowers, which can almost completely cover the attractive fleshy foliage. The most familiar colors for fall-flowering sedums are shades of pink, purple, and red.

Sedum spectabile 'Carmen' *(above)*, recently reclassified as *Hylotelephium spectabile*, is a herbaceous plant up to 1½ ft (45 cm) high with pale gray-green leaves and fluffy, bright carmine-pink flowers.

Other sedums in flower in early fall are *S.* 'Autumn Joy' with pink flower heads deepening to copper-red, and *S. maximum* with flowers in shades of red and pink. *S. maximum* 'Atropurpureum' has pink flowers and purple-red tinted leaves and stems.

Other early-fall flowers Many perennials are still in full bloom at this time of year. Some selections that you can try as partners for sedums are New York asters with starry flowers in shades of blue, purple, pink, red, or lilac, or African lilies *(Agapanthus)*, with long-stemmed, rounded clusters of funnel-shaped flowers in shades of blue or white. Korean chrysanthemums have an enormous range of flower forms and colors, including pink, white, yellow, and orange.

Late-season red-hot pokers *(Kniphofia)* have flowers in shades of red, orange, and yellow, while goldenrod *(Solidago)* has plumes of vivid yellow flowers.

Dahlias are an important plant for early fall color. There are also bulbs, such as pink fall crocus *(Colchicum)*, white or pink *Dierama,* and deep pink *Nerine bowdenii.*

---

last time this season, but leave hedging plants that flower on new shoots in spring, such as barberry and forsythia.

Remove any remaining weeds around the base of a hedge before they set seed, and put them on the compost pile. Do not leave hoed-up weeds on the surface.

The fruit garden
Prepare storage places for apples and pears, checking that they are free of mice and that flats are clean. Pick fruit in cool conditions before it is fully ripe. Exposed fruit at the tops of trees ripens first, followed by that on the sides. Inside fruit is the last to ripen. Wrap apples in paper for long storage. Complete the pruning of apples and pears. Continue to pick peaches and nectarines, prune old shoots, and tie in new growth. Pick and use all types of plums; they do not keep well.

Continue to pick blackberries, loganberries, and hybrid berries when ripe. When harvesting is complete, cut out old growth and tie in new shoots.

Pick early-fall-fruiting raspberries. Continue to protect fall-fruiting strawberries against birds and slugs, and cover during passing frosts.

The vegetable garden
Sow lettuce in a cool spot indoors to plant out as a fall crop. In the South this is the best time of year to start salad greens; these cool-loving crops will often continue to produce right through the winter. This is also the time to sow brussels sprouts, broccoli, cauliflower, and cabbages in the South. Sow carrot seed on ground that was dug and fertilized for the previous crop; protect with cloches.

Harvest squashes for immediate use. If they are to be stored for use during the winter, leave them on the plants until midfall.

In moderate regions, such as zone 7, cover crops with clear-plastic tunnels. This extends the harvests of cool-loving crops such as lettuce or spinach into late fall, and of truly cold-hardy plants, such as kale, right into winter.

Herbs In zone 8 and south, sow parsley and chervil for a spring crop. Take cuttings of bay and rue, and root them in a frost-free, protected spot.

MIDFALL

Make the most of good weather to dig the ground, clear fallen leaves and fading annuals, and divide perennials.

Throughout the Southeast and central South, this is the busiest time of the gardener's year, as the winter flowers and vegetables begin to take root. In the Southwest, seeds sown a few weeks previously start to sprout and demand care. In southern California the November rains begin a new growing season.

In the North, however, midfall is a time for gardeners to enjoy nature's spontaneous displays.

The blazing foliage colors of deciduous trees and shrubs are the garden's main ornament now; across much of the central states winter is setting in as plants retreat into dormancy.

Like spring, midfall is an unpredictable season in the North. It brings many clear, golden days. But these pleasant spells can change in a matter of hours to tempests. Nights are likely to be foggy, and if clear they are often

LAWN MAINTENANCE

Apply fall fertilizer to all lawns. To improve drainage in areas prone to flooding or waterlogging — particularly where heavy soil has become compacted — use a hollow-tined fork to open up the surface, making holes about 4 in (10 cm) deep and 2-3 in (5-7.5 cm) apart. Apply a good quantity of sharp builder's sand and gypsum, working them thoroughly into the surface of the turf. Try to avoid walking on the lawn during wet weather.

Lay turf in midfall to give the grass time to root before winter. Prepare a weed-free turf bed in advance, and allow it to settle for a few weeks. Apply fertilizer at the rate of 2½ oz (70 g) per sq yd/m and lightly rake it into the surface before laying the turf.

quite cold. So during good weather, try to do your fall digging. Soil dug over now benefits from winter frosts and will break down in time for spring planting. Rake up fallen leaves and stack them in a heap until they have decomposed into leaf mold.

Beds and borders

In all but extremely cold regions (zones 1 to 4) midfall is the best time for planting most herbaceous perennials; the only exception is northern gardens with heavy, wet soils. Especially in the South, planting now allows plants to sink their roots well into the soil before summer, where they find moisture during droughts. When it is wet, however, lay short planks over the beds and step only on these. Also, plant out hardy perennials raised from seed.

Clean up beds and borders, but cut back faded growth only if it looks unsightly. Continue deadheading, and keep down seedling weeds by hoeing in dry weather.

Divide and replant herbaceous perennial clumps that flowered in early summer, but leave soft-leaved types such as pyrethrum and achillea until early spring.

◀ **Fall tints** The flame-colored foliage of a Virginia creeper (*Parthenocissus quinquefolia*) trails above the small golden and red leaves of a deciduous barberry (*Berberis*). On the right, the sweet gum (*Liquidambar styraciflua*) has begun its transformation into a dome of brilliant orange and scarlet.

STORING DAHLIA TUBERS

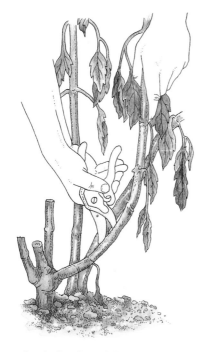

1 After the first frost, dahlia foliage becomes limp and black. When this happens, cut the stems back to 6 in (15 cm) and lift the tubers with a border fork. Stand them upside down to drain.

2 When the stems have dried out, put the tubers right side up in shallow boxes. Cover with slightly damp potting soil, keeping the crowns above the surface. Store in a dry, frost-free place.

3 For outdoor storage (zone 7 and South), place the tubers on a 3-in (7.5-cm) layer of vermiculite. Cover the tubers with more vermiculite to a depth of 3-4 in (7.5-10 cm) and then with a plastic sheet held in place with bricks.

With new beds and borders planned for planting in spring, dig the ground thoroughly.

To overhaul old beds, dig up all growth and shake the earth off the roots. Discard all but healthy plants or any divisions that are to be replanted. Then dig deeply and enrich the soil as if preparing a new bed, destroying the roots of any perennial weeds. Dig green annual weeds into the ground, upturning them and covering with at least 9 in (23 cm) of soil.
Annuals and biennials If frosts are late and the weather is mild, leave summer bedding plants such as marigolds, begonias, and pelargoniums until there are no more flowers on them. Otherwise, remove them as soon as possible.

Remove annuals to make room for biennials for spring display, such as wallflowers and forget-me-nots. Plant these while the soil is still warm. Do not add manure or chemical fertilizers to beds or borders for spring-flowering bedding plants. When planting, work bonemeal into the top 6 in (15 cm) of soil at a rate of 4 oz (100 g) per sq yd/m.

Continue sowing annuals in the South. This season may also produce a crop of "volunteers" — new plants that spring from seeds of annuals that bloomed the previous spring and summer. These will not bear blossoms as impressive as their hybrid parents but can still provide cheerful and unpredictable garden color. A distinct advantage of the self-sown seedlings is that they sprout only in favorable natural conditions and so are typically more self-sufficient than those sown by hand.
Bulbs, corms, and tubers Finish planting spring bulbs, and start planting tulips and hyacinths. Hoe beds of newly planted daffodils, except in mild areas, where shoots have begun to grow. You can also kill weed seedlings with a contact herbicide.

Lift tender summer-flowering bulbs, such as acidanthera, chincherinchee, schizostylis, and sparaxis. In cold-winter regions, move containers of amaryllises, crinums, and nerines indoors.

Place lifted bulbs in shallow boxes to dry. A few days later, separate the bulbs and corms from any debris and store them in a cool, dry, frost-free place.

Cut down dahlias to about 6 in (15 cm) above the ground as soon as the first frost blackens the plants. Lift the tubers carefully, remove as much soil as possible, and then stand them upside down in a frost-free place for about a week to allow the sap on the stems to dry out. Dust the crowns with sulfur before storing them.

Lift gladiolus corms when the leaves brown. Cut the main stem down to ½ in (12 mm), and leave the corms to dry for a week in flats in a dry, frost-free place.

Plant lilies; stake late-flowering types that are prone to wind damage. Bury the bulbs to a depth of two and a half times their height. If the soil is alkaline or very heavy, plant less deeply.

Rock gardens
Plant alpine seedlings or rooted cuttings by the third week of midfall, except for pot-grown plants, which can go in at almost any time. When moving established plants to a new site, keep plenty of soil on the roots. Protect hairy-leaved plants for winter by covering them with sheets of glass supported on wires.

Set out slug pellets or beer-traps if it is damp, particularly close to evergreen, trailing, and shrubby plants, or rough grass.

Water gardens
Toward the end of midfall, thin out underwater oxygenating plants and remove old water-lily leaves. If the water is brackish, replace half with fresh water.

While the pool is half drained, remove debris from the bottom but leave most of the mud.

Roses

Do not plant in regions north of zone 7; in zone 7, plant with care. In the South and Southwest, fall planting is preferable because it allows the new shrubs to overcome the trauma of transplanting before the stress of summer.

Prepare beds for new roses by double-digging. Incorporate plenty of organic matter, and add bonemeal at the rate of 2-4 oz (50-100 g) per sq yd/m. If the topsoil is not as deep as two lengths of the spade's blade, add more topsoil. If the soil is strongly acidic, spread a handful of lime per sq yd/m of soil.

Continue to watch for insect pests such as aphids, spraying with insecticidal soap or a recommended pesticide if their numbers increase. In areas prone to fungal diseases, continue to spray with recommended fungicides.

Shrubs and trees

Toward the end of midfall, start planting hardy deciduous shrubs and trees in dry weather in well-prepared ground. Support new trees with stakes, but leave some slack in the ties, as freedom to sway with the wind strengthens the young plants' trunks.

If bare-root plants are delivered during bad weather, unpack them and stand them in a dry shed with straw or burlap around the roots. If you cannot plant within a few weeks, insert the shrubs in a V-shaped trench. Cover the roots with soil and firm down. Leave until spring.

First fall frosts Midfall brings the first crisp layer of frost to the ground and signifies the end of the growing season. Gardeners must now finish the tasks of clearing debris from the garden, protecting tender plants and preparing beds and borders while the ground is still soft enough to be worked.

The map below gives average first frost dates throughout the U.S. Identify this date in your region, then plan your fall tasks accordingly. Local geography can also create "frost pockets" — for instance, if your garden is located in a depression, or far from the moderating influence of a large body of water.

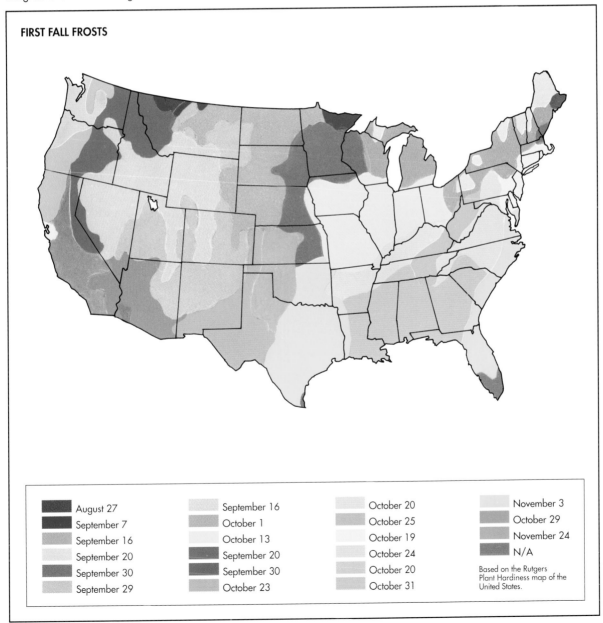

FIRST FALL FROSTS

August 27	September 16
September 7	October 1
September 16	October 13
September 20	September 20
September 30	September 30
September 29	October 23

October 20	November 3
October 25	October 29
October 19	November 24
October 24	N/A
October 20	
October 31	

Based on the Rutgers Plant Hardiness map of the United States.

When moving evergreens, spray the entire plant with an antidessicant. This coating protects against dehydration through the winter but breaks down by the next growing season. Also spray deciduous trees that have to be moved while they are still in leaf.

Take hardwood cuttings 1 ft (30 cm) long of *Aucuba japonica*, *Buddleia davidii*, deutzia, escallonia, spring-flowering honeysuckle, mock orange, spirea, tamarisk, and weigela. Root in sandy soil in a cold frame or in the open. Propagate *Daphne cneorum* and fothergilla by layering young shoots in pots of well-drained, organically enriched soil.

Separate rooted suckers of bittersweet, *Forsythia suspensa*, *Rhus typhina*, robinia, and snowberry from their parent plants. Replant in their permanent growing sites, staking where needed. Divide and replant overgrown *Euonymus fortunei* and spirea.

The fruit garden
Order fruit trees and bushes for immediate delivery and prepare the planting sites.

Inspect bases of peach, cherry, plum, and apricot trunks for holes exuding gum and "frass" (shredded wood) — symptoms of peach tree borers. To eradicate them, scrape away the grass and top few inches of soil from around tree bases, and remove gum deposits. Then encircle the trunk with a band of moth crystals: ¼ lb (115 g) for a small tree; up to 1½ lb (680 g) for a large tree. Keep moth crystals 1-3 in (2.5-7.5 cm) from the trunk, and cover with 1 ft (30 cm) of garden soil. Leave for 1 month for saplings; 6 months for mature trees.

Some varieties of apples and pears will not mature on the tree, but leave them as long as possible. After harvest, store them in closed, but not sealed, plastic bags and keep at an even temperature of 36°-39°F (2°-4°C).

Right after leaf drop, spray peach and nectarine trees with Bordeaux mixture or another approved fungicide to help to control peach leaf curl next season.

With damsons and other plums prune roots after leaf fall for any trees that regularly fruit badly. Sever vigorous roots, but leave the fibrous feeding roots intact.

With blackberries, loganberries, and hybrid berries, cut out canes that have fruited and train new shoots onto the supporting framework. Propagate gooseberries by taking 10-12 in (25-30 cm) cuttings from well-matured wood of the current season's growth.

Pick fall strawberries; protect ripening fruit with tunnels of clear plastic held on wire hoops pushed into the soil. Replant runners for fruiting next year.

The vegetable garden
Pick the last of the tomatoes, including green ones, which can continue ripening indoors.

Continue sowing fall lettuces after raking in bonemeal at the rate of 4 oz (100 g) per sq yd/m. Space the plants 9 in (23 cm) apart in rows 1 ft (30 cm) apart.

In mild areas, plant out spring cabbages early in midfall. In cold weather, protect young plants with caps cut from plastic soft-drink bottles or with clear-plastic tunnels; cover the ends of the rows on cold nights.

In the North, protect emptied beds by sowing "green manure," a winter crop that prevents soil erosion over the winter. In spring, turn the crop into the soil.

Cut any remaining squashes, and store in a dry, frost-proof place. Clear away the top growth of peas and beans once harvesting is over. Dig manure or garden compost into empty beds, leaving the soil surface rough.

PLANT OF THE MONTH

Staghorn sumac *(Rhus typhina)* provides brilliant fall foliage interest when its large, toothed leaflets turn from midgreen to vivid shades of orange, red, yellow, and purple.

A small tree or large shrub with a spreading, rather gaunt frame, it grows up to 15 ft (4.5 m) high. In midsummer it bears upright greenish flower clusters, replaced in early fall (on female trees only) by clusters of dark red, felted fruits, which last on the branches until early winter.

Staghorn sumac can be cut back to the ground each year from late winter to midspring to obtain a thicket of lush foliage. The female cultivar 'Laciniata' has deeply cut leaflets, giving a ferny effect and rich fall tints.

Other midfall trees include maples *(Acer)* with an outstanding range of fall tints in shades of red, orange, and yellow. The multistemmed *Parrotia persica* develops beautiful amber, crimson, and gold tints, while crab apples *(Malus)* have decorative fruits in shades of red and yellow, as well as fall tints in a range of colors.

LATE FALL

Use the last mild days before winter sets in to plant shrubs and perennials and clear up the garden.

As the days shorten and sunshine weakens, temperatures drop across the country. This effect is more pronounced in the North and in the interior sections of the country, where there is no moderating influence from the oceans.

Average daily temperatures go down to the mid-40's F (around 7°C) in Bridgeport, Connecticut, in November; in St. Cloud, Minnesota, the average for the same period is slightly less than 29°F (–2°C). Frosts are common even in the Southeast during this period. The coldest weather typically comes on still, clear nights, and temperatures may be 10°-15°F (5°-8°C) cooler in low-lying areas than on adjacent uplands.

Throughout the Southwest there are modest rains. It is the beginning of the wettest season of the year in the Pacific Northwest.

In the North, take full advantage of the few days suitable for outdoor work. Continue clearing up the ground; fallen leaves are excellent material for compost, but keep diseased material (such as rose leaves that are infected with black spot) out of the heap.

Beds and borders

Finish digging new beds and borders for winter, and clean up existing borders, cutting down tall herbaceous plants. Cut plant tops into 6-12 in (15-30 cm) lengths for composting. Use fallen leaves as leaf mold or to protect the crowns of tender plants against frost. In established borders, take precautions against slugs and snails. Put away stakes and wire supports in a dry place.

In the middle of late fall, begin winter digging between plants in heavy soil. Do this when the weather is fine and the soil is not sticky. Winter frost will break up the soil, improving its texture.

Use a flat-tined digging fork, and insert it at an angle so that its wide tines turn over a neat wedge of surface soil, burying any

LAWN MAINTENANCE

In the North, it's still not too late to sow seed of cool-season grasses or to fertilize.
In the South, for a green lawn through winter, scarify its surface with a power rake (available at rental centers), clear off debris, and sow with annual ryegrass at a rate of 10-15 lb (4.5-6.8 kg) per 1,000 sq ft (90 sq m).
In the West, if you overseed with annual ryegrass, continue to irrigate through the winter.

weeds such as annual grasses or chickweed. However, deep-rooted perennial weeds should be dug up completely, and their roots disposed of off-site.

New herbaceous perennials that have been delivered late and hardy perennials raised from seed can still be planted out in their permanent sites during good weather. If it is too cold to plant

▼ **Last fall colors** A waterside planting in fall dress includes the browning fronds of a royal fern *(Osmunda regalis)* beside the brilliant red of a deciduous euonymus. In the foreground pale hostas, purple-leaved bugle, and faded astilbe spires carpet the ground below a tall silver grass *(Miscanthus)* and yellow-variegated evergreen euonymus.

or the soil is too wet, heel plants in or set them in a cold frame and delay planting until early spring.

If soil around chrysanthemums overwintering outdoors is water-logged, improve drainage by piercing the soil around the roots with a garden fork. Clear beds of fallen leaves and weeds, which can conceal pests such as parasitic nematodes.

Bulbs Finish planting tulips and hyacinths as soon as possible. If stored dahlia tubers are shriveling, leave them overnight in a bucket of tepid water, then remove and dry them carefully. Using a sharp knife, cut off any parts that show signs of rotting and dust the cuts with sulfur. Replace the tubers in vermiculite or slightly damp potting soil.

After gladiolus corms have dried off, they can be cleaned at any time until just before planting out in spring. Remove the bulblets from around the base of the new corms, and store them separately in paper bags if they are to be used for propagation. Break away and discard old shriveled corms, and remove the tough outer skins from the new corms. If thrips are a problem, dust the corms with malathion or another recommended insecticide.

Annuals In the North, dig next year's beds for hardy and half-hardy annuals, incorporating a dressing of well-rotted manure or compost. Leave the soil rough; winter weathering will break it down, leaving a fine tilth suitable for seed sowing. Fall digging is particularly helpful if you have clay soil, but it is important to complete this task before winter makes the soil too sticky to work.

Send for seed catalogs to allow plenty of time to plan next year's bedding displays.

In the frost-free or nearly frost-free regions of the South (zones 9 and 10), this is the season to sow hardy and half-hardy annuals such as alyssums, calendulas, nasturtiums, annual phlox, snap-dragons, and sweet peas.

In the South, this is also the time to transplant young plants of fall-sown biennials to their permanent sites. A light mulch will protect plants from the occasional frost, but do not bury the crowns; a thick blanket of damp leaves or pine needles will make them rot.

Rock gardens

Finish trimming and deadheading alpine and rock plants, saving any seeds for propagation. Clear away fallen leaves, and mound beech or oak leaves over tender plants to protect them during the winter. Hold the leaves in place by laying sticks over them.

Plant out shrubs, heathers, and alpines that were started in pots. On clean, level ground between the plants, spread a layer of fine gravel or crushed stone ½-1 in (12-25 mm) deep. This will suppress most weed seedlings, making hoeing unnecessary.

Elsewhere, turn over the surface between plants with a small, flat-tined hand fork. Carefully remove all perennial weeds.

Water gardens

Finish drastically thinning out underwater oxygenating plants,

WEEPING STANDARD ROSES

To train a weeping standard rose with stiff growth, secure the stem to a stout stake about 6 in (15 cm) higher than the head of the rose. Fix a training frame to the top of the stake — a wire frame used for hanging baskets will work. Pull the rose shoots through the top, tie them down, and trim the ends to shape.

and continue to remove dead leaves from the water. Leave the foliage on marginal plants such as reeds and rushes to provide some protection during severe weather.

If leaves and other debris are likely to fall into the pool, cover it with small-gauge wire mesh or fencing on a frame. This cover is easy to remove for cleaning.

Service pumps used for waterfalls and fountains, and store them in a dry place.

Stop feeding any fish when the days become colder.

Shrubs and trees

In mild weather continue to plant deciduous trees and shrubs as

---

PREPARING GLADIOLUS CORMS FOR WINTER STORAGE

1 After gladiolus corms have dried off, gently break off the cormels. If the cormels are to be used for propagation, store them separately in paper bags in a cool, dry place.

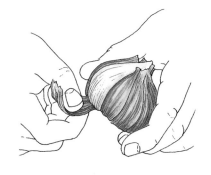

2 At the base of each new corm formed in the current year there will be the old shriveled corm. Break off the old corm gently, using a slight twisting action, and discard it.

3 Peel away the tough outer skin of the new corm. If there are thrips on the corm, or if there has been an attack of thrips during the growing season, dust with a recommended insecticide.

▲ **Fall berries** Evergreens continue to provide color, and berrying trees and shrubs are at their finest in late fall. Huge clusters of red and orange berries adorn a windbreak of tall-growing fire-thorns *(Pyracantha)*, interspersed with variegated hollies *(Ilex x altaclarensis)*, backdrops for variegated euonymus.

well as heathers. Examine those planted during midfall, and re-move any weeds. Gently firm in-to place any plants that have been loosened by frost.

Protect any tender trees and shrubs in severe weather, includ-ing *Campsis, Caryopteris, Cistus, Garrya, Hydrangea, Hypericum,* and *Spartium.* For a windbreak, insert several stakes around the plant and staple a skirt of burlap to the stakes. To prevent snow damage to young plants, stretch burlap over the windbreak too.

Take hardwood cuttings of *Elaeagnus pungens,* ivy, poplar, *Ribes,* and willow *(Salix).* Select strong, firm shoots about 1 ft (30 cm) long, and insert them in-to sandy soil in a cold frame or in a sheltered spot in open ground. Plant out the cuttings in their permanent sites the following spring. Take hardwood cuttings of winter jasmine, and root them in a covered cold frame or on a cool windowsill.

To propagate actinidia, layer firm young shoots in pots of soil sunk into the ground around the parent plant. The following spring, when the layers have made enough roots, sever them from the parents and plant out.

Examine cuttings in cold frames and in open-air nursery beds, and firm in any that have been heaved or loosened by frost.

Hedges Prepare the sites where hedges are to be planted; com-plete planting as soon as possible.

If the site is not ready when your stock is delivered, separate the plants in the bundles and bury the roots in shallow trench-es. Lay the plants at an angle, so they are not blown about too much before they are planted.

The fruit garden

Clear weeds from the soil around the bases of established fruit trees and bushes. With heavy soil, take care not to trample and com-pact the earth around plantings.

In zone 7, you can still plant fruit trees, as the soil remains workable and warm enough for the roots to establish themselves. From zone 8 southward, fruit trees may be planted out all through the winter, provided the soil is neither waterlogged nor frozen below the surface.

If trees arrive from the nursery and cannot be planted immedi-ately, store them in a frost-free shed, covering the roots with leaves or straw to prevent drying out or frosting. Alternatively, heel them in with the tops leaning over at an angle; tread the soil down around them firmly.

Prepare the holes immediately before planting. If the roots are dry, soak them for a few hours. Cut off any broken roots with pruning shears.

Provide stout stakes for dwarf-ing rootstocks — many of which cannot support a tree adequately by themselves — and for trained trees and bushes. Drive stakes in-to the ground before planting to prevent damage to the roots. With short-stemmed trees, insert the stake at a slant to the trunk with its top pointed toward the prevailing wind.

Plant fruit trees and bushes at the same depth as they were in the nursery. Spread out the roots in the prepared planting hole, and refill with layers of topsoil, firming in each layer with your fingertips. Repeat until the soil in the planting hole reaches the lev-el of the surrounding soil. Firm the soil in thoroughly, unless it is wet and sticky. Water well.

Fasten all trees and bushes se-curely to stakes, but leave some slack in the ties. When planting trees on windy sites, set them

PLANT OF THE MONTH

Beauty berry makes a colorful sight in late fall, when its leafless stems bear profuse clusters of purplish berries. In mid- to late summer it bears small pink to lilac flowers; in fall, the leaves turn purplish pink. Plant several together for a good show of berries.

If you have room, choose *Calli-carpa bodinieri* 'Profusion,' which grows up to 8 ft (2.4 m) high and 6 ft (1.8 m) wide and bears rose-violet berries. For a smaller garden, plant *C. japonica* with lilac-mauve berries. The cultivar 'Leucocarpa' has unusual, decorative white fruits. Northern winters may kill these shrubs to the ground, but new growth will fruit the next fall.

With raspberries, cut out all fruiting shoots that have carried this season's crop. Tie new canes to the supporting framework. Remove weak and surplus shoots at ground level. As soon as possible, finish pruning the blackberries, loganberries, and hybrid berries. Train new growths onto the supporting framework.

Prune established black currant bushes by removing some of the old wood — leave as much new growth as possible. Do not prune bushes at the end of their first season of growth.

With established gooseberry, red currant, and white currant bushes, prune by shortening the leaders by a half and shortening the laterals to 2 in (5 cm).

From zone 8 south, plant new beds of strawberries now. Use runners taken from old plantings.

The vegetable garden
Remove all leftover debris, and chop it into the compost pile — be sure to add plenty of animal manure or some other source of nitrogen to the pile as well. This helps to heat up the compost sufficiently to destroy insect eggs and weed seeds. Cultivate empty beds, turning over the top few inches of soil to expose overwintering insect eggs and larvae to winter's killing frosts.

In mild-winter regions (zone 8 and south), it is time to sow another crop of cold-tolerant plants such as spinach, lettuce, turnips, mustard greens, and parsley. Sow leeks and scallions now indoors in seed flats filled with sterile seed-starting mix.

In the extreme South (zones 9 and 10), this is also the planting time for crops that cannot tolerate this region's long, hot summers. Sow carrots, beets, peas, and celery now for picking in late winter or early spring.

In mild-winter regions, cut globe artichokes right back; at the northern end of this plant's range (zones 6 and 7), cut them back to 15-20 in (38-50 cm). Then bend the remaining stems over, mulch heavily around them with leaves, and cover the stems with plastic secured with rocks.
Herbs In the North, remove the frost-killed remains of annual herbs such as basil, chervil, and dill, as well as any biennials, such as fennel and parsley, at the end of their second season of growth.

with their best shoots growing into the prevailing wind to help form a well-balanced tree.

Prune fruit trees after planting: this can be done at any time from now until spring, except during a hard frost. First trim back or remove branches that were broken or damaged during shipping; then prune to shape the tree and form a framework of branches. With one-year-old trees, prune only enough to shape the tree and form the framework. In general, train apples, pears, and cherries with a central leader or trunk and well-spaced limbs; train peaches, nectarines, and plums for open centers with several scaffold limbs spreading upward from a low trunk.

Winter-prune established trees, but don't prune established cherries, peaches, nectarines, or damsons and other plums except to remove damaged branches — tidy up ragged wounds with a pruning knife but do not paint the wounds.

To winter-prune fruit trees, cut off the tips of leaders or shoots that will extend the branch framework, and remove badly placed shoots. Thin out spur systems (the stubby shoots that bear the flowers and fruit) on older trees. Stop tip-pruning the leaders after 4 or 5 years; then restrict winter pruning to removing crossing and rubbing branches and dead or diseased wood.

If birds are attacking the fruit buds, do not prune until the spring. Check that ties running to stakes are not cutting or chafing the bark. Rake up and remove fallen leaves to prevent overwintering spores of apple scab or other fungal disease from reinfecting trees in the spring — a light dressing of nitrogen fertilizer will speed the decomposition of any fallen leaves that remain.

Inspect stored fruit. To ripen pears, remove them from storage and keep them at room temperature until they are ready to eat.

EARLY WINTER

The dormant season, when trees and shrubs are bare of foliage, is the ideal time for pruning.

If fall has been mild, plants have not yet had a chance to harden off. The effects of a cold spell in early winter can be devastating. Fortunately, the most severe winter weather has yet to come in most parts of the country.

In the North, this is a good time to clean up the garden. The respite from regular garden tasks, such as weeding and dead-heading, provides an opportunity to catch up with pruning.

Roses

Rake up and remove all the fallen leaves from beneath rosebushes; otherwise, black spot, rust, and mildew spores may remain there over the winter and infect new growth the next spring. Do not compost these leaves, as fungal spores may survive even the heat of composting. Instead, bag and dispose of them with trash.

To the north of zone 7, hybrid tea roses are more likely to survive the winter if you build up 10 in (25 cm) circular hills made up of a mixture of soil and compost around the bases of the bushes. Wait for consistently cold weather to do this, and remove the hills in early spring as soon as the rosebuds begin to swell.

Ensure that cuttings planted out in early fall are still firm in their open trenches.

Beds and borders

Continue tidying beds and borders and digging between plants. If beds are close to tall-growing trees, shrubs, or hedges, cut back invasive tree roots, using a sharp, deep-bladed spade. Push it deeply into the edge of the bed to sever outgrowing roots. Cut large, thick roots with a mattock or ax. Also prune overhanging branches of deciduous trees or bushes.

If the ground freezes and then

LAWN MAINTENANCE

In the North and West, if you are planning to sow an area of new lawn next spring, prepare the site now. Dig over the ground and apply well-rotted stable manure. It is always a good idea to have a small area of turf specially sown to use for patching up any damaged areas of lawn.

Do not walk on the lawn when it is wet or frozen. Lay down boards on which to wheel heavy loads over the grass.

Clean and service mowing machines and other lawn maintenance equipment. Oil them well before putting them away in a dry place until the spring. **In the South,** continue mowing and other routine turf care if the lawn was overseeded with annual rye. Dormant warm-season grasses should be protected from excessive foot traffic now, as the turf cannot repair itself at this time.

▼ **Early-winter color** Shrubs trained up this wall — yellow-flowered winter jasmine and red-berried cotoneaster — bring cheer to dull days. At ground level the frosty gray carpeting foliage of cerastium and the glossy bergenia leaves provide evergreen ground cover.

PLANT OF THE MONTH

Holly is a good-looking specimen tree or bush with dense growth and glossy, prickly leaves. Female hollies bear shiny berries in fall and winter, as long as there is a male nearby.

Hollies are very diverse. There are northern species such as the meserve holly (Ilex x meserveae), which is hardy through zone 5, or the American holly (I. opaca), hardy through zone 6. There are also southern species such as I. alta-clarensis (above), which flourish in the heat and humidity of zones 8 and 9.

thaws out as the weather warms up, refirm the ground around chrysanthemums that are overwintering outdoors and check for waterlogging around crowns.

Bulbs Periodically check tender bulbs that have been stored indoors for the winter. This will help prevent the spread of fungi. If you find any gladiolus corms marked by water-soaked spots, for instance, that is probably a symptom of fusarium dry rot. Dispose of the corms right away, before the infection spreads.

If stored dahlia tubers are shriveling, leave them in tepid water overnight. Cut off any parts that have rotted, and dust the cuts with sulfur.

Annuals In the North, plan your seed requirements for the season to come and send off mail orders as early as possible. In the South, continue usual maintenance: deadheading and watering as necessary. Fertilize only during periods of active growth; cold spells can force even hardy annuals into semidormancy.

Rock gardens

Remove fallen leaves, and fork over vacant spaces between the plants. Remove perennial weeds.

Sow slow-germinating seeds and seeds that need a period of chilling to promote germination. Use clay pots or pans, or shallow wooden or plastic flats. Line the container with a clean sheet of newspaper and fill with a commercial seed-starting mixture. For easier handling, mix very small seeds with clean dry sand before you sow them.

Distribute the seeds evenly, and sprinkle sand over them so that they are just covered. Sink the pots or flats into a well-drained bed outdoors. The seeds should begin to germinate by the end of early spring, when the pots or flats should be moved to a protected spot, such as a cold frame or unheated porch, and watered regularly to keep the seedlings from drying out.

Water gardens

Float a log in the pool to create a break in the ice, so that toxic gases formed by the decomposition of organic debris can escape from the water. In addition, the break will relieve pressure that expanding ice would otherwise exert on the pool's walls, perhaps cracking them. If an unbroken skin of ice forms over the pool, stand a pot of

boiling water on it to melt a hole, but be careful not to touch any fish with the boiling water.

Shrubs and trees

Check trees and shrubs that were planted in fall, and refirm any soil that was loosened by frost. Water these plants deeply during periods of thawing.

Gather fallen leaves into a pile to make leaf mold to use for topdressing the garden next spring.

In cold regions, bring tubgrown hydrangeas and fuchsias into a cool greenhouse or frost-free garage or shed.

The fruit garden

When fruit trees and bushes are dormant and the temperature is over 40°F (4.5°C), spray with a dormant horticultural oil to kill pest eggs and overwintering insects. Also remove annual weeds at or below ground level.

Check stakes and ties on newly planted trees. Pull mulch away from their bases, and wrap the bottoms of the trunks in plastic tree guards to discourage rodents from gnawing tender young bark. Check framework supports and wires for trained trees. Tie in branches where necessary.

Begin winter pruning. Paint fruit tree trunks white to prevent sunscald — mix 1 part white latex paint with 3 parts water, and spray or brush on trunks up to the first major limb.

Regular fertilization is unnecessary in most cases for mature fruit trees, though those growing on limy, alkaline soils may benefit from a dose of potassium sulfate. Espaliered trees will also benefit from an annual fertilization with some balanced, slow-release organic fertilizer.

The vegetable garden

In the South, continue weeding around crops that were planted in fall. Drape old bedsheets or plastic painters' dropcloths over beds at night to protect plants against the occasional frost.

Herbs In the North, bring pots and tubs of half-hardy perennial herbs such as bay or rosemary into the greenhouse or into a frost-free, glass-enclosed porch or sunroom to overwinter them without damage. South of zone 7 these should overwinter without damage if left outdoors in a fairly well-protected spot.

MIDWINTER

**Most gardens now lie dormant,
making this the perfect time to overhaul
equipment and plan for spring.**

At lower elevations in Arizona and along the southern California coast, midwinter is the greenest and most pleasant time of year, with abundant rainfall and mild temperatures. In southern Florida, rainfall is at its lowest, but if you irrigate, blooms will abound.

The coldest nights are usually at the end of midwinter, so even in the South be on the watch for frosts. Temperatures may drop in gardens away from the moderating influence of large bodies of water. Gardens in cities are often several degrees warmer than those in rural areas.

The frigid cold and snow in the North and the South's raw winds and rain make outdoor gardening nearly impossible. Fortunately, many tasks can be done in the shelter of a shed or greenhouse.

Routine tasks

To destroy fungal disease, wash old pots and plastic seed flats with a mild detergent. Paint wooden flats with a copper-based wood preservative. Sharpen cutting tools, such as pruning and hedge shears, knives, and mower blades, or bring them to a service center for sharpening and repair.

During good weather, check all fences, gates, trellises, pergolas, and other wooden structures for decay or breakage. If they are weak, repair them immediately; a heavy snowfall or high wind could bring them down. Apply several coats of wood preservative to bare wood. Paths and paving stones may also need attention.

Mail-order catalogs begin arriving in midwinter, a good time to order vegetable and flower

LAWN MAINTENANCE

In the North, inspect the lawn during winter thaws for evidence of pink or gray snow mold — fungal diseases that thrive in wet and near-freezing conditions and often develop beneath a blanket of snow. Pink or grayish-white circles up to 8 in (20 cm) in diameter spread over the lawn, killing the turf underneath. These diseases can occur as the result of too much high-nitrogen fertilizer applied in late fall. Control the mold with an approved fungicide, or scratch up fungal growth with a spring rake. In spring, reseed brown spots and fertilize the entire lawn to restore vigor.

In the South, the growing season is beginning in warmer regions. Lawns benefit from an early application of a complete turf fertilizer rich in slow-release organic or water-insoluble nitrogen (check the label for the W.I.N. number).

In the West, in southern California or Arizona, sow grass seed. Temperatures are mild, and gentle rains moisten the soil without washing the seed away. This type of weather, however, promotes fungal diseases such as leaf spot (which marks grass blades with reddish or purplish semicircular spots). Treat with an approved fungicide, but keep in mind that this disease is often a symptom of excessive fertilization.

seeds, gladiolus corms, onion sets, shallots, and bare-root perennials and shrubs. Cultivars in short supply may be sold out unless you order in good time.

Beds and borders

Regularly inspect all plant stakes and ties, especially after windy or snowy weather, securing or replacing them if necessary.

After hard frosts, check newly planted perennials, biennials, and heathers. If they haven't grown good anchorage roots, frosts can heave them out of the ground and they will need refirming.

In the South, insulate half-hardy plants from severe cold spells with a mulch of leaves or

◀ **Midwinter color** Although snowdrops and golden winter aconites are hardy to zone 4, these bulbs are most welcome farther south — in zone 7, where they bloom in midwinter if they are protected. Clumps of hellebores introduce somber purple tones to this pale winter scene.

pine needles. Don't tread on the dormant crowns of plants that have been cut all the way down.

Cut or snap off remaining dead stems of herbaceous perennials. Tops pull away cleanly in light soil if the ground is frost-bound. Because clearing is easy at this time of year, you may prefer to clean up all your borders now rather than in the fall. However, your compost will not benefit from the dried-out tops and dead stems you remove.

Shrubs and hedges

Thin out dead and diseased branches from established shrubs and trees. Prune wisteria by cutting back all young shoots not needed to increase the plant size. Cut them to within 3 in (7.5 cm) of the old wood. Protect rhododendrons with a generous mulch.

Plants usually survive under a complete cover of snow, but heavy snow can break branches and so must be brushed or shaken off. Push upward on the branches' undersides; pushing downward may snap off limbs.

Fruits and vegetables

Inspect stored fruits and discard any that have rotted. Winter is the traditional season for pruning fruit trees in the orchard, in part because the absence of foliage allows the pruner to examine the branching structures with greater ease.

The type of cuts made when pruning will depend on the result you wish to achieve. A tree that is being trained to have an open center, with a number of main limbs radiating outward from a short trunk, demands different treatment from a tree being trained with a central "leader" — one main trunk reaching all the way to the top of its growth with secondary branches sprouting outward at regular intervals.

In either case, this is the time to inspect trees, and decide whether the growths of the past year enhance the structure you seek. New shoots that rub against or crowd established branches should be removed. So should water shoots — long, thin new branches that shoot directly upward through the tree's scaffold of limbs. Fruit-bearing branches that spread outward from the main limbs, or laterals, may be shortened now, and the last season's growth cut off at the tips to encourage heavier flowering and fruiting the following year.

This is also a good time to begin renovating any fruit trees that have been neglected. First, remove all diseased or dead wood. Then start pruning to create an open, airy branch structure; this structure is essential to the health of the tree. First, cut out one branch from any pair of branches that cross each other. Then remove any branches that run back toward the center of the tree rather than outward. If you find that you must remove many branches, divide this work over a couple of winters, so that the tree is not overly traumatized.

In mild-weather regions, cover established rhubarb crowns with a generous layer of well-rotted manure or garden compost to encourage early growth. You can also cover the crowns with upturned containers that keep out the light.

In the South, sow peas for an early crop. You can plant shallots now in well-drained soil, although most gardeners prefer to wait another month or two before completing this task.

PLANT OF THE MONTH

The Christmas rose (Helleborus niger), with its white or pink-tinged flowers, 2-5 in (5-13 cm) wide, is a midwinter gem in protected spots in zone 7. The flowers are long-lasting and cold resistant. In colder locations, protect the opening buds with caps made from tops cut from plastic milk containers or soft-drink bottles.

Other midwinter flowers Several flowering shrubs enliven the midwinter garden in milder locations. These deserve a position where they can be seen from indoors.

Chinese witch hazel (Hamamelis mollis) makes a large shrub, or small tree with age, and its leafless branches are decked with clusters of fragrant, spidery golden or sulfur-yellow flowers. For a similar effect, try the fragrant yellow wintersweet (Chimonanthus) or the cornelian cherry (Cornus mas), which has clusters of tiny yellow flowers.

The silk tassel bush (Garrya elliptica) is an unusual wall shrub, producing masses of silver-gray catkins, which are eye-catching after a white frost or sprinkling of snow. Crocus tomasinianus, one of the earliest crocuses, gives a pretty display of slender lavender blooms beneath the winter-flowering shrubs.

LATE WINTER

**Early-spring bulbs signal the
end of winter, and preparations for the coming
season can begin on mild days.**

Late winter sometimes brings spells of intense cold and freezing winds, which dehydrate and damage plants, including dormant ones. However, sunshine is now increasing and mixed with the bitter weather are milder periods in which gardeners may prepare their plots for the next growing season. In the South (zones 8 to 11) the new garden year is beginning and it is time to sow seed.

Beds and borders
Late winter is your last opportunity to clear the dead tops from last year's herbaceous perennials.

Prepare the ground for spring planting, but only if the soil has dried sufficiently. Digging in wet soil destroys its structure, causing compaction. Lightly hoe or fork over the top 2-3 in (5-7.5 cm)

of soil. At the same time, work in bonemeal and wood ashes. These organic fertilizers supply, respectively, the phosphorus and potassium that perennials need for the best flowers.

Lightly fork over beds that have been dug the previous fall and reserved for sowing and planting annuals. If manure or compost has not been applied earlier, rake or hoe in a dressing of bonemeal, using 4 oz (100 g) per sq yd/m. In the South, this is the season to sow seeds of tender and half-hardy annuals indoors.

Firm the soil around loosened border or rock plants. Remove small tufts of grass and seedlings of annual weeds, which often germinate unnoticed during the fall but become more prominent during a mild late winter.

LAWN MAINTENANCE

In the North, watch during thaws for grass patches that remain flooded. These poorly drained spots will benefit from aeration as well as a topdressing of compost and sharp sand later in spring.
In the South, apply a preemergent herbicide for weeds. Do not treat newly seeded or reseeded lawns, because these herbicides prevent grass seed germination.
In the West, during clear, dry weather, apply preemergent herbicides in warmer regions of the Southwest and Northwest.

Roses, shrubs, and hedges
In the South, plant roses and other shrubs if the soil is dry or moist, but not if it is wet and sticky.

Buds are beginning to swell in warmer regions of zone 7 and southward. It is time to prune *Callicarpa, Campsis, Spiraea,*

▼ **Red against the snow** Dramatic in the shape of its curious flowers, the red witch hazel *(Hamamelis* x *intermedia* 'Ruby Glow') turns a flaming bright copper-red in late winter. Its foliage is equally spectacular in the fall.

and *Tamarix ramosissima* back hard by cutting away the previous year's growth to within 1 in (2.5 cm) of the old wood to encourage the development of new, vigorous shoots.

Prune summer-flowering clematis back hard, either to 1 ft (30 cm) above ground or within two buds on young growth.

Cut back all shoots that have completed flowering on chimonanthus and winter jasmine, but wait until early spring if they are still in bloom. Thin out climbers such as celastrus and potato vine by removing any weak growths, and shorten or pinch the tips of main shoots.

To encourage new growth, cut back overgrown hedges near the end of late winter. Cut top growth at least 1 ft (30 cm) lower than the height ultimately required, so that any new growth will have space to hide the old skeleton.

Fruits and vegetables
Prune newly planted espaliered peaches, nectarines, cherries, and plums, cutting back shoots to 1-1½ ft (30-45 cm). Spray peaches with a recommended fungicide at the bud-swelling stage to prevent peach leaf curl.

Prune established fall-fruiting varieties of raspberry close to the ground. Cover strawberry plants that have been planted for early fruit with clear-plastic tunnels supported on wire hoops.

In the upper South, sow early crops of green and edible podded peas. Wait until early spring in cold, northerly areas unless seedbeds can be covered with plastic.

To grow early potatoes, buy the tubers now. Arrange them in one layer in shallow boxes, with their eyes, or embryo shoots, uppermost. Put them in a light, frost-proof place to promote sprouting.

Carrots, such as 'Baby Finger' or 'Golden Ball,' sown in late winter in light, fertile soil in a cold frame, should be ready to harvest in early summer. Keep glass and plastic covers closed for a week or two to warm the soil, then sow the seed thinly. Keep the frame closed until the seed has germinated, then give some ventilation.

Plant onion sets as soon as the soil can be worked; soil in raised beds warms and dries a couple of weeks earlier than in conventional beds. Dig the site in preparation for planting out asparagus.

Winter-flowering mahonia (*Mahonia x media* 'Charity') is one of the most elegant shrubs, especially during late winter. Its upright branches carry huge evergreen leaves made of leaflets shaped like holly. Tapering sprays of yellow flowers scented like lily of the valley crown the branches in late winter. Tassels of berries then develop, which ripen blue-black with a gray bloom. At maturity this imposing shrub reaches a height of 8-10 ft (2.4-3 m).

Other late-winter flowers Winter jasmine (*Jasminum nudiflorum*), a delightful wall shrub, has green stems showered with bright yellow trumpet flowers over a long winter period.

For rich purplish-pink flowers on upright bare branches, choose *Daphne mezereum*. As the flowers mature, tufts of bright green leaves unfurl at the tips of the branches. For a low display of late-winter blue or mauve flowers, grow chionodoxa and *Iris reticulata*.

Gardening indoors

Moving your plants indoors, whether to a greenhouse, sunroom, windowsill, or simply under the protection of a cold frame or plastic-covered tunnel, affords you new opportunities in any region. In the North, of course, it extends the growing season so that you can grow plants year-round. With the help of supplemental indoor lighting, for instance, gardeners can cultivate tropical orchids even in the coldest regions. By starting seedlings indoors, Northerners can also grow flowers and vegetables that normally require a long, warm growing season. Southerners gain an opposite advantage by growing plants indoors. There, an air-conditioned environment makes it possible to start fall crops of cool-loving vegetables and annual flowers weeks earlier.

Installing a greenhouse can be expensive, but the benefits can be enormous. A greenhouse lets you experiment with the tremendous diversity of hybrids and species that are available as seed but are not supplied as plants at garden centers. Even a modest windowsill unit with a plastic-covered frame can provide a sheltered environment for sowing early seeds and rooting cuttings.

When you garden indoors you are in control of the growing conditions — you can regulate temperature, humidity, ventilation, and the amount of light that your plants receive. You can be sure to grow plants in the most suitable soils; you can water and fertilize them only when necessary; and you can help to combat pests and diseases by maintaining strict hygiene. It is even possible to combat greenhouse pests in an environmentally friendly way by the introduction of beneficial pests and parasites.

Indoor harvest Raising young tomatoes and other plants from seed is economical.

GREENHOUSE KNOW-HOW

**In a well-equipped greenhouse, the choice
of plants and produce extends from the half-hardy
all the way to near-exotic types.**

A greenhouse can free you from the tyranny of the weather; under cover, plants flourish that would normally suffer outdoors. Many commercial greenhouse kits are available, complete with framing, glazing, and shelving. Before erecting a greenhouse, discuss with a building inspector or other qualified professional whether you will need to install a foundation — even if it is just concrete blocks. Then choose your site carefully according to the criteria given on the following pages.

Light

Select an open, sunny site so that the greenhouse gets as much light and warmth as possible. In the winter the plants will need full sunlight for most of the day.

Whenever possible, a greenhouse should be away from any large buildings, tall hedges or trees, and fences. If only a shady spot is available, your choice of plants will be more limited. Also avoid sites prone to waterlogging and frost pockets and those exposed to strong, cold winds.

Remember that shadows cast in winter are much longer than those in summer. Also, a tree or wall on the north side of the greenhouse will cast a smaller shadow than a similar plant or structure elsewhere.

Even if a nearby tree does not directly overshadow the greenhouse, falling branches may break the glass during a storm, and roots can damage the foundations. However, small trees up to about 12 ft (3.6 m) high can help to provide shelter.

Orientation

The orientation of the greenhouse — the direction in which the ridge of the roof runs — will affect the amount of light and heat available to it at different times of the year.

East-west axis Most gardeners prefer a freestanding greenhouse to run on an east-west axis. This provides the best light in winter for plants such as orchids, flowering annuals, winter bulbs, and alpines. It is also useful for raising batches of half-hardy annuals from seed. However, temperatures may rise too high at midday during the summer, especially in the South.

North-south axis A freestanding greenhouse with the ridge running north-south is best in

▼ **Freestanding greenhouse** Ideally, choose a site that gives good light but also shelter. Here, shade is cast during the hottest part of the day over vegetables grown in the ground inside the greenhouse, while the flowering plants on the greenhouse benches receive full sun.

cool northern regions for summer and fall crops. A greenhouse built at this orientation heats up quickly in the morning during the summer and retains its warmth well into the night.

If space is scarce, consider a lean-to greenhouse against a wall of your house. It will get less light than a freestanding greenhouse, but the insulated house wall will collect and store solar radiation, and thus help to heat the greenhouse after dark. It is also easier and cheaper to install water, gas, and electricity in a lean-to.

South-facing wall A lean-to greenhouse with an east-west ridge on a south-facing wall receives maximum heat in summer and maximum light throughout the year — a plus in cool and cloudy northern regions but too much in the South. This is the perfect arrangement for Northerners who want to ripen long-season, warmth-loving crops such as melons, eggplants, or peppers.

North-facing wall A lean-to greenhouse running east-west on a north-facing wall is in shade for much of the time, even in summer, making it a haven for many shade-loving foliage plants and ferns, especially in the South.

West-facing wall A north-south lean-to on a west-facing wall is shaded in the morning, but warmth lingers after nightfall, making it useful between fall and spring. However, on winter mornings it is chilly and shaded.

East-facing wall With a north-south axis, a lean-to on an east-facing wall receives morning light, but otherwise is shaded for much of the day, especially in winter. It retains little natural heat.

Shelter

Although an open site is important, shelter from winds — particularly the cold northern winds of winter — is essential. Strong, cold winds lead to rapid heat loss and hence large heating bills, while even gentle breezes can cause chilling drafts inside the greenhouse. A storm can rip a polyethylene-covered greenhouse and break glass panes.

If your garden does not have a suitable sheltered site, plant a hedge or a row of shrubs to filter the wind, or build a wall or fence to act as a windbreak. Position the windbreak so that it does not cast shade over the greenhouse.

Access

Plants grown under glass need daily care, so make sure that the greenhouse is within easy reach, especially in bad weather. Build it as close to the house as possible, given the considerations of light and shelter, and provide access to it via a firm path wide enough for a wheelbarrow.

Water Greenhouse plants need constant watering, particularly at the height of the growing season, so you will need access to a water main — automatic watering systems may require more than ordinary household pressure to operate successfully.

If your water is "hard" (rich in minerals), consider installing a cistern near the greenhouse to collect rainwater or investing in a water-softening system.

Electricity If you have an electrical main close to the greenhouse, you can install an electrical system. This would be more expensive to operate than a gas or oil system, but electricity is also essential to provide power

---

SITING A GREENHOUSE

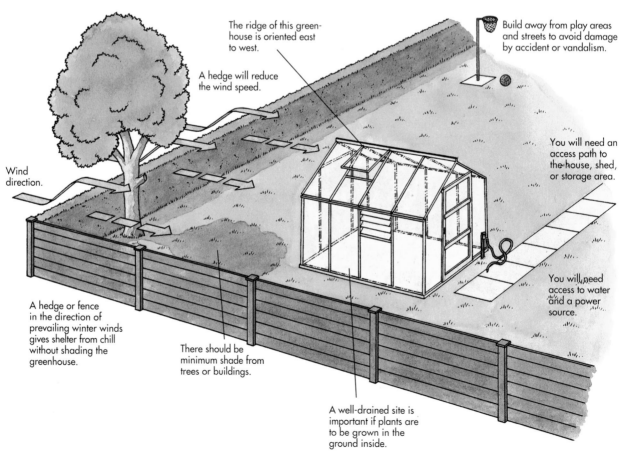

The ridge of this greenhouse is oriented east to west.

A hedge will reduce the wind speed.

Build away from play areas and streets to avoid damage by accident or vandalism.

Wind direction.

You will need an access path to the house, shed, or storage area.

A hedge or fence in the direction of prevailing winter winds gives shelter from chill without shading the greenhouse.

There should be minimum shade from trees or buildings.

You will need access to water and a power source.

A well-drained site is important if plants are to be grown in the ground inside.

for ventilation systems in summertime, and you can work into the evening if you have electric lights. Electric lights also extend the daylight hours and bring into bloom so-called long-day plants.

Sloping gardens

If your property is on a grade, stand the greenhouse on a leveled foundation. If you grow plants in containers, a sloping site does not pose a problem once the greenhouse is built. But if you want to grow plants in the ground within the greenhouse, the slope will create drainage problems. Take measures to prevent the drainage of soil moisture down the slope before even installing your greenhouse. Remember also that frost pockets often occur at the base of a slope.

Unheated greenhouses

An unheated greenhouse will keep out frost in the South. In the North it will create warmer conditions for heat-loving plants. Unheated greenhouses can also be useful for overwintering plants that are not quite hardy in a particular zone. The most valuable function of a greenhouse in the North, however, is to lengthen the growing season. Plants can be encouraged to grow early in the spring and then either kept indoors or planted out in the garden. In the greenhouse, plants will grow well into the fall.

For instance, an unheated greenhouse makes it possible to ripen a crop of tomatoes even in northern New England or the upper Midwest, and to bring to bloom late-flowering chrysanthemums in fall, when the tomato plants have been discarded.

For the northern gardener who is interested in producing top-quality blooms, an unheated greenhouse is invaluable for growing a range of half-hardy shrubs, fruits, and annuals, as well as lilies, gladioli, and many other bulbs. In intermediate zones such as northern zone 8, an unheated greenhouse will let you cultivate lettuces, carrots, string beans, radishes, and other vegetables in wintertime.

By installing equipment for ventilation, shading, and watering, you can control the environment of even an unheated greenhouse — some of the more expensive systems are semi- or even fully automatic.

Staging

By installing staging — benches and shelves — in your greenhouse, you can expand the growing area and at the same time raise the plants to an easier working height. Sun-loving plants, including seedlings and young plants, can be placed higher up, while plants that prefer some shade can be put underneath the

▼ **Greenhouse staging** Aluminum or wooden shelves along the greenhouse walls increase the growing space for potted plants and seedlings and provide a convenient working space. Ferns and other shade lovers beneath this staging benefit from the humidity of an enclosed environment.

staging or on low shelves. Similarly, trailing plants can be placed on high shelves to tumble to eye level, and tall upright plants can be put lower down. Where space allows, stepped or tiered staging is useful for displaying plants.

A benefit of filling the greenhouse with plants is that it will increase the humidity — essential to plant health, especially during summer's high temperatures.

The simplest type of staging is made of wooden slats. Many wooden-frame greenhouses come complete with prefabricated wooden staging, or you can build your own. Manufacturers of aluminum-frame greenhouses usually offer a range of aluminum shelves and benches to match the greenhouse structure. These screw or bolt onto the framework. Some brands have a top surface of wire mesh.

To provide extra humidity in summer, cover your staging with a sheet of plastic, then spread a 1 in (2.5 cm) layer of moist sand, gravel, or vermiculite over the top. Prevent the sand from falling over the edges by fastening a wooden lip along the edges of the staging, under the plastic. Alternatively, cover the staging with commercial "capillary mats," which absorb water.

Potted plants set on the moist sand or mats will draw up water through their drainage holes by capillary action. Keep the sand moist — but not flooded — at all times. You can do this by watering or by installing an automatic irrigation system. In winter, when high humidity is not required, remove the sand or mats to allow good air circulation around the plants and to better distribute the heat.

Whenever you have more than two tiers of staging, set plants on trays or polyethylene sheeting to prevent water from splashing down onto the plants below when you irrigate.

Ventilation
To keep your greenhouse from overheating in the summertime, it should have at least two vents in the roof as well as additional vents in the side walls. Make sure the side-wall vents are staggered; otherwise, opening them even a crack in cool weather can create drafts that are lethal to plants. As a general rule, the total surface

TYPES OF STAGING

aluminum staging

wooden staging

aluminum shelving

suspended shelving

Staging — benches and shelves — can be made from wood or metal (usually aluminum). Manufacturers usually supply benches and shelves to fit each of their greenhouse models, or you can construct your own. Staging can be freestanding or permanently fixed to the greenhouse framework, and can incorporate watertight trays or consist of slatted wooden shelves.

Aluminum shelf brackets can be secured easily to aluminum glazing bars using bolts or self-tapping metalworking screws. Many types of specialized hardware are available to secure high-level shelves to the glazing bars of the sloping roof.

area of the roof vents should be at least equal to one-sixth of the floor area. Hot air rises, so the roof vents are very important.

Fungus diseases flourish in a warm, stagnant atmosphere. When top vents and side vents are open at the same time a rapid change of air takes place, keeping the air as fresh as possible — hot air escaping through the roof vents pulls cooler air in through the low side vents. You can increase ventilation as necessary simply by propping the door open.

An additional benefit can be gained by installing sliding side vents at ground level — they allow access to the area under the staging, for cultivation and adding or removing stock.

Top vents and most hinged side vents can be fitted with automatic openers in glass greenhouses. A special liquid compound inside the unit expands or contracts with

temperature changes and drives a piston system of levers. These units are quite expensive, but once installed they free you from the necessity of adjusting your greenhouse vents every time the weather changes.

An alternative form of ventilation is by an electric exhaust fan controlled by a thermostat. The fan is best placed in the apex of the roof, at the end of the greenhouse opposite the door. As the fan sucks air out of the greenhouse, sufficient air will usually come in under the door and through gaps between glass panes. But during very hot weather the door or vents at a distant point from the fan should be left open.

Shading
In some cases, plants need to be protected from strong, direct sunlight. Ferns, orchids, and tropical

INDOOR THERMOMETER

Keep a check on the temperature in a greenhouse, and take action to regulate it within an acceptable range by adjusting the ventilation and shading. Provide ventilation when the inside temperature reaches 70°F (21°C).

Hang a thermometer in the greenhouse so that it is out of direct sunlight and away from the door or vents. The type that records a minimum and maximum reading between resettings is the most useful — you can see at a glance how low the temperature falls at night. Reset such a thermometer daily.

jungle plants definitely need such protection, but other plants generally do not.

The most efficient method of shading the greenhouse is to use specially designed roller blinds. These are usually made of wood, bamboo, or aluminum slats, or some woven plastic fabric. The blinds can be lowered on sunny days and rolled up on cloudy days. They can be fitted to the inside or outside of the roof, and should be set on rails 1-2 in (2.5-5 cm) away from the glass. More expensive automatic blinds are also available. These are usually operated by photo-electric cells, which respond to light intensity.

Ordinarily, you need only install blinds across the greenhouse roof, although they are available to cover the sides as well. A greenhouse where the ends face east and west should be shaded on the south side of the roof. A

greenhouse running north and south should be shaded on both sides of the roof.

An effective and less expensive alternative to blinds is specially formulated electrostatic shading paint. This compound is available in a concentrated form from greenhouse supply companies and must be diluted with water before use. Use either a brush or sprayer to apply the paint to the outside of the glass. If you cannot reach all parts of the roofing glass easily from a stepladder, attach the brush to a long pole or use an old soft broom to apply the paint. Never attempt to climb on a greenhouse roof — you may damage the glazing, buckle an aluminum frame, or even fall into the greenhouse. Shading paint is waterproof, so it will not be washed off by rain, but it is easily

wiped off with a dry cloth at the end of the season.

You can also apply shading paint to the sides of the greenhouse as well as to the roof. If the house runs north-south, paint the south, east, and west sides, and both sides of the roof.

Because shading paint reduces the amount of sunlight that penetrates into the greenhouse, it may also be used for reducing the interior temperature in summertime. But beware of applying too thick a coat, since that may lead to spindly, light-starved plants.

Water supply

Unless your greenhouse is being built alongside an existing garden faucet, a permanent water supply should be installed. This is a job for a professional plumber, but the expense is justified by the

VENTILATION SYSTEMS

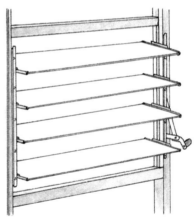

1 Side-louver vents can be opened fully and occupy little space on a horizontal plane. They are usually designed to replace a standard 2 ft x 2 ft (60 cm x 60 cm) pane of glass.

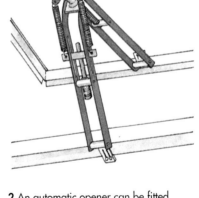

2 An automatic opener can be fitted to almost any type of hinged vent. A special piston operates via levers to open or close the vent, expanding or contracting with temperature changes.

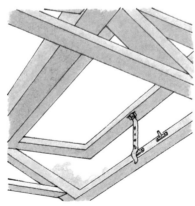

3 Ordinary window latches provide the simplest and cheapest means of supporting a hinged vent in a fully open or partially open position. Ensure they are secure to prevent wind damage.

4 An electric exhaust fan can be set into a pane of glass or mounted onto chipboard or exterior-quality plywood. It is controlled by a thermostat and gives draft-free ventilation.

SHADING SYSTEMS

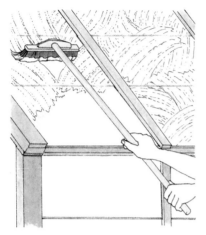

1 White electrostatic shading paint is the simplest and cheapest means of shading a greenhouse during the summer months. It can be wiped off easily when it is no longer needed.

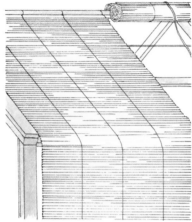

2 Roller-type wooden or plastic slat blinds can be bought for use inside or outside the greenhouse. Those positioned on the outside are the easiest to install, but may be damaged by weather.

3 Roller blinds, with an aluminum frame, are made from a strong decay-resistant synthetic fabric. Extra rollers can be purchased that allow blinds to be pulled over the side panes as well.

savings in your work and time later. And, running a hose out to the greenhouse may simply be impossible in freezing weather.

Once a supply line and faucet have been installed, you can water your plants by hand, with a long-spouted watering can or a hose, or you can put in an automatic system. The amount of water you need depends on the plants, time of year, and temperature. During active growth, plants need more water than during dormancy. Aim to keep the soil just moist, neither waterlogged nor dry — on a hot summer's day, tomatoes, for example, may need watering several times.

Automatic watering

An automatic system has several advantages. It is often more reliable than hand-watering, especially where plants are crowded and difficult to reach, and it promotes steady plant growth. It also saves time and enables you to leave the greenhouse unattended for a period of up to several days, provided ventilation is controlled automatically.

A popular method of supplying automatic irrigation is to purchase a small commercial unit consisting of a plastic tray or sheeting, a tank or reservoir, and a constant-level float valve. If the staging is covered with plastic and a capillary mat or a layer of sand mixed with a nontoxic algicide, the system can maintain a consistent level of moisture.

The float valve regulates the

level of water in the tray and hence the degree of wetness of the sand or matting. Use plastic pots with large drainage holes for capillary-bench work. Do not put gravel or other drainage material inside the pots. Press the pots down firmly on the moist mat or sand, so that the soil makes contact with it through the pots' drainage holes.

Water the pots well before setting them on the bench or mat. This will ensure continued uptake of water.

TRICKLE IRRIGATION

Trickle irrigation This system of watering consists of a plastic pipeline with spaghetti tubes and nozzles fitted to the main tubes at intervals. Water drips slowly out of these tubes into the pots or flats. The irrigation flow is controlled as water is siphoned from a tank fitted with an automatic valve or electronic timer. You can also adjust the water flow by adjusting the nozzle aperture. Nozzles can be held over the pots by wire staples or by special weights attached to the tube ends.

A regular supply of water is essential at all stages of plant growth, but watering by hand is not always possible.

Trickle irrigation, in which a pipe fed from a tank brings water for the plants via spaghetti tubes and drip nozzles, irrigates slowly and steadily and is an ideal system for plants of all sizes. The nozzles can be adjusted to regulate the flow of water to suit each plant's needs.

Provided the tank is higher than the supply nozzles — the system is gravity-fed — plants can be watered on several levels of staging at once. Water-soluble fertilizer can be added to the tank, so that plants are watered and fed at the same time.

HEATED GREENHOUSES

**Artificial heat is needed to preserve tender shrubs,
young seedlings, and exotic houseplants through all but
the most southerly winters.**

Even unheated greenhouses protect overwintered plants, shielding them from rain, snow, and freezing winds. However, they do little to protect plants from low winter temperatures — for example, an unheated greenhouse of all-glass or glass and wood construction will probably stay only a few degrees warmer inside than the air outside. If the outdoor temperature falls dramatically below freezing, so will the temperature inside the greenhouse.

An unheated greenhouse is useful principally for extending the growing season for warmth-loving plants, though as far north as zone 7 the minimal protection it provides is useful for overwintering more delicate plants or for enjoying blooms that can survive

a slight frost, such as ericas, camellias, winter pansies, polyanthuses, and primroses.

Heating a greenhouse, even just enough to keep it frost-free, enormously widens the range of plants that you can grow. You can sow seeds early to produce bedding plants by spring, and many tender shrubs, climbers, and houseplants will flourish in that heated, controlled environment.

Unfortunately, glass, fiberglass, and plastic all allow heat to escape, so heating a greenhouse, however small, can be costly. Consider whether it is worth heating the entire greenhouse or just part of it — it may be that you can divide the structure into two or more compartments, heating just one area

in the center of the greenhouse.

In an open site, the winter sun provides free warmth to the greenhouse. However, a windbreak of trees or tall shrubs that protect the greenhouse from winter gusts can also substantially decrease your heating costs. Makeshift double glazing may be installed in glass houses by stretching sheets of clear plastic across the inside edges of the glazing bars during winter. This reduces heat loss, but remember that it also greatly cuts down on light transmission and can create problems with condensation and ventilation.

Calculating heat

The importance of installing a heating system with adequate capacity is obvious — one night of frost can destroy all your months of work. But installing a heater that is unnecessarily large can be expensive and lead to inflated fuel bills. It is therefore important to calculate the exact energy needs of your greenhouse before shopping for a heater.

Fortunately, this is a straightforward process. Manufacturers rate gas, oil, and kerosene heaters according to the number of BTU's (British thermal units) they can produce. Before investing in a heater you must first calculate the BTU's necessary to ensure that your greenhouse interior never drops below a minimum temperature of 45°F. (Note that BTU's are calculated based on degrees Farenheit.)

To calculate BTU's, you must examine three factors and establish a numerical value for each. The first factor is the total surface area of the greenhouse: the area of all four walls and the roof, measured in square feet. To

◄ **Year-round blooms** A heated greenhouse creates a sheltered place for plants even through the coldest winters. A lean-to greenhouse such as this can often be warmed by means of an extension of the household system or with an inexpensive gas or electric heater.

GREENHOUSE AIR-WARMING HEATERS

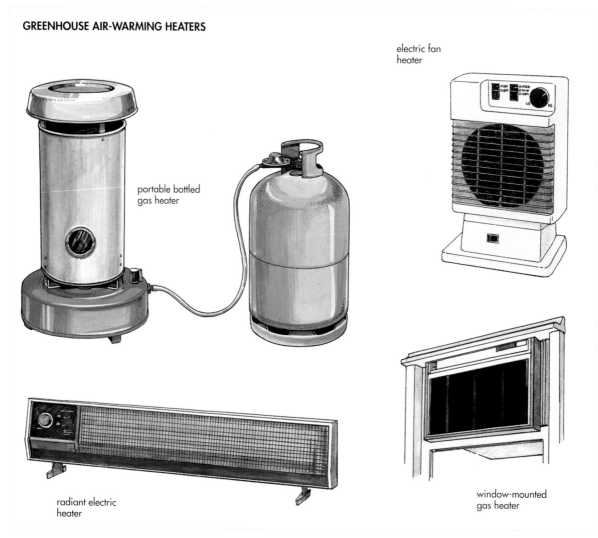

electric fan heater

portable bottled gas heater

radiant electric heater

window-mounted gas heater

determine this, you must multiply the length of each surface by its width. For example, if a wall is 12 ft long and 8 ft high, the surface area of that wall is 96 sq ft. Repeat this process for the remaining walls and the roof and add the resulting figures together to obtain the total greenhouse surface area.

Next you need to calculate the difference between the coldest outdoor temperature you may expect and the minimum temperature you need to maintain inside the greenhouse. Consult a USDA (United States Department of Agriculture) plant hardiness zone map to determine the average minimum temperature for your area. If you live in USDA zone 7, for instance, that temperature is 0°F. Remember that your goal is to maintain the greenhouse at a minimum of 45°F — a temperature adequate for starting bedding plants and also for overwintering most tender plants. The difference between this coldest minimum outdoor temperature and the minimum indoor greenhouse temperature is therefore 45°F.

The final value you need is the heat-loss factor (known as the U factor) of the glazing material. This expresses the heat loss in BTU's per hour per square foot of surface for each degree that temperatures are colder outside than in. Listed below are U factors for common glazing materials:

❑ Glass — 1.1
❑ Fiberglass — 1.0
❑ Polyethylene film (single layer) — 1.1
❑ Polyethylene film (double layer), double acrylic sheet, or polycarbonate sheet — 0.6

If you are unsure about the U factor of your glazing material, consult the manufacturer.

Once you have determined all three of these values — total surface area, temperature difference, and U factor — you must multiply them together to establish the BTU capacity you require.

Suppose you own a glass-covered greenhouse with a total surface area of 300 sq ft, you live in zone 7 (where the lowest winter temperature is typically 0°F), and you wish to maintain your greenhouse at a temperature of 45°F, your calculations will be as follows:

$$300 \times 45 \times 1.1 = 14,850$$

In this case, you would require a heater with a rating of at least 14,850 BTU's.

If you intend to heat with an electrical heater, you can convert BTU's to watts by multiplying the BTU value (14,850) by 0.293. In the above example, the result is approximately 4,300 — the minimum wattage of the electrical heater you require.

These calculations give only approximate heat requirements — individual greenhouses vary according to site, construction,

ELECTRICAL SAFETY

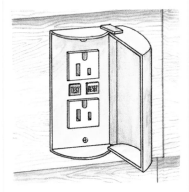

If properly installed, electric heat is both safe and clean. However, electricity can be dangerous in a greenhouse, especially because of the presence of water there.

Take precautions when you work with electricity. Have any permanent installations done by a qualified electrician. Permanent cables should be encased in conduit and weatherproof sockets should incorporate a faceplate to shield the terminals when not in use. Screw-lock shielded plugs prevent moisture from touching the terminals when equipment is in use. A GFCI outlet *(above)* will protect against serious electric shocks.

Always use electrical equipment designed for the greenhouse. Equipment designed for domestic use may be hazardous.

and climate. In general, it is wise to buy a heater that will give slightly more heat than the minimum required, rather than less.

Types of heaters

In practice there is little difference between the costs of oil or natural gas as fuels, though prices vary from year to year and from region to region. Electricity is usually more costly than the two fossil fuels, though its price also varies from region to region.

Electricity Despite the expense, electricity has advantages: it is most likely to be trouble free, gives excellent automatic control, produces no harmful fumes, and does not raise humidity in winter. Winter storms may bring down power lines, though, so it is prudent to have an alternative heat source such as a kerosene heater in case of blackouts.

For a small greenhouse, an electric fan heater is ideal. These are portable and easy to install — you simply plug them in. Fan heaters usually incorporate a thermostat, which controls the fan and the heat output simultaneously. The air circulation is good for the plants and minimizes fungal diseases. A disadvantage is that if the fan breaks down, the resulting heat loss will be total.

Convector heaters, which produce a current of warm air without a fan, are fairly inexpensive and easy to install, but heat distribution is not as good as with a fan. If you are using convector heaters, install one at each end of the greenhouse.

Bottom heat Cuttings root slowly if the rooting medium is cold, and seeds are slow to germinate in cold soils. To heat the rooting medium or soil in a propagation box by air warmth takes time. And a high air temperature in winter or spring can produce unwanted top growth in plants; in fact, most seedlings grow best with warm soil and cool air.

One way to achieve this is with commercial soil-warming cables. These cables come in various lengths to provide the correct amount of heat and are usually connected to a thermostat. The cables are fully insulated and have a braided metal grounding sleeve for safety. The heating section is usually a distinctive color and must never be cut.

Soil-warming cables can be connected directly to the wall outlet, or special low-voltage cables can be operated via a transformer. The latter is safer if there is any risk of damage to cables from gardening tools.

Another option is a propagation root zone mat — essentially heating cables enclosed in a waterproof plastic or rubber mat. These mats may be placed underneath seed flats, eliminating the need for a propagation box. Most types come with a thermostat.

Kerosene heaters A range of these heaters are available in different styles and sizes. You should buy a model that meets UL safety and performance requirements and incorporates such features as push-button ignition, fuel siphon pumps, and a shut-off feature that turns off the flame if the heater tips over.

It is important to use no. 1 grade kerosene because low-grade kerosene, when burned, can give off sulfur fumes, which may damage plants. However, with larger

SOIL-WARMING CABLES

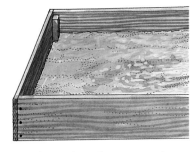

1 For a bottom-heated propagation box, begin by spreading a 2-in (5-cm) layer of sand in the base of a wooden or galvanized metal tray — there should be several drainage holes in the bottom.

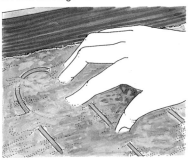

2 Snake the heating cable backward and forward over the sand. Avoid sharp bends, and lay it no less than 4 in (10 cm) and no more than 8 in (20 cm) apart. It must never cross itself.

3 Cover the cable with a further 1 in (2.5 cm) of sand and 3 in (7.5 cm) of moist rooting medium. Install a thermostat with its sensor rod lying 1 in (2.5 cm) above the cable.

4 Plant cuttings directly into the rooting medium, or sink pots into it so that each base is in contact with the sand. Ensure that the rooting medium remains evenly moist at all times.

and more sophisticated kerosene heaters, there is a flue that takes the fumes outside the greenhouse. Condensation is reduced by the heated flue, creating a drier atmosphere in winter.

Kerosene heaters are most useful as emergency heating or to supplement the normal heating system. However, you should consult with local authorities about fire and safety codes before purchasing a kerosene heater, as they are not approved for use in all states and localities.

Gas heaters Controlled by a manual valve, these provide a lot of heat. Both portable models and units that are installed in a window frame are available. The gas supply bottle is connected to the heater unit by a neoprene hose. Gas heaters are inexpensive, but the gas bottles, which are cumbersome and heavy, need to be regularly refilled. These heaters also produce water vapor and require free ventilation.

Hot-water pipes Heated by an oil or gas boiler, hot-water pipes can be used for heating a greenhouse. They can be installed relatively easily in a lean-to greenhouse or conservatory, where they form an extension to the main house's central heating system, but if the greenhouse is far from the house these pipes are costly to install. Thermostatic control is possible, but the pipes retain heat and do not respond quickly to temperature changes.

Thermostatic control

Any thermostat that you use with a greenhouse heating system should be easily adjustable, graduated in degrees, and be able to regulate the temperature by as little as 1 or 2 degrees.

Set the thermostat according to readings taken from a minimum/maximum thermometer in the greenhouse. In addition to recording the current temperature, this thermometer records high and low temperatures reached since the previous day. Adjust the thermostat so that the minimum temperature does not drop below the desired level.

A thermostat can also help provide better atmospheric control within the greenhouse. If connected to an electric fan ventilator, it will continually adjust air flow (and thus humidity) to best suit temperature fluctuations.

HEATED PROPAGATORS

Electrically heated propagators provide adequate warmth for rooting cuttings or raising seeds at a much lower running cost than heating an entire greenhouse.

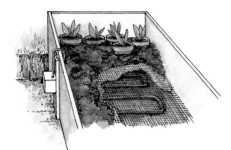

Single-compartment propagators with a fixed temperature thermostatic cutout are the least expensive propagators, and they are suitable for raising small quantities of seedlings or cuttings. Adjustable vents in the top allow some regulation of humidity.

Soil-warming cables Although more difficult to install than a ready-made propagation box, a thermostatically controlled soil-warming cable enables the gardener to adjust bottom heat to suit the needs of different seeds.

Propagation root zone mats are made of Mylar plastic and provide bottom heat up to 100° F (38°C). The mats may be connected to a thermostat fitted with a sensor rod; all mats connect to an electric outlet. Always place a metal grounding screen over the mat.

GROWING FRAMES

Growing frames are less expensive than a heated greenhouse for raising seedlings and cuttings, and they can be installed inside an unheated greenhouse or in the open. They consist of an aluminum framework with removable trays, covered with clear plastic, which can be rolled up and down. The roof can be lowered to adjust the size of the unit. Some incorporate a built-in soil-warming device.

THE GREENHOUSE YEAR

**With careful planning and good hygiene,
flowering potted plants and many food crops can fill
the greenhouse year-round.**

The greenhouse adds an extra dimension to gardening, enabling you to grow tender plants that would not survive outdoors in the garden and providing you with an all-weather retreat. A greenhouse is also invaluable for raising bedding annuals and for propagating various plants.

It is important to plan your use of the greenhouse. A year-round growing program is possible in all but the hottest climates, assuming you choose suitable plants and crops and follow a meticulous routine of cultivation. For obvious reasons, avoid plants with widely differing needs, although you can house shade and sun lovers within the same greenhouse and create a microclimate on capillary matting for plants that require extra-moist growing conditions.

Midwinter
This is the season when seed catalogs start arriving, and you should plan now which plants you will grow throughout the succeeding year. By ordering through the mail you have access to a huge range of species and cultivars that do not appear in local garden centers.

Start bringing pots or bags of bulbs — tulips, hyacinths, narcissi, and crocuses — out of cold storage and into the greenhouse for forcing. Keep them in a dark, cool place until shoots reach a height of 3-4 in (7.5-10 cm), then move them to a well-lit but fairly cool bench.

When watering, do not splash the flowers or leave water lodged in the crowns of the plants, as this may lead to rotting when temperatures are low. Avoid overwatering tender or young plants, or the fine roots may be damaged.

Take cuttings of zonal pelargoniums from stock plants moved indoors the previous fall. When roots reach ½ in (1 cm) in length, pot up and pinch back the top buds to encourage bushiness.

If you have a propagation box and can maintain a temperature of 60°-65°F (15°-18°C) during germination, sow wax begonias, pansies, impatiens, gloxinias, and Cape primroses toward the end of midwinter.

Late winter
Move dormant heliotropes, fuchsias, and hydrangeas onto the greenhouse staging, if possible in a warm spot where a temperature of 50°F (10°C) can be maintained. Move azaleas in from the cold frame, and set them in a cool spot. Spray these plants with water on sunny days, and give them increasing amounts of water as they begin to grow actively.

Sow seeds of slow-growing annuals such as celosia, coleus, periwinkle (*Catharanthus roseus*), and scarlet sage. Place the seed flats in a propagation box heated to 60°-65°F (15°-18°C). When the seedlings are large enough to handle, prick them out and grow them on at normal greenhouse temperatures. Apply dilute liquid fertilizers on a regular basis as plants come into active growth.

If you want to plant tomatoes in greenhouse beds during mid-spring, sow the seeds in late winter at 61°F (16°C).

Prune greenhouse climbers, such as plumbagos and passion-flowers, by cutting back the growths made last summer to within one or two buds of their point of origin. Keep watering to a minimum, and ventilate freely on mild days.

Increase your stock of ferns by dividing old plants. Use the vigorous pieces from the outsides of the old plants, and discard the woody centers. Pot on any other pot-bound ferns.

▶ **Greenhouse summer** A glazed aluminum-frame greenhouse is fairly easy to erect. With good planning it will support a wide range of tender and semihardy ornamental plants and food crops. It also offers the gardener a warm and sheltered workplace.

GREENHOUSE PLANTS THROUGH THE SEASONS

Midwinter
Azalea (*Rhododendron* Indica, Kurume, or Rutherfordiana hybrids)
Cineraria (*Senecio x hybridus*)
Narcissus (*Narcissus tazetta* cvs.)
Poinsettia (*Euphorbia pulcherrima*)
Primrose (*Primula obconica*)

Late winter
Azalea (*Rhododendron* Indica, Kurume, or Rutherfordiana hybrids)
Cineraria (*Senecio x hybridus*)
Florist's cyclamen (*Cyclamen persicum* cvs.)
Hippeastrum/amaryllis (*Hippeastrum* hybrids)
Hyacinth (*Hyacinthus orientalis*)
Narcissus (*Narcissus* cvs.)
Primrose (*Primula obconica*)

Early spring
Cineraria (*Senecio x hybridus*)
Freesia (*Freesia x hybrida*)
Hippeastrum/amaryllis (*Hippeastrum* hybrids)
Kaffir lily (*Clivia miniata*)
Mimosa (*Acacia* spp.)
Primrose/primula (*Primula x kewensis, P. malacoides, P. obconica*)

Midspring
Cineraria (*Senecio x hybridus*)
Hippeastrum/amaryllis (*Hippeastrum* hybrids)
Mimosa (*Acacia* spp.)
Primrose/primula (*Primula x kewensis, P. malacoides*)
Slipper flower (*Calceolaria crenatiflora* hybrids)

Late spring
Butterfly flower (*Schizanthus hybridus*)
Cineraria (*Senecio x hybridus*)
Primrose (*Primula obconica*)
Regal and zonal pelargonium (*Pelargonium* cvs.)
Slipper flower (*Calceolaria crenatiflora* hybrids)

Early summer
Begonia (*Begonia* spp. and cvs.)
Cape primrose (*Streptocarpus* hybrids)
Gloxinia (*Sinningia speciosa*)
Monkey-faced pansy (*Achimenes* cvs.)
Regal and zonal pelargonium (*Pelargonium* cvs.)
Slipper flower (*Calceolaria crenatiflora*)

Midsummer
Begonia (*Begonia* spp. and cvs.)
Black-eyed Susan vine (*Thunbergia alata*)
Bougainvillea (*Bougainvillea* spp.)
Busy Lizzy (*Impatiens* cvs.)
Cape primrose (*Streptocarpus* hybrids)
Cockscomb (*Celosia cristata*)
Fuchsia (*Fuchsia hybrida*)
Glory bush (*Tibouchina urvilleana*)
Gloxinia (*Sinningia speciosa*)
Heliotrope (*Heliotropium arborescens*)
Italian bellflower (*Campanula isophylla*)
Lily (*Lilium* spp. and cvs.)
Monkey-faced pansy (*Achimenes* cvs.)
Slipper flower (*Calceolaria crenatiflora*)
Zonal and ivy-leaved pelargonium (*Pelargonium* cvs.)

Late summer
Begonia (*Begonia* spp. and cvs.)
Cape primrose (*Streptocarpus* hybrids)
Cockscomb (*Celosia cristata* cvs.)
Columnea (*Columnea* spp.)
Flowering maple (*Abutilon* spp.)
Fuchsia (*Fuchsia hybrida*)
Glory bush (*Tibouchina urvilleana*)
Gloxinia (*Sinningia speciosa*)
Heliotrope (*Heliotropium arborescens*)
Italian bellflower (*Campanula isophylla*)
Monkey-faced pansy (*Achimenes* cvs.)
Passionflower (*Passiflora caerulea*)
Smithiantha (*Smithiantha* spp. and vars.)
Zonal and ivy-leaved pelargonium (*Pelargonium* cvs.)

Early fall
Begonia (*Begonia* spp. and cvs.)
Canna (*Canna* hybrids)
Columnea (*Columnea* spp.)
Flowering maple (*Abutilon* spp.)
Fuchsia (*Fuchsia hybrida*)
Glory bush (*Tibouchina urvilleana*)
Heliotrope (*Heliotropium arborescens*)
Italian bellflower (*Campanula isophylla*)
Plumbago/Cape leadwort (*Plumbago auriculata*)
Scarborough lily (*Vallota speciosa*)
Zonal pelargonium (*Pelargonium* cvs.)

Midfall
Flowering maple (*Abutilon* spp.)
Fuchsia (*Fuchsia hybrida*)
Glory bush (*Tibouchina urvilleana*)
Italian bellflower (*Campanula isophylla*)
Plumbago/Cape leadwort (*Plumbago auriculata*)
Zonal pelargonium (*Pelargonium* cvs.)

Late fall
Capsicum/pepper (*Capsicum annuum*)
Cineraria (*Senecio x hybridus*)
Florist's chrysanthemum (*Dendranthema* spp.)
Florist's cyclamen (*Cyclamen persicum* cvs.)
Flowering maple (*Abutilon* spp.)

Early winter
Azalea (*Rhododendron* Indica, Kurume, or Rutherfordiana hybrids)
Cineraria (*Senecio x hybridus*)
Florist's carnation (*Dianthus* spp.)
Florist's chrysanthemum (*Dendranthema* spp.)
Florist's cyclamen (*Cyclamen persicum* cvs.)
Poinsettia (*Euphorbia pulcherrima*)
Primrose/primula (*Primula x kewensis, P. obconica*)

Poinsettias that have finished flowering should be cut back slightly and laid on their sides underneath a greenhouse bench.

Early spring
To encourage sturdy growth of tomato plants grown from a late-winter sowing, give them extra space. If you aim to plant tomatoes in late spring, sow the seeds now in a heated propagation box.

In a cool greenhouse, prepare the bed for planting tomatoes in midspring. Dig in plenty of well-rotted manure or compost as well as a dressing of bonemeal, 1 cup (240 ml) per sq yd/m.

Sow the seeds of half-hardy annuals — ageratum, sweet alyssum, cosmos, annual phlox, snapdragon, stock, and the like — in flats of seed-starting mix. Maintain the seeds at a temperature of 50°-65°F (10°-18°C).

Take cuttings of fuchsias and coleuses, rooting them in compost at a temperature of 50°-61°F (10°-16°C). Also take cuttings of chrysanthemums and zonal pelargoniums to produce plants for flowering next winter.

Plant hippeastrum (Dutch amaryllis) bulbs in 6 in (15 cm) pots. Provide a temperature of 50°-55°F (10°-13°C), and water sparingly until buds appear.

Ventilation becomes especially important as temperatures rise both inside and outside the greenhouse. Apply a light coat of shading paint or use roller blinds to filter sunshine that reaches sun-sensitive plants such as orchids and ferns.

Midspring
Complete the greenhouse sowings of half-hardy annuals, and sow seeds of vegetable seedlings for planting outside after the last frost. Apply shading to the entire greenhouse now, and pay special attention to ventilation: clouds moving past the sun in this most changeable season may make it necessary to close and then

▶ **Glass protection** Unaffected by rain or wind, tender ivy-leaved pelargoniums and trailing fuchsias tumble from baskets in a riot of color. Potted half-hardy annuals — black-eyed Susan vines and petunias — cover the benches.

reopen vents several times a day. Move established half-hardy annuals into a cold frame so that they can harden off.

Give increasing amounts of water to plants repotted in early spring. Continue to apply liquid fertilizers to established plants such as pelargoniums, as well as seedlings. Hydrangeas in pots are now in active growth and need a temperature of 50°F (10°C) and generous watering.

Pot up rooted cuttings and move them if possible to a cold frame. Propagate dahlias by potting up tubers and using sprouts to make cuttings.

By now, increasing light intensities and temperatures will probably make it necessary to water more than once each day. But take care: moisture requirements vary tremendously from plant to plant, and overwatering is just as damaging as underwatering. Try to keep soil evenly moist — that is, neither wet nor dry.

In a cool greenhouse, plant tomatoes in the bed that you prepared last month and provide suitable supports. Sow seeds of outdoor tomatoes at a temperature of 61°F (16°C). Sow melon and cucumber seeds at 61°-65°F (16°-18°C), setting them individually, about 1 in (2.5 cm) deep in 3 in (7.5 cm) pots.

Late spring
Move flats and pots of annuals sown in midspring to a cold frame for hardening off. Apply a liquid fertilizer if the leaves show signs of yellowing.

Sow cineraria seeds at a temperature of 50°-55°F (10°-13°C) to produce plants that will flower in early winter. Sow cucumbers and melons if not done already.

On warm days, provide shade for plants now in flower, such as calceolarias, pelargoniums, cinerarias, primulas, and hydrangeas. Increase the humidity by hosing down the staging and the floor. Provide adequate ventilation. Give plenty of water and a weekly liquid fertilizer to vigorously growing plants.

When fuchsias reach a height of 4-5 in (10-13 cm), pinch back the growing points to encourage bushy growth. Later, pinch the side shoots as necessary.

With cucumbers grown in large pots or in inside beds, pinch off side branches at two leaves beyond the first or second developing fruit. Remove tendrils and male flowers — those without an embryo fruit behind them (modern cultivars typically bear only female flowers).

Train tomatoes that are being grown as a greenhouse crop by twisting stems around the support strings, or tie the stems to stakes. Pinch off side shoots regularly. Feed the plants every week or 10 days from the time the first fruits begin to swell.

For an early harvest or in cold-weather regions, plant out into cold frames melons that were raised from a midspring sowing.

Bring poinsettias out from under benches, cut branches back hard, and give the plants a good soaking; set them on top of the bench and water regularly, keeping the soil on the dry side.

Early summer
Plants that have finished flowering — such as azaleas — can be put into the open garden for the rest of the summer to make more room in the greenhouse. Young cyclamens, seedling cinerarias, calceolarias, primulas, and solanums can be moved to a cold frame or protected spot outdoors.

Pay particular attention to watering — plants in clay pots may need two or more applications daily during hot weather. Maintain a humid atmosphere by frequently damping down the shelving and the floor. Syringing plants — wetting them with a fine spray of water — not only cools the leaves in hot weather, it helps protect them against spider mites, which often attack during hot weather.

If the weather is very warm, leave open the top ventilators on the sheltered side of the greenhouse at night. Beware of leaving plants exposed to a late cold snap.

Sow cineraria seeds if this was not done in late spring; also sow *Primula malacoides*.

Pot on *Streptocarpus* plants, raised from a winter sowing, in pots that are 5-6 in (13-15 cm) wide. Make a further sowing at 61°-65°F (16°-18°C) to provide flowering plants next year.

Plants that are now flowering,

such as pelargoniums and fuchsias, must be deadheaded regularly and given liquid fertilizer every 10 days.

Propagate African violets *(Saintpaulia)* and *Begonia rex* from leaf cuttings, rooting them in a propagation box at a temperature of 61°-65°F (16°-18°C).

Examine the stems of tomato plants. If they are becoming thin, give them some liquid fertilizer containing extra nitrogen.

Midsummer

Continue wetting down the greenhouse beds, paths, and staging at least once a day during warm weather, and syringe plants during really hot weather. Unless the plants are standing on continuously moist capillary matting, most require watering at least once a day during hot spells.

Tomato plants should be producing well, with a few fruits to pick almost every day. Continue to feed and twist the stems around the supporting strings, or tie them to stakes, and pinch off side shoots regularly.

There should be cucumbers to harvest, too. Continue picking off

any male flowers as soon as they show. If white roots appear on the surface of the bed, apply a 2 in (5 cm) deep dressing of well-rotted manure or leaf mold.

To encourage prolonged blooming of potted plants now in full flower, shade the plants during sunny weather and give ample ventilation, especially in early morning. Except during cold or windy weather, leave the roof ventilators on the sheltered side of the greenhouse open all night.

Take 4 in (10 cm) cuttings from nonflowering shoots of regal pelargoniums — the best will come from stock plants that were cut down by about half in early summer and are now producing lots of fresh growth. Take cuttings from new growth on old poinsettias. Root both types in a propagation box.

Late summer

Renew shading if necessary, and wet paths and beds during hot weather. Continue to feed plants and watch for pests and diseases.

This is a good time to repair and paint the greenhouse in readiness for the winter. Wooden

▲ **Dual-purpose greenhouse** A well-organized house can support ornamental plants as well as food crops. Here the bed along one side is occupied by tomatoes, while the bench opposite supports potted plants such as coleuses, begonias, fuchsias, and pelargoniums.

A small room at the far end can be closed off from the house by an insulated door. This room is kept warmer in winter to accommodate delicate plants.

greenhouses must be painted before heavy fall dews soak into the wood. If you have a heating system, service it now before you need to turn it on.

Hippeastrums should have died down by now and can be stored just in their pots, under the greenhouse staging, until required again in early spring.

Continue to take cuttings of regal pelargoniums. Also propagate cuttings of zonal pelargoniums at this time. Select only firm, healthy, nonflowering growths of average size. Cut them with 3 in (7.5 cm) of stem.

During the second half of late summer take 3 in (7.5 cm) fuchsia cuttings from sturdy young growths if young plants are

YEAR-ROUND GREENHOUSE HYGIENE

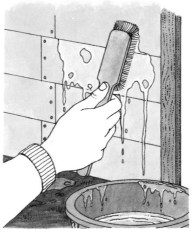

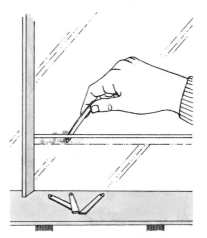

1 Keep the glass or plastic glazing clean at all times, especially at the onset of fall, when the amount of natural daylight lessens. Wash off algae and dirt with mild detergent, commercial glass cleaner, or strongly diluted ammonia.

2 Using a scrubbing brush and a mild detergent, remove dirt from any masonry or wooden walls and from the benches, shelves, doors, and framework of the greenhouse — dirt may harbor fungal disease spores.

3 Scrape out any algae and dirt that has accumulated in gaps between overlapping panes of glass, reducing the transmission of light. To avoid scratching the glass, a plastic tool such as this plant label is ideal.

4 Maintain a regular prevention campaign against greenhouse pests and diseases — infestations are hard to control once they are well established. Use insect traps and predators, good hygiene, and insecticidal soap.

5 A soil drench such as PCNB is one means of combatting the fungal pathogens that may eventually build up in greenhouse beds, but home gardeners will probably find it easier to simply replace soil periodically.

6 Empty old soil out of pots and flats, and scrub the containers with a mixture of bleach and water (1:9) before storage or reuse — dirty containers harbor diseases and defeat the purpose of using sterile potting soil and seed-starting mix.

---

required for growing on as standards next summer. Sow cyclamen seeds at a temperature of 61°F (16°C) for flowering the winter after next.

Pinch off the growing tips of tomatoes to encourage rapid development of the fruits on the tops of the vines. A few weeks later, stop feeding and reduce watering to keep fruits from splitting. If the nights turn chilly, close the vents early in the evening.

As they root, pot up poinsettias into 4 inch (10 cm) pots, or pot three or four cuttings together into an 8 in (20 cm) pot.

Early fall
Annuals such as clarkias, cornflowers, nemesias, schizanthuses, godetias, antirrhinums, and pot marigolds, sown in early fall and grown in pots in a cool greenhouse, make a colorful display during spring and early summer. Sow the seeds in flats of seed-starting mix at a temperature of 55°-61°F (13°-16°C).

Continue to take cuttings of fuchsias, regal and zonal pelargoniums, coleuses, heliotropes, *Plumbago auriculata,* and impatiens. Root them in pots or in a propagation box.

Be careful not to overwater at this time, as cooler temperatures reduce plants' water needs.

Toward the end of early fall, remove any permanent shading from the glass. In sunny weather provide local shading for seedlings and cuttings. Before the nights turn cold, bring into the greenhouse cinerarias, primulas,

cyclamens, ornamental peppers, regal pelargoniums, and begonias that have been in frames outside.

Do not to expose poinsettias to artificial light at night, since this may delay bud formation.

Midfall
Bring into the greenhouse any tender plants still outdoors in cold frames. In the greenhouse, reduce syringing, damping down, and watering. Where possible, carry out any irrigation in the morning hours.

Thin out the shoots of climbing ornamentals, such as plumbago, passionflower, and *Tibouchina urvilleana,* to give them more light and air during the winter.

Clean the glass inside and out, then line the greenhouse with clear plastic sheeting, to within 1 ft (30 cm) of the ridge, to conserve heat during the winter. Cover the ventilators separately, so that they can still be opened.

Check any heating system during the evening to make sure it is working properly and that its thermostat is operating.

Late fall
Ventilate the greenhouse freely on all sunny days, but avoid cold drafts and close the ventilators fairly early in the afternoon to

trap some of the daytime warmth. Keep the greenhouse closed during damp, foggy weather.

Complete any outstanding potting as early as possible. Annuals raised from seeds sown in early fall will now be ready for moving to 3 in (7.5 cm) pots. Cuttings of pelargoniums, heliotropes, fuchsias, and campanulas will now be rooted and also ready for potting up into 3 in (7.5 cm) pots of the appropriate potting soil.

Dry off fuchsias, begonias, heliotropes, and hydrangeas that have flowered during the summer and early fall. Store the pots under the benches in a cool greenhouse or in a frost-free shed, but do not let the soil dry out.

Pinch back new growth on ornamental peppers, so that it does not hide the berries. When the earliest cinerarias begin developing their flower heads, give the plants extra space to allow them to grow freely and ensure that they get as much light as possible.

Keep poinsettias a bit drier now and stop fertilization — this hardens growth and will help them hold their bloom longer once in the house.

Early winter
Plants grow very slowly or else remain dormant in early winter

▲ **Greenhouse spring** Pots of forced narcissi, eye-catching multicolored cinerarias, and dainty yellow-flowered *Primula* x *kewensis* announce the arrival of spring even when it is still winter outdoors in the garden.

because of the relatively brief hours of daylight. Don't try to make them grow faster by raising the temperature — you will just encourage soft, weak, and straggly growth.

At the beginning of early winter give extra attention to plants that you hope to have blooming in the next few weeks. Select the warmest spot for any cinerarias, cyclamens, or primulas that are developing too slowly. In contrast, move plants to a cooler spot to delay the opening of blossoms you wish to keep for later.

Open ventilators a little on sunny days, but close them again quite early in the afternoon. Most plants — except those actually in flower — must be kept fairly dry. But do not allow them to dry out so much that the soil begins to shrink from the sides of the pot.

If the floors and paths need damping down to increase humidity, do this during the early part of the day. Discontinue overhead spraying of the plants.

GREENHOUSE BEDS

Pots are an obvious choice for greenhouse growing, but the roots of large or heavy-cropping plants are less restricted when grown in ground.

Most greenhouse gardeners want to grow a variety of plants, both ornamental types and food crops. Most ornamental plants do well in containers set on staging — benches and shelving — perhaps with capillary matting. In containers, the individual needs of these plants can be carefully monitored and regulated — for instance, you can move them around the greenhouse as light or temperature conditions demand.

The single biggest limitation of growing plants in containers is the restriction imposed on root growth and hence water and nutrient uptake. It is vital to irrigate and fertilize container plants during the growing season in order to avoid loss of vigor. Even so, some fruit and vegetable crops can suffer badly from restricted root growth. When roots are overcrowded, the plant may run to seed, give reduced yields, or produce tough-textured fruit or flowers. Therefore, it is common practice to grow crops and large plants in open greenhouse beds.

Greenhouse beds are suitable for growing tomatoes, cucumbers, melons, lettuces, sweet peppers, eggplants, radishes, spinach, spring onions, beans, strawberries, grapes, citrus fruits, and all climbing or shrubby ornamentals. Ideally, you should use a crop rotation system, growing tomatoes, for example, in the east bed one year and in the west bed the following year.

Preparing the soil

In a newly erected greenhouse that has not been put on a solid concrete slab, you may be lucky enough to already have good-quality soil as a floor. In this case, all that is needed for the first season is routine digging and the same application of organic material and fertilizer that you would use for an outdoor plot.

It is unlikely that the foundations for the outer walls of the greenhouse will be deep enough to impede the natural drainage of the soil inside, but on very poorly drained sites it is advisable to incorporate a drainage layer of gravel while double-digging the greenhouse beds.

Plants grown under the protection of glass or plastic tend to grow more quickly than in the garden. In so doing, they take up nutrients rapidly from the soil, often depleting ordinary soils well before the end of the growing season. You must take special care to keep the greenhouse bed soil enriched. Well-rotted manure, garden compost, or leaf mold should be dug into the soil at a rate of one bucketful per sq yd/m a few weeks before planting.

Before planting, water the bed thoroughly and when any excess moisture has drained away, scatter a general-purpose fertilizer over the surface at a rate of one generous handful per sq yd/m, and rake it in.

If the greenhouse has been built on poor soil, dig out the soil entirely to one spade's depth and replace with a loamy garden soil, mixed with compost, peat moss, and coarse builder's sand at a rate of 4 parts loam, 2 parts compost, 2 parts peat, and 1 part sand. If you do not have access to a sufficient quantity of loam, you may fill your beds with a ready-

◀ **Greenhouse tomatoes** For high-yield crops, tomatoes need a constant supply of water and nutrients. These can be easily furnished when the plants are grown in a greenhouse bed. An edging of marigolds helps to ward off harmful whiteflies.

SOIL PREPARATION AND CARE

1 If the soil at the base of your greenhouse is of poor quality, prone to waterlogging, or infested with pests and diseases, dig it out entirely to at least one spade's depth and discard it.

2 Where the site is poorly drained, add a layer of coarse sand or gravel across the bottom of the excavated ground. A more labor-intensive solution is to install plastic or ceramic drainage pipes.

3 Refill the site with good-quality sterilized garden soil or commercial topsoil, incorporating one bucketful per sq yd/m of well-rotted manure, garden compost, or leaf mold.

4 Leave the bed to settle for a few weeks before planting. Just before you plant, soak it through, sprinkle on some granular general-purpose fertilizer, and rake it into the top 1 in (2.5 cm) of soil.

5 Throughout the growing season, apply liquid fertilizer to the soil around plants using a watering can, or apply granular fertilizer by hand. For amounts, follow the manufacturer's instructions.

6 Once a year, after you have cleared away the plants, sterilize the bed soil using an approved liquid pesticide, fungicide, or disinfectant, or dig out and replace the soil entirely.

---

to-use potting soil available from most garden centers and nurseries. If you buy a sterilized product (that is, one that has been steam-pasteurized), your beds will start off entirely free of soil-borne diseases.

Raised beds
On a site where the greenhouse bed soil is poorly drained, an alternative to digging the soil out and replacing it is to construct a raised bed over the broken-up subsoil. Build an outer framework of wooden timbers — either naturally rot-resistant, such as cedar, or treated with a wood preservative that is not toxic to plants. You can also use bricks or concrete to form the sides. A height of about 9-12 in (23-30 cm) should be adequate for most greenhouse plants.

Fill the bed with the soil mix-ture described previously to within about 1-2 in (2.5-5 cm) of the top. You can, of course, also use a commercial potting mixture to fill the raised bed.

Planting and care
The principles of growing plants in a greenhouse bed are identical to those for growing outdoors, except that you must be especially diligent with watering and feeding — regulation of the greenhouse environment depends entirely on your constant attention. Soil dries out very quickly under glass, and you may wish to install some form of automatic watering system, especially when growing salad crops, which tend to run to seed when they are excessively hot and dry.

Pests and diseases must be kept under strict control — minor outbreaks can rapidly turn into a major epidemic in a confined environment. Before using any chemical pesticide or fungicide on food crops, check that it is approved for this use and follow the directions on the label faithfully. Releasing predacious insects such as ladybugs or lacewings (which may be purchased from mail-order companies) is often a highly effective alternative to chemical controls, especially as some greenhouse pests, notably spider mites and whiteflies, have now become resistant to many commercial pesticides. Before releasing these beneficial predators, install screens in vents, windows and doors to keep the insects from migrating outside. These barrier screens also help prevent the entry of undesirable pests into the greenhouse.

Controlling soil-borne pests and diseases can be more of a

challenge in the greenhouse bed, because they build up unnoticed. Prevention is the best policy: use sterilized soil wherever possible and maintain scrupulous hygiene at all times throughout the greenhouse. Alternatively, try to incorporate homemade garden compost into your beds — recent research indicates that it may contain microorganisms that inhibit the spread of many pests and diseases.

Spray a dilute solution of household bleach (1 part bleach to 9 parts water) on paths to clear them of algae and moss. The same solution can also be applied to the glass and framework as a disinfectant. Take care not to let it touch any parts of your plants,

however, and use it with great caution around aluminum, because bleach has a corrosive effect on this metal.

Ring culture

Ring culture is a specialized growing system, which is best suited to tomatoes. Plants are grown in bottomless cylinders filled with sterilized potting soil. The plants' roots grow into an inert medium that holds plenty of water and provides stability. This growing medium is free from pest and disease problems (as with plants grown in sterilized soil in a pot), yet allows roots to extend without any restriction. Thus, ring culture combines the advantages of growing plants in open bed soil with those of growing in individual containers filled with sterilized potting medium.

Begin preparations for ring culture by digging a trench to one spade's depth. Remove the soil from the greenhouse — you won't need it. Line the trench with a single sheet of heavy-duty plastic. This will act as a watertight membrane and isolate the plant roots from the garden soil underneath (which may contain pests or disease organisms). Fill the trench with coarse gravel.

Transplant tomato seedlings singly into 8 in (20 cm) fiber or plastic cylinders— filled with a loam-based sterilized potting soil. Sink each container into the gravel to a depth of about 1 in (2.5 cm) to aid stability.

Fibrous feeding roots will eventually fill the container, while anchorage and water-absorbing roots will grow into the gravel. Water plants by watering the gravel, but feed them by applying liquid fertilizer to the soil in the container. Because the gravel bed has an open structure with plenty of air trapped in tiny pockets, the plant roots can be kept permanently moist without fear of waterlogging — tomatoes are quickly damaged by periods of water shortage in normal all-soil growing systems in a greenhouse.

Grow bags

Commercially available plastic bags of so-called soilless growing medium — typically a blend of peat moss, perlite, or vermiculite, sometimes bark, and a dose of complete fertilizer — provide a simple, though expensive, means

RING CULTURE

1 Do not use a natural bed soil for ring culture. Dig a trench the full length of the greenhouse, or to whatever size you have allocated for the greenhouse bed — there are no rules for size.

2 Discard the soil dug from the trench. Line the trench with a single sheet of heavy-gauge plastic, then fill with gravel. This will form a water reservoir and anchorage medium for the plants.

3 Tomatoes are suited to this form of culture. Plant them singly in 8 in (20 cm) bottomless pots filled with good-quality sterilized potting soil. Stand each pot on the gravel. Water via the gravel, but give liquid fertilizer via the pots.

RAISED BEDS

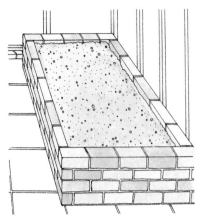

1 A raised bed, constructed from bricks, wood, or concrete, provides an ideal means of growing plants where greenhouse bed soil is poorly drained or where low walls of the greenhouse framework shade the floor.

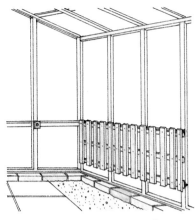

2 With a little ingenuity you can hinge slatted wooden or aluminum shelving so that it can be lowered during summer, leaving the bed soil available for use, but can be secured horizontally to hold containers at other times.

USING GROW BAGS

1 It's cheaper to cultivate bed soil than to buy grow bags, so use them only where the soil is unworkable or on a solid floor. Lay the grow bags on any flat surface; cut holes as needed in each bag.

of growing tomatoes, eggplants, cucumbers, sweet peppers, and other heat-loving, heavy-cropping plants. These grow bags offer the advantage of a naturally sterile growing medium, which is useful where soil-borne pests and diseases are a problem. Unfortunately, the bags can be used for only one growing season, after which the contents are suitable only for mixing with fresh soil as a texture conditioner.

The grow bags can be laid directly on a concrete or pavement floor, or on uncultivated soil in the greenhouse bed. The bag must be of sufficient capacity to give a long root run for large plants — a bag that is at least 3 cu ft (.08 cu m) works well.

Plants cultivated in grow bags must be carefully supported because they do not form deep root structures and the growing medium has little substance. As a result, plants fall over easily unless they are tied in. Do not push garden stakes through the bottom of the bag — you will reduce its water-holding capacity.

You can insert tall stakes into a grow bag, however, and prevent them from falling over by securing the top end to a fixed structure within the greenhouse, such as a roof glazing bar. Tie tall plants to wires, strings, or netting secured to the framework of the greenhouse. Alternatively, stakes may be inserted around a grow bag and strings tied between.

SUPPORT SYSTEMS

2 Grow bags arrive from the supplier dehydrated, which lessens their weight. Open the bags and fully moisten the contents with water, following the instructions — hot water is absorbed much more easily by dry peat moss.

1 Ordinary bamboo or wooden stakes make adequate supports for tall bed-grown greenhouse plants such as tomatoes. Loosely tie plants to the stakes using soft garden string — paper and wire ties may injure stems.

2 Tomatoes can be supported on a line hung from the greenhouse roof — nylon string is the strongest. Simply tie the bottom end of the line loosely around the base of the plant. As the stem grows, twist it around the string.

3 Water carefully — never overwater, but ensure that the growing medium remains moist at all times. New bags contain enough nutrients for a couple of weeks, but liquid fertilizer must be added regularly from then on.

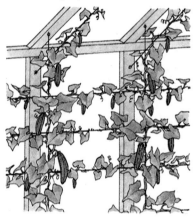

3 Cucumbers are heavy croppers and thus need careful support to prevent the stems from breaking. Fix wires across the glazing bars for the side branches, and vertical strings or wires for the main stem. Tie in each fruit's stalk.

4 For climbing ornamental plants or cucumbers grown against a vertical wall, use nylon netting secured to wooden battens mounted on the wall. Alternatively, erect a wooden or plastic trellis framework.

POTTED PLANTS

**Greenhouse plants that spend their entire life
in containers must be correctly potted and repotted
to maintain health and vigor.**

The concept of potting seems a simple one — merely bedding a plant in some sort of soil in a pot. To be successful, however, you must use the correct type and size of container, choose an appropriate soil type, and pay attention to the seasonal and cultural demands of each plant.

There are three basic methods of potting:

❑ Potting up — moving a seedling, rooted cutting, or plant division into its first container.

❑ Potting on — moving a plant that has outgrown its container into a slightly larger one.

❑ Repotting — providing a mature plant that is not likely to grow any bigger with new soil without increasing the pot size.

Choosing the pot

Most gardeners now use plastic pots rather than ceramic ones, especially for potted plants bought in shops and nurseries. They have a number of advantages, but also several disadvantages compared with unglazed clay, glazed ceramic, and china pots.

Plastic pots are generally quite cheap, easily cleaned, and light to handle and store. They come in a vast range of sizes, colors, and patterns. In addition to clay-colored types, plastic pots come in green, black, white, buff, red, and even mixed colors.

The fact that clay is more porous than plastic is important. Plastic pots are nonporous, so the potting soil can easily become waterlogged. Where the pots stand in a bed of moist gravel or capillary matting to provide constant moisture and extra humidity, plastic pots are essential. Porous types would soak up the water and short-circuit the movement of water up into the soil.

Plastic pots have smooth surfaces, so roots don't cling to them, which makes the removal of plants from their pots much easier. If the root ball does get a grip, the walls of a plastic pot are usually flexible, allowing the bond to be eased apart. However, plastic pots can become brittle, especially when exposed to sun, and then break easily.

Clay pots allow water to evaporate from the side walls as well as the top, so soil dries out more quickly. They are good for plants that enjoy dry conditions, such as cacti, but less suitable for moisture lovers, such as ferns. If you are unsure of a plant's particular water needs, however, there's less chance of waterlogged soil in a clay pot. In areas where the water has a large mineral content, lime deposits build up on the outsides of clay pots as water evaporates, and these can look unsightly.

Clay is much heavier than plastic, so pots are less likely to fall over, especially when tall, unstable plants are grown in a lightweight potting soil. Obviously, this also makes larger sizes more difficult to move around. Cost, too, can be restrictive — clay pots are often at least twice the price of plastic, and glazed ones can be 10 times as expensive.

Pot sizes

A standard pot is measured by

▶ **Potting up** The process of moving young seedlings and rooted cuttings to their first pot is known as potting up. Do not handle seedlings by the fragile roots; instead, hold them gently by the leaves.

POTTING UP

1 Make sure the pot is thoroughly clean: scrub it in a mixture of water and mild detergent to remove old soil and lime deposits, which could harbor disease. Add a few crocks to the bottom if necessary to stop potting soil from falling out through large drainage holes, then partly fill the pot with potting soil.

2 Settle the potting soil by gently bumping the pot on a solid surface, but don't compress it too much or you may encourage waterlogging. Hold the plant in the pot with its neck level with the rim of the pot, then fill with potting soil around the roots. Try to keep the roots well spread out, so that the plant is stable and grows upright.

3 Firm the potting soil by gently bumping the pot against a surface. Don't use your fingers to compress the potting soil, as you can damage the roots of young plants (though with spongy potting soils this is less likely to occur). Fill the pot to within ½-1 in (1-2.5 cm) of the rim. Water well, but don't saturate.

the diameter of its rim or by its height — both are the same. So-called pans, however, are substantially shallower than they are broad, making them ideal for plants with shallow roots and those with a low habit — they give a better-balanced appearance to the potted plant and use less potting soil.

Standard pots range from 2 in (5 cm) all the way up to bucket size or even larger. It is possible to buy all sizes in about ½ in (1 cm) increments, but the most popular sizes for house plants are 4 in (10 cm), 6 in (15 cm), and 8 in (20 cm). Large plants, shrubs, and climbers may need correspondingly larger pots.

Be sure that all pots have adequate drainage holes. (You can use containers with no drainage holes, but you will have to water very carefully to avoid waterlogging; ideally, put a drainage layer of pebbles or crocks — pieces of broken clay pot — in the bottom.)

Round shapes are the most common, but plastic pots in particular come in several other shapes as well, including square. Matching saucers and drip trays are usually available. Some plastic pots and hanging baskets even have built-in or clip-on drip trays.

Potting up

Before use, scrub all pots thoroughly in warm, soapy water. Scrub off encrustations of lime, especially from clay pots. It's best to soak clay pots thoroughly before use, since they absorb a lot of water and quickly dry out.

In general, plastic pots need no drainage material in the bottom because they have several small drainage holes that allow free passage of water without a corresponding loss of potting soil. Clay pots usually have only one drainage hole, but it's quite large, so potting soil can fall through. First cover the drainage hole of a clay pot with a few crocks or clean pebbles. However, if you plan to stand the pot on a capillary watering mat or sand bed, never add crocks — they will only impede the uptake of water.

Begin potting by placing moist potting soil in the bottom of the pot. Firm it down gently. Hold the plant in the pot so that its roots are resting on the potting soil and the base of the plant comes to about 1 in (2.5 cm) below the rim of the pot.

Position the plant carefully, and sprinkle more potting soil around it, filling the pot up to about 1 in (2.5 cm) from the rim

POTTING SOILS

African violet potting soils are rich in humus, moisture retentive, and yet loose enough to accommodate the violet's fine fibrous roots. Mix equal parts of garden loam, leaf mold or peat moss, and sand, and add 1 tsp (15 ml) of bonemeal per quart (liter). This mix works equally well for begonias and many other tropical plants. For use with ferns, add charcoal to keep the soil "sweet."
Bromeliad potting soil is spongy, very porous, and free of lime.
Cactus potting soil should be free-draining. Mix 1 part garden loam with 1 part peat moss or compost and 2 parts coarse builder's sand.
Loam-based potting mixtures have substance and weight — ideal for large, top- or crop-heavy plants. These mixtures retain water and nutrients well. There are many formulas, but a good mix for general use contains 2 parts loam, 1 part leaf mold or peat moss, and 1 part coarse builder's sand. Blend the ingredients, and add 1 lb (½ kg) of bonemeal per bushel (35 liters).
Orchid potting soil (formerly made principally of osmunda fiber but now

more likely to be fir or pine bark) is usually available from nurseries that specialize in growing orchids.
Perlite is a heat-expanded volcanic mineral that holds water very well and also drains freely.
Soilless potting mixtures are based on peat moss, but may include a number of other ingredients, most commonly bark, perlite, and vermiculite. They are clean and light to handle, and save work because they arrive premixed. In addition, because they contain no soil, they do not harbor soil-borne pathogens. However, soilless mixtures lack the nutrients found in soil, so any plants potted into them require heavier and more frequent fertilization. They commonly turn acidic after a few months — as a result, they are most suitable for the cultivation of annuals or vegetable seedlings or other crops that will be transplanted out of their containers while still young.
Vermiculite is a pale, spongy, granular material manufactured from a silicate mineral. It retains a lot of water and air.

POTTING ON

1 Gently remove the plant from its pot. Cover the soil with the palm of one hand, turn the plant over, and then lift off the pot with the other hand. To loosen a plant that is stubbornly stuck in its pot, tap it against a table or run a knife around the rim.

2 Partly fill the new, slightly larger pot with moist potting soil as for potting up. Prepare an exact-size hole for the root ball by using the old pot as a mold, gently firming the potting soil down around the mold by hand. Add more potting soil until the pot is full.

3 Carefully lift out the empty pot — the potting soil should stay in place if it is sufficiently moist. Then insert the plant into the hole and firm it in by tapping the pot down on the table. Fill with more potting soil if necessary, and water the plant well.

(tiny pots can be filled a little fuller). Settle the potting soil by gently tapping the pot on the table or bench. Resist the urge to pack the potting soil in too firmly with your fingertips, as this may damage the roots or eventually lead to waterlogging.

Once potted, water the plant, but don't give it too much — any damaged roots quickly rot if the potting soil is very wet.

Potting on

Container-grown plants must be potted on when they become pot-bound (or repotted if you don't want them to increase in size). A plant is pot-bound when it has filled its pot with roots and exhausted the soil. Under such conditions it makes little or no new growth and dries out rapidly, even when watered frequently. Roots often grow through the drainage holes in the bottom of the pot, giving an obvious indication that the plant is pot-bound.

Young plants and those that you wish to increase in size should be potted on into larger pots every year, preferably in spring or early summer.

To dislodge a pot-bound plant, place one hand over the potting soil with your fingers on either side of the main stem. Lifting the pot from the table, turn it over carefully and tap it firmly on the base with your other hand to shake out the soil ball. If it won't come free, tap the upturned rim of the pot against the edge of the table or shelf.

POT-BOUND PLANTS

A pot-bound plant *(above)* in need of potting on often has roots growing through drainage holes in the pot. You may have to cut these off to release the plant from its pot, or even break open the pot. Fleshy roots often coil around the bottom, but aren't evident until you remove the plant from its pot *(top right)*, so inspect regularly. Gently tease coiled roots away from the ball and trim them back before potting the plant again *(right)*.

If the soil ball still sticks, as can happen with clay pots, use a knife with a long, thin blade (an old kitchen knife works well) to slice carefully around the edge of the soil. Poke a stick through the drainage hole to apply extra pressure if necessary.

Select a new pot that is slightly larger than the plant's previous container — approximately 1 in (2.5 cm) larger for small to medium-size plants, or up to 3 in (7.5 cm) larger for bulkier ones. Depending on the depth of the root ball, put a 1-2 in (2.5-5 cm) layer of potting soil in the base of the new pot.

Set the root ball on the soil so that the top is about ½ in (1 cm) below the base of the broader rim of the pot. Hold the plant in the center, and sprinkle more potting soil into the space between the root ball and pot. It is possible at this stage to straighten a plant that is listing to one side.

Cover the top of the ball with potting soil. Gently bump the pot down on the table to settle the potting soil, then fill to within ½-1 in (1-2.5 cm) of the top with more potting soil. Water the plant well and leave it to drain.

When potting on fragile plants or those with a spreading habit, it may be difficult to fill in the new potting soil without damaging the foliage or stems. To avoid this problem, prepare a mold of potting soil by first "potting" the old, empty pot in the new one.

Repotting

Established plants that have reached their required size still need new soil every year or so to remain healthy, but the pot size need not be increased.

First, remove the plant from its pot as before and thoroughly clean the pot. If the soil ball and roots are fairly loose, gently tease away some of the spent potting soil and sever a few old roots completely. This allows space for new potting soil to be added. Return the plant to its pot as before.

If the soil ball is hard and crammed with matted roots, simply slice some of the ball off with a sharp knife. Root pruning, however, does weaken the plant somewhat, and renewed growth will be quite slow.

Topdressing

This is a simpler method of revitalizing an established plant. This method is suitable for mature plants in heavy, unwieldy containers. Instead of removing the plant from its pot, tilt the pot and scrape out the top surface of the old soil with a small fork or spoon. Do not damage the stem or any large, essential roots. Then fill with fresh potting soil, firm it down gently, and water as before.

Incorporating a moss pole

Moss poles are long plastic tubes bound with moss — held in place with nylon thread — suitable for supporting climbing plants with aerial roots such as Swiss-cheese plant (*Monstera*), syngoniums, and certain philodendrons. Unlike other forms of support for pot plants, they are bulky in cross section and cannot simply be pushed into the potting soil. Instead, they must be incorporated when the plant is potted.

Position the root ball off-center in the new pot, and stand the moss pole in place behind the plant before filling the pot with

REPOTTING

1 Reduce the size of the root ball by teasing away loose soil and severing some old roots. Slice solid, matted root balls with a knife if necessary.

2 Partly fill the original pot — or a new one of the same size — with fresh potting soil. Position the plant, and fill in around the root ball. Water the plant.

TOPDRESSING

1 Without removing the plant from its pot, scrape the old surface soil away, taking care not to damage the base of the stem or major roots. An old kitchen fork is an ideal tool.

2 Clean away mineral deposits from the rim of the pot, then refill it with fresh potting soil up to the original level. Firm it in gently, and water well. Restake and trim the plant if necessary.

the new potting soil. Ensure that the pole is upright and securely firmed in. Tie stems to it with soft thread at first — aerial roots will eventually grow into the moss and support the plant.

Finishing touches

An additional topdressing of gravel or marble chips improves the appearance of potted plants and helps to reduce water evaporation from the potting soil. This is particularly beneficial to cacti and many hairy-leaved plants, which dislike having moist potting soil in contact with their leaves. Gravel and stone chips are available in many different colors and sizes to suit all purposes.

Outdoor pots can be given a topdressing of wood bark chips to reduce water loss, improve appearance, and deter weeds.

HANDLING PRICKLY CACTI

The spines of many cacti are very sharp, making handling during potting difficult and dangerous — some are barbed and can even cause infection if lodged in flesh.

Make a strap from a piece of rolled-up paper or thin cardboard. Pinch it firmly around the base of the cactus, and you will be able to maneuver the plant quite easily.

GREENHOUSE PROPAGATION

**A greenhouse is the ideal setting in which
to experiment with new plants — growing them from seed,
cuttings, divisions, and offsets.**

A small unheated greenhouse can provide ideal conditions for rooting cuttings, germinating seeds, and carrying out most other types of plant propagation. If you can install some form of heating — even if it is only a small heated compartment — within the greenhouse, the scope for raising new plants is even wider.

In order to germinate or root well, most seeds or sections of material taken from indoor plants and from soft-stemmed garden plants need warmth. And although many hardy, woody garden plants will germinate or root at lower temperatures (easily provided in a cold frame or outdoor nursery bed), a constant, controlled greenhouse environment will ensure much better results.

It is usually possible to keep plant material suitably warm and moist in an inexpensive plastic-topped propagation box or improvised unit placed on an indoor windowsill. But space is invariably a limiting factor indoors, so if you want to propagate large numbers of plants — especially if you enjoy growing annual bedding plants — you will need to set

aside a section of the greenhouse.

Another problem associated with raising new plants in the house is lack of light. Although a windowsill may be bright, the light comes from one direction only and seedlings are drawn toward it, producing leggy, thin-stemmed plants. Devices such as aluminum foil reflecting screens can be set up to reflect light back onto the young plants, but they are cumbersome and ugly. In any case, shade seedlings and cuttings on a windowsill from direct sun, or they will dry out, wilt, and die.

A greenhouse eliminates these problems. If properly sited, natural sunshine keeps the plants well lit all day and from all angles, so that new growth is even, compact, and upright.

The air temperature increase caused by sunlight through the greenhouse glass or plastic glazing is used to beneficial effect. With better air circulation and the means to maintain much higher humidity, high temperatures no longer dry out the soil and kill the plants. Instead, high, constant temperatures encourage better plant metabolism and

hence improve germination, rooting, and subsequent growth.

Essential conditions
Taking cuttings or sowing seeds and merely placing the flats or pots in a greenhouse will not ensure success — you must get all the growing conditions right and make appropriate allowances for different types of plants.

Humidity For most plants, a humid atmosphere is essential for vegetative propagation (that is, using cut sections of shoot, stem, or leaf). Humidity helps to prevent water loss from a cutting, which is temporarily unable to take up moisture readily because it has been severed from its roots.

Loss of moisture is greatest where leaves are included in the cutting, because the leaves continue to transpire — give off moisture from their pores. Leafless stem-section cuttings, on the other hand, don't transpire very much or at all. But if the rooting medium in which they are set dries out, they will soon wither and eventually die.

Maintaining high humidity in the air is more effective than watering as a means of maintaining an optimum amount of moisture in the rooting medium. This is because watering — even if carried out on a very regular basis — is intermittent, so there are fluctuations in the water content of the medium. Where frequent regular watering is not possible, the medium can go through severe fluctuations of wetness and dryness, doing great damage to the emerging roots or discouraging rooting in the first place.

However, humid air is not a requirement for the rooting of cuttings taken from fleshy-

◀ **Vegetative propagation** By planning the timing of softwood cuttings, flowering and foliage plants can be kept at a continuous stage of growth. The light shade that is cast by flowering begonias and fuchsias is beneficial to young pelargoniums and flats of rooted cuttings waiting to be potted up.

PROPAGATION BOXES

1 An improvised single-pot case can be made simply by inserting a wire hoop in the seed-starting mix or rooting medium and covering it with a clear-plastic bag. Use string or a rubber band to secure the bag, and punch a few holes for aeration.

2 Unheated ready-made propagators have a rigid plastic cover over an ordinary seed flat. They come in a range of sizes and have ventilation holes in the top. Individual pots or small flats are placed beneath the cover.

3 More elaborate heated boxes have thermostatically controlled electric heating cables buried in the base below the rooting medium. This allows the temperature to be regulated to suit any special needs of each batch.

stemmed plants, such as cacti and other succulents and certain perennials and subshrubs, including pelargoniums.

Even where high humidity is required, the secondary effect it has of encouraging fungal diseases can be a major problem unless good ventilation is maintained. Always make sure that fresh air circulates around cuttings or seedlings — at least from time to time.

Temperature Most cuttings and seeds start growth best at a temperature of at least 66°F (19°C). Tropical plants generally require higher temperatures — above 75°F (24°C). Use a minimum-maximum thermometer to monitor the temperature during the night and day, and take steps to ensure that the heating remains as constant as possible.

Rooting powder This powder contains a synthetic plant rooting hormone, identical to the one normally produced by plants. Soft-stemmed plants usually root swiftly without the assistance of extra hormones, and a thick coating of powder on the base of the stem or leaf can actually form a barrier against successful rooting. If you want to use a rooting powder on soft-stemmed cuttings, make sure the dusting is light.

Woody stems root more slowly, and the process can be speeded up by dusting the base of the cutting with hormone rooting powder. Buy fresh powder every year — it

becomes less effective with age.

Propagating media Standard potting soils are not suitable for cuttings or seeds. The texture of such mixtures is too heavy, and they contain too much nutrient, which may scorch delicate young roots. All that is required of the propagating medium is that it holds moisture well, yet prevents waterlogging.

For germinating seeds, it is best to buy one of the commercial seed-starting mixes, though you should make sure that the product has been steam-pasteurized.

An effective blend for rooting and one that it is easy and inexpensive to make is composed of equal parts coarse builder's sand and peat moss. First remove any

CREATING THE RIGHT ENVIRONMENT

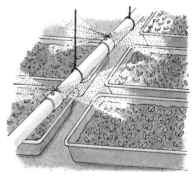

1 Maintain humidity around newly sown seeds by covering the flat with glass, rigid transparent plastic, or clear plastic film. For surface-sown seeds that need darkness to germinate, sandwich pieces of newspaper under the glass.

2 During direct hot sunshine, provide shade for cuttings or seedlings in a propagating case by covering them with a semi-opaque fabric. A piece of burlap, plastic shading cloth, or the sacking used to contain root vegetables is ideal.

3 A spray tube fitted with mist nozzles at intervals and connected to a water supply is the ideal means of maintaining high humidity around seedlings or cuttings. The system can be manually operated or automatic.

MIST PROPAGATION UNIT

LABOR-SAVING UNITS

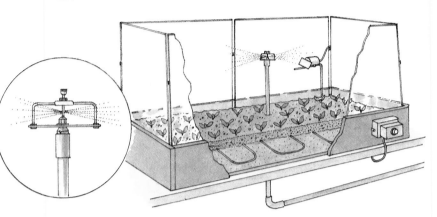

The specially constructed mist unit provides a fine spray of water in the air above the cuttings or seedlings. An electronic humidity sensor monitors evaporation from an artificial leaf. The sensor automatically assesses when to switch on the mist nozzle, and a time switch or light/moisture sensor controls a cut-off valve in the water supply pipe. In this way, the real plant material never dries out, nor does it get too wet.

A probe thermostat controls electric heating cables that have been buried in the sand in the base of the unit. Cuttings can be rooted directly in rooting medium laid on top of the sand; seedlings can be raised in flats bedded in the medium. Shade the mist unit from hot, direct sun.

1 Special multiple dibble plates can be bought to speed up and simplify the sowing of large seeds and the spacing of seedlings. Level the seed-starting mix in the flat, then firm the dibble plate into the surface to make equally spaced holes. Press lightly to make shallow holes for small seeds.

impurities from the peat moss by passing it through a sieve made of ¼ in (6 mm) wire mesh, also known as hardware cloth.

Such a mixture is naturally sterile (peat contains antiseptic properties) and well drained but moisture retentive. The fact that it tends to stay moist makes it ideal for tropicals and many other leafy plants, but less than ideal for rooting plants that need dry conditions. Such plants, pelargoniums, and evergreen trees and shrubs (yews, junipers, and arborvitaes) root better in clean coarse sand.

Various other materials such as perlite or vermiculite may be incorporated into rooting media, but remember that whatever you use, it must be sterile — the presence of fungal spores leads to rot diseases. For this reason, never use garden soil or old potting soil.

Germinated seeds and rooted cuttings soon need more food than is provided by seedling/cutting mixtures. They should be transplanted into potting soil or a soilless mix that contains fertilizer as soon as they are large enough to handle. Liquid feeding with a weak solution of ordinary houseplant fertilizer provides a good temporary alternative if you must delay transplanting for any amount of time.

Propagation boxes

The simplest way to maintain high humidity for greenhouse propagation is by means of a plastic-topped case or frame. These can be bought from most garden centers and catalogs and come in a range of sizes and shapes.

It may seem odd to put a miniature greenhouse within a greenhouse, but unless you are able to hose down the floor and staging every few hours, or invest in a humidifying system, this is the best method, especially for small amounts of cuttings or seeds. You can also use ordinary plastic containers with transparent lids designed for storing foods.

For individual pots of cuttings or seeds, the simplest covering is a transparent plastic bag. A few sticks or hoops of wire inserted in the rooting or seed-starting mix will hold the bag upright.

Once rooting has occurred, high humidity is less essential, so remove the cover to let more air reach the leaves and prevent fungal diseases. With the propagation boxes, this can be done in easy stages with the aid of one or more adjustable vents in the cover. If you are using a plastic bag as a cover, slice open one side of the bag at first, and remove the bag entirely only after a few days of acclimatization.

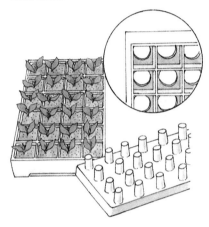

2 Special polystyrene slabs with small, pot-shaped insulated cells are ideal for bedding plants. By putting seedlings one to a cell, the roots of adjacent plants don't grow together and form knotted masses. A studded drip tray serves as a soil-compressing tool and is later used to push the plants out of their cells.

3 Miniature grow bags can also be used for rooting cuttings. Simply lay the bag flat, cut holes in the top, and moisten the soilless mix inside. Insert the cuttings through the holes and into the mix. Because they are enclosed, the bag's contents remain more constantly moist than the soil in a pot.

SUMMARY OF PROPAGATION TECHNIQUES

Vegetative propagation methods are those that involve cutting and growing on sections of plants:

Division is used to propagate plants that grow in clumps. After you have removed the clump from its container, break the clump apart or cut it into pieces, each with roots and top growth attached. Replant the pieces.

Layering is when roots and shoots are encouraged to develop on stems buried in a rooting medium but still attached to the parent plant. Air layering is a special technique where roots are encouraged to sprout from a stem above ground.

Leaf cuttings are taken by detaching individual leaves and inserting their stalks in rooting medium. In a few cases, you can cut the leaf into pieces without any stalk, each of which you insert, cut edge down, in the medium. Or you can peg a whole leaf down flat and encourage shoots to sprout by making slices across the veins.

Offsets are small replicas of the parent plant that spring directly from the base of the parent's stem; you can detach these offsets and pot them up. Many bulbs also produce offsets, which can be grown on.

Plantlets are replicas that some plants naturally produce by themselves. You can detach these and pot them up individually.

Shoot-tip cuttings are taken by cutting off the tips of shoots, with two or more leaves attached, and inserting them in rooting medium.

Stem-section cuttings are similar to tip cuttings, but older stem material from lower down the plant is used. Trim away the soft tip growth and discard it.

Propagation from seed
Large numbers of new plants can be raised from seed, and this is the most common way for gardeners to propagate annuals.

HANDLING SEEDLINGS

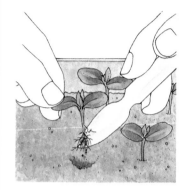

When pricking out a seedling, make sure always to handle it gently by a leaf — either a seed leaf or a true leaf. Never hold it by the stem, because if you injure the stem, the seedling may rot and die. Though you may slightly damage the leaf by holding it, the growing tip and stem will not be affected, and the seedling will survive.

Heated boxes have a heating element incorporated in the plastic base or in separate heating trays. You will need a professionally installed and grounded electrical outlet in the greenhouse if you choose this type.

Small electrically heated cases have a built-in pre-set thermostat, which is set to a moderate temperature suitable for the propagation of most plants. Larger cases have an adjustable thermostat. Carefully consider your needs before you buy — the larger cases often give more value for money and provide greater scope for raising a selection of plants.

There is no need to operate the case at high heat. Most seeds will germinate at a maximum temperature of 66°F (19°C), and cuttings root readily at around 70°F (21°C). Excessive temperatures can inhibit seed germination.

To prevent scorching of the plant material, all propagation boxes should be shaded lightly during periods of direct sunlight.

Mist propagation
Intermittent mist spraying is an expensive but more efficient alternative to keeping cuttings or seedlings in a closed case or in a bag. A thin film of moisture is maintained over the leaf surfaces using a water jet controlled automatically by an electronic sensor.

With this method, propagation can be carried out in full sunlight or with just very light shading, and normal plant growth and food production within the leaves can take place efficiently.

Heat from underneath the cuttings or seedlings — known as bottom heat — is usually needed to balance the cooling effect of moisture passing through the rooting medium and to encourage healing, callus formation, and rooting of cuttings.

With mist propagation, rooting is more rapid and certain. Also there is less risk of disease because spores of fungal organisms are washed away.

However, cuttings rooted by mist propagation need to be weaned gradually to drier air.

Small mist units, with a transparent surrounding screen to keep the mist within bounds, are available, but cost more than a heated propagator.

Alternatively, you can build your own mist unit. In addition to basic materials for making the case, you will need PVC pipe, mist nozzles, heating cables, a thermostat and humidity sensor, and a control unit. Seek advice from a greenhouse supplies dealer and from a licensed electrician before starting such a project.

PREVENTING FUNGAL DISEASES

1 When sowing seeds under glass, always use a sterile seed-starting mix. Read the label — most commercial mixes are sterilized before being sealed into their bags and are fine-textured enough for even tiny seeds.

2 Take care not to overwater seedlings, especially in a cool greenhouse — seedlings must not be kept continually wet. Drenching the soil with an approved fungicide helps prevent fungal diseases such as damping-off.

GREENHOUSE PESTS

The warmth and humidity of a greenhouse promote growth, but they also encourage pests and diseases.

▲ **Greenhouse aphids** The many species of aphids are among the most common and troublesome greenhouse pests. They make shoot tips and flowers sticky, deplete the plants' energy, and frequently transmit virus diseases.

The best way to keep greenhouse plants healthy is to give them the right growing conditions. Often pest troubles are due to inadequate care and attention.

Many diseases result from poor cultivation — periods of excessive dryness or unduly humid air, lack of air movement among crowded plants, and overwatering. It is generally easy to deal with such problems once they are spotted.

Pests are harder to guard against. Some live all year in the greenhouse, and others come in through windows and doors or are introduced on new stock.

Try to keep newly acquired plants in isolation until you are sure they are healthy — if there are eggs or spores concealed on the plant, they can soon spread.

Examine all plants regularly for signs of trouble. The succulent shoot tips are usually the first to be attacked by sap-sucking pests. Fungal diseases often appear on mature leaves. Any unusual leaf or flower disfigurement or discoloration can be a sign of trouble. Turn leaves back to check the undersides.

Also check the pots and potting soil. A white crust on the surface of the soil or around the rim of clay pots may simply indicate that you are using very hard water, but it can also result from overfertilization. Collected rainwater, provided it is clean, is softer and more suitable than tap water for watering potted plants. A green scum of algal growth on the soil or around the rim of the pot indicates overwatering or poor drainage.

There are many liquid and mixable greenhouse insecticides and fungicides. Follow the manufacturer's instructions exactly for handling and applying these chemicals — be sure always to wear rubber gloves and any other recommended protective gear.

Biological controls

Some pests have become resistant to chemical pesticides but can be treated by biological controls. These controls are a plant's natural enemies — its predators, parasites, or diseases. They are introduced into the greenhouse in order to control the pest. Such beneficial controls must be put on the host plants before the infestation becomes heavy, and they need a temperature of 70°F (21°C) for at least part of the day if they are to breed fast enough to overcome the pests. The most effective period is midspring to midfall, though root weevil nematodes should be applied in late summer when young grubs are present. The caterpillar bacterium *(Bacillus thuringiensis)*, or Bt, can be used at any time and can also be applied to some outdoor plants such as cabbages.

Most insecticides are harmful to natural pest controls, and you should not apply them in conjunction with biological controls. Even a mild insecticidal soap is as lethal to a beneficial insect as it is to a pest.

◄ **Tomato late blight** This fungal disease can eventually lead to rotting of the fruit. Plant resistant cultivars, or spray your plants with Bordeaux mixture to prevent the disease from taking hold.

APHIDS

Plants affected Most plants.
Symptoms Colonies of small, round-bodied green, pink, reddish, yellow, or black insects, mostly wingless but often with some winged individuals present. Leave sticky excretions on leaves.
Danger period Any time.
Treatment Use biological controls, or spray with insecticidal soap or horticultural oil. For serious infestations spray with acephate, malathion, permethrin, or neem (except on food crops).

BLACKLEG

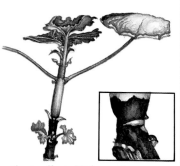

Plants affected Pelargoniums.
Symptoms A black rot develops at the base of cuttings or at the stem base, and the affected tissues become soft. Leaves turn yellow, and eventually the whole cutting or stem dies.
Danger period Soon after cuttings are taken.
Treatment Destroy badly affected plants. Use sterilized potting soil; maintain strict greenhouse hygiene.

CATERPILLARS

Plants affected Carnations, chrysanthemums, and many greenhouse plants.
Symptoms Petals eaten; caterpillars often visible inside the blooms. Irregular holes in leaves.
Danger period Any time.
Treatment If relatively few plants are affected, remove the caterpillars by hand. For larger infestations of caterpillars, use biological control (*Bacillus thuringiensis*) or spray with carbaryl or pyrethrin.

DAMPING-OFF

Plants affected Any seedlings, especially fast-growing species, which tend to have the softest stems. Bedding plants are susceptible.
Symptoms Seedlings rot and collapse at soil level. The disease may affect a small group of seedlings or spread rapidly through an entire flat or pot of seedlings.

Danger period Soon after germinating seedlings emerge.
Treatment Maintain good greenhouse ventilation, and space seedlings the appropriate distance apart. Remove collapsed seedlings immediately. Water remaining seedlings with soluble-powder copper sulfates or copper oxychloride.

BIOLOGICAL PEST CONTROL

The following biological controls are commercially available from specialist suppliers. They are best used from midspring to midfall.
Aphids
Ladybugs, lacewings, and midge larva *Aphiodoletes aphidimyza.*
Caterpillars
Bacterium *Bacillus thuringiensis* (Bt).
Greenhouse spider mite
Predatory mite *Phytoseiulus persimilis.*
Greenhouse whitefly
Parasitic wasp *Encarsia formosa.*
Mealybugs
Ladybug predator (*Cryptolaemus montrouzeri*) and convergent lady beetle (*Hippodamia convergens*).
Root weevil grubs
Pathogenic nematodes *Steinernema carpocapsae* and *Heterorhabditis bacteriophora.* (Application depends on life cycle of the target pest.)
Scale insects (soft scale, hemispherical scale) Predatory midge larva *Aphiodoletes aphidimyza.*

GRAY MOLD (botrytis blight)

Plants affected All types.
Symptoms Gray velvety mold on rotting leaves.
Danger period Growing season.
Treatment Remove and destroy affected parts when plants are not wet. Water early in the day. Remove all debris. Avoid crowding plants to enhance air circulation. Spray with thiopanate-methyl; nonfood crops with benomyl. Clean greenhouse with bleach and water solution.

LEAFHOPPERS

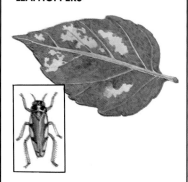

Plants affected Many types, especially pelargoniums, primulas, and tomatoes.
Symptoms Coarse white flecks on leaves; insect skins present on the undersides. Small yellowish-green insects leap from leaves.
Danger period Any time.
Treatment Spray thoroughly with insecticidal soap. For serious infestations spray with rotenone, malathion, or pyrethrin.

LEAF MINERS

Plants affected Many types, especially chrysanthemums.
Symptoms Whitish-brown twisting lines on leaves trace tunnels mined in the inner tissues by small fly maggots. Growth is weakened.
Danger period Any time.
Treatment If numbers are few, pick off and destroy each affected leaf. Spray more serious outbreaks with horticultural oil, neem (on nonfood crops), or chlorpyrifos.

LEAF MOLD

Plants affected Tomatoes.
Symptoms Purple-brown mold on undersides of leaves; yellow blotches on upper surfaces.
Danger period Summer.
Treatment Grow resistant cultivars. Ventilate and space plants properly. Spray with thiophanate-methyl or mancozeb. Disinfect greenhouse with chlorine bleach and water.

MEALYBUGS

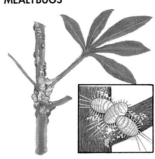

Plants affected Many types.
Symptoms Colonies of pink bugs covered with white mealy or waxy wool, usually concentrated around buds and leaf axils.
Danger period All year.
Treatment Remove insects with tweezers or toothpicks, and wash plants with 2 tsp (10 ml) of mild dish detergent in 1 gal (4.5 lit) of water. Use biological controls or spray with insecticidal soap, neem (on nonfood crops), or malathion.

SPIDER MITES

Plants affected Many types, especially impatiens, fuchsias, vines, cucumbers, and tomatoes.
Symptoms Fine mottling of upper leaf surfaces, yellow discoloration, and silk webbing between leaves.
Danger period Any time.
Treatment Maintain high humidity. Use biological controls, or spray with insecticidal soap, horticultural oil, or malathion.

SCALE INSECTS

Plants affected Many types, especially camellias, bays, citruses, poinsettias, and ferns.
Symptoms Flat or rounded, yellow or whitish-brown scales, mainly on the undersides of the leaves and lying alongside veins.
Danger period Any time.
Treatment Spray with insecticidal soap (half normal dilution for ferns), acephate, or pyrethrin + rotenone. Use biological controls.

SCORCH

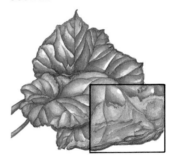

Plants affected Most plants growing in greenhouses.
Symptoms Pale brown spots appear on the leaves or affected plants, but sometimes entire leaves become papery.
Danger period Mainly summer, during prolonged spells of hot sunshine.
Treatment Shade the greenhouse with blinds, shading cloth, or shading paint. Ensure that the potting soil does not dry out.

TARSONEMID MITES

Plants affected Begonias, fuchsias, gerberas, cyclamens, amaryllises (*Hippeastrum*), ferns, and others.
Symptoms Very small, slow-moving mites, similar to spider mites, but feeding in concealed parts of the plants — for instance, protected in buds or in the crevice of a sheathing leaf. New growths are checked and distorted by severe infestations, and leaf edges are slightly curled, thick, and brittle. Flower buds may be killed; those that open are discolored and often very distorted.
Danger period Any time.
Treatment No chemical treatment gives effective control. Destroy infected plants.

87

TOMATO GREENBACK AND BLOTCHY RIPENING

Plants affected Tomatoes.
Symptoms Flattened brownish-gray blotches develop on green fruit, remaining gray or turning yellow as fruit ripens. Cut fruit shows dark brown tissue in vascular walls. Greenback may be associated with scorch.
Danger period As the tomato fruit swells and ripens.

Treatment Grow resistant tomato cultivars such as 'Count II,' 'Duke,' 'Floridade,' and 'Walter.' In order to maintain even growth of the fruit, never allow the soil to dry out. Also avoid high soil moisture, as well as high humidity and high-nitrogen, low-potassium fertilizers. Shade and maintain good ventilation during hot weather. Don't let the greenhouse temperature rise excessively, but maintain steady warmth.

VINE WEEVILS

Plants affected Begonias, cyclamens, gloxinias, and others.
Symptoms Legless white grubs, up to ⅜ in (8 mm) long, eat roots, tubers, and corms. Leaves wilt. Adults eat notches from plant leaf edges.
Danger period Any time.
Treatment Remove dead leaves and debris from around the base of potted plants. Spray with chlorpyrifos; use biological controls at larval stage.

VIRUSES

Plants affected Pelargoniums and many other plants.
Symptoms Variable, according to plant affected — color changes in leaves and stems; wilting, crinkling, and stunting of leaves.
Danger period Any time.
Treatment No chemical treatment available. Maintain good greenhouse hygiene; control aphids and leafhoppers, which spread viruses; destroy and dispose of any affected plants.

WHITEFLIES

Plants affected Many, especially cucumbers, fuchsias, pelargoniums, and tomatoes.
Symptoms Small white mothlike flies take off from the undersides of leaves when disturbed. Leaves are discolored and sticky.
Danger period Any time.
Treatment Use biological controls or yellow sticky traps. Treat serious infestations with spray of insecticidal soap, horticultural oil, neem (on nonfood crops), or acephate.

OTHER TROUBLES

Earwigs eat irregular, tattered holes in the leaves of many plants, or they may bite flower petals. They are active at night from late spring to midfall. These small brown insects hide during the day under pots and among debris on the floor or benches. Trap them in rolled newspapers, and shake into soapy water every morning; for serious infestations spray with malathion.
Fungus gnat larvae feed primarily on fungi, but occasionally attack roots of growing plants and can be destructive to young ones. Midgelike adults up to 3/16 in (5 mm) long often swarm over the surface of moist potting mixes, especially soilless mixes. Repot plants into sterile media, eliminate stagnant water (as in plant saucers), and spray with Bt.
Rust disease affects many plant types. Brown, orange, or yellow powdery masses of fungal spores develop on affected leaves and stems during the

growing season. Remove diseased tissues. Maintain good air circulation, and ventilate the greenhouse to reduce humidity. Apply sulfur when greenhouse temperature is below 85°F (29°C).
Slugs and snails crawl into the greenhouse, eating irregular holes in plant leaves in summer and fall. Characteristic slime trails mark their paths. Maintain good greenhouse hygiene. Sprinkle slug baits around the floor.
Thrips attack tomatoes and many ornamental plants, causing fine, light-colored mottling on leaves, giving them a silvery appearance. Avoid underwatering and overheating the plants. Use biological controls, or spray with acephate, neem, or chlorpyrifos — but only if specifically recommended for affected plant.
Tomato late blight is a serious fungal disease of outdoor tomatoes, but may also occur in cool greenhouses. Brownish-black blotches develop on

the leaves; dark streaks and spots develop on green fruits, and brown discoloration spreads over ripening fruits until they shrivel and rot. Plant resistant cultivars. Spray with Bordeaux mixture or fixed copper after blossoming (not on young plants).
Tomato leaf mold occurs in early summer to midsummer. Light yellowish-green patches develop on upper leaf surfaces, yellowing further as purple or olive-green mold spreads over lower leaf surface. Leaves eventually wither and die. Plant growth is checked and fruit is slow to develop. Remove infected leaves or entire plants. Plant resistant cultivars, maintain good ventilation, and avoid high temperatures with high humidity. Spray with fixed copper, mancozeb, or thiophanate-methyl as a preventive measure. Disinfect the greenhouse at the season's end with chlorine bleach and water.

GROWING ORCHIDS

**Many orchids will flourish in a cool greenhouse
or conservatory, and with a little extra care and heat,
some tropical ones can also be grown.**

Orchids are members of the Orchidaceae family. There are some 30,000 species, originating in almost every country, making this one of the largest families of flowering plants. Orchids' natural habitats vary from up among the leafy canopies of tropical forests, through woodland floors, to heaths, grasslands, marshes, and even semideserts.

Orchid flowers vary widely in size, shape, and color. Most are specially adapted for pollination by insects and other animals. They produce vast numbers of dustlike seeds, which are dispersed by wind in the wild. Orchid seed may not germinate under artificial conditions, however, so gardeners propagate them by division of the bulbs or cuttings. Commercially, orchids may be increased in a laboratory by meristem tissue culture, a special micro-propagation technique.

Though several types of orchids will survive on a windowsill, this situation is rarely ideal. If you want to grow a wide range of these exquisite plants, you really need a cool greenhouse or shelving equipped with fluorescent lights. Since low humidity is fatal to most tropical species, a greenhouse certainly provides the best growing space for them.

Choosing orchids

Hundreds of modern hybrids and a wide range of natural species suitable for home gardeners are available from specialist nurseries. Beginners should choose among *Angraecum, Brassia, × Brassolaeliocattleya, Cattleya, Coelogyne, Cymbidium, Dendrobium, Laelia, × Laeliocattleya, Lycaste, Miltonia, × Odontioda, Odontoglossum, Oncidium, Paphiopedilum, Phalaenopsis, Pleione, Vanda,* and *× Vuylstekeara.* Most orchids can be divided into either cool greenhouse types, such as *Coelogyne, Cymbidium,* and *Pleione,* or warm greenhouse (tropical) types, such as *Miltonia* and *Phalaenopsis.* (See pages 95–98.)

Growing conditions

The ideal growing conditions for the majority of orchids include humidity of 40-60 percent and fairly strong light for 12-14 hours a day. These needs can be met indoors by a humidifier and banks of 4 ft (1.2 m) fluorescent lights (keep these 6 in/15 cm from the tops of the plants and include both warm and cool tubes). Most serious growers, however, eventually opt for some sort of greenhouse as well — if only a small unit that mounts on the outside of an ordinary window.

Tropical orchids need very warm conditions, but can be grown economically in a cool greenhouse by keeping them in a fairly tall glass frame (a sort of terrarium) set up on the benches. At least six tropical orchids will fit into a frame 2 ft × 2 ft (60 cm × 60 cm) square and 3 ft (90 cm) tall. A heating cable on the frame's floor should provide enough heat, but if necessary the walls can be lined on the inside with clear-plastic film for extra insulation during winter.

Fix the plastic sheeting to wooden supports around the sides and top of the frame, leaving a 1 in (2.5 cm) space between plastic and glass. In summer remove the plants from the frame and keep them in the greenhouse or move them outside into the shade of trees if the temperature inside the greenhouse rises much above 85°F (29°C).

Another alternative is to construct a glazed partition at the end of the greenhouse, forming a cubicle that can be kept warmer and more humid. This can provide quite a large area for tropical

◀ **Lady's slipper orchids** The numerous species and hybrids of *Paphiopedilum* are characterized by their exotic, waxy-textured flowers, each with a pronounced slipper-shaped pouch. The colors vary from yellow, green, and brown to violet, purple, and deep crimson, striped, speckled, or marbled. Some lady's slipper orchids (*P. insigne*) can be grown as houseplants.

Cymbidium
'Rincon Clarisse'

Cattleya 'Pink
Debutante'

Dendrobium
wardianum

pansy orchid
Miltonia 'Hamburg Stonehurst'

tiger orchid
Odontoglossum 'Natrium Mont Millais'

orchids. During the winter, line the area with plastic sheeting mounted on wooden frames. Remove the plastic in spring, when maximum sunlight is needed.

A window-mounted miniature greenhouse offers another excellent place for growing tropical orchids if it is equipped with a humidifier. If possible, keep the frame in a north- or east-facing window in summer, and in a south- or west-facing window in winter. Cultural requirements are the same as for greenhouses, but ventilation is crucial as temperature changes are more rapid in a small space.

Providing heat
The cool greenhouse orchids need a minimum temperature of 45°F (7°C) in winter and 57°F (14°C) in summer. Tropical orchids need a minimum temperature of 61°F (16°C) in winter — although they will tolerate brief cooler periods

— and 72°F (22°C) in summer. However, many commonly grown orchids, such as *Cattleya, Dendrobium, Odontoglossum,* and some *Paphiopedilum* species tolerate temperatures intermediate between these two ranges.

To provide heat, an electric fan heater with a thermostatic control is ideal as it keeps the air moving. A 3-kw heater will keep a 10 ft × 8 ft (3 m × 2.4 m) greenhouse warm enough for cool-house orchids. A 4.5-kw heater is needed in the same-size greenhouse for tropical orchids.

If you are growing tropical orchids in a separate section of a cool greenhouse, you will probably need an additional smaller heater in this section.

Providing humidity
In their natural habitat, many orchids grow in areas where water vapor rises from the damp ground or foliage around them. These

lady's slipper orchid
Paphiopedilum 'Chipmunk Vermont'

moth orchid
Phalaenopsis schilleriana

Vanda
'Rose Davis'

TYPICAL ORCHID FLOWER STRUCTURE

petal

sepal (dorsal)

column

petal

anther cap with pollen sac (pollinia) beneath

sepal (lateral)

sepal (lateral)

lip or labellum (modified lower petal)

An orchid flower has three outer sepals, which are often colored to match the petals, alternating with three inner petals. The lower petal (lip or labellum) is modified in shape and contrastingly colored or marked. The lip serves as a showy landing platform for pollinating insects. The plant's fingerlike column carries the reproductive organs.

a ventilator at the bottom of the greenhouse can be opened to increase air flow in hot weather.

Fans can be connected to a thermostat, so that they come on automatically when the temperature becomes too high.

The least expensive way to ventilate is with traditional ventilators fitted to the top and bottom of the greenhouse on both sides. It is preferable to have one top vent and one bottom vent on each side of the orchid house for every 4 ft (1.2 m) of its length. Bottom ventilators should be at least 1 ft × 2 ft (30 cm × 60 cm), and covered with fine-mesh screening to keep out pests.

During summer, open the top vent on the leeward side by 4-6 in (10-15 cm) day and night. On very hot days also open the bottom ventilators on the same side. With below-average temperatures, close all ventilators.

In winter close the top ventilators to retain the warm air, and open the bottom vents on the leeward side to allow fresh air into the greenhouse.

plants absorb moisture through both their leaves and roots.

This level of humidity must be produced in the greenhouse by spraying water frequently on the flooring and on the staging where the plants stand. Light but frequent damping is more effective than occasional flooding.

In summer, dampen the orchid house at least once a day — in the morning — and preferably again in the late afternoon or evening. If the weather is particularly hot, three or four dampings may be necessary, as well as mist spraying of the foliage. In winter, two or three dampings a week are sufficient, before midday. Do not dampen if the outside temperature is below freezing.

The easiest method of damping the benches and shelving is to apply tap water through a hose with a fine-spray nozzle. Do not spray the water on the flowers or bulb bases. To avoid this, stand the plants permanently on upturned flower pots. When tropical orchids are grown in a frame, dampen with a hand-held plastic sprayer or atomizer filled with clean water.

Automatic misting systems provide a fine mist at intervals from a spray line, according to instructions received from computerized humidity sensors, but they are expensive to install.

Providing ventilation

Fresh air is essential to all orchids, but it must be provided without causing a draft or lowering the temperature or the humidity. A close, muggy atmosphere encourages fungal diseases.

A 10-12 in (25-30 cm) exhaust fan will draw in enough air through gaps around the door to ensure adequate ventilation, and

Providing shade

To prevent the temperature inside the greenhouse from rising too high in summer, the greenhouse must be shaded.

The best but most expensive form of shading is provided by roller blinds made of wooden or plastic laths. Plastic fabric roller blinds, which are rolled up and down the roof, are less expensive.

Leave an air space between the glass and the blinds to allow air to circulate over the surface of the glass, keeping the temperature

TWO TYPES OF PSEUDOBULB

Pseudobulbs are thickened portions of the stem adapted to storing water and food — they are not true bulbs. Cymbidiums (*above*) have stout pseudobulbs, measuring 3-4 in (7.5-10 cm) long and covered with leaves. The old, leafless bulbs are called back bulbs. The pseudobulbs of *Coelogyne* (*above*) grow along a creeping horizontal rhizome.

SUPPORTING STEMS AND FLOWERS

1 With cattleyas and other top-heavy orchids, provide support after potting or repotting. Wind soft garden string around the upright growths, and tie them to a thin stake.

2 Upright stems and slender flower stalks, such as those of lady's slipper orchids, can be supported with a piece of galvanized wire shaped into a U and pushed into the potting mix.

3 For a long, arching flower spike, insert a bamboo stake at an angle and tie the spike to it with fine twine or string. This will maintain the plant's natural curves and grace, but prevent breakage.

---

even inside the greenhouse. Unroll the blinds on the sunny side of the greenhouse whenever the sun shines brightly during late spring and summer.

A less satisfactory method of shading is to paint the greenhouse glass with a special electrostatic shading paint, which can be removed in fall.

Growing supplies

Potting mixes for growing orchids were formerly made from the root fibers of osmunda ferns, mixed with sphagnum moss and leaf mold. All of these ingredients are still used, but resourceful growers today are also making use of such abundant and inexpensive items as pine or fir bark chips, dry oak leaves, polystyrene packing nuggets, perlite, rock wool, and even wine corks.

Packaged mixes of excellent quality are also available from orchid nurseries. But if you want the best-quality potting mix in large quantities, it is far less expensive to make it yourself than to buy it ready-made. The savings will be considerable even if you choose to include special ingredients, such as New Zealand sphagnum moss, which can be bought only from specialist nurseries.

A good basic mix consists of half a bucket of medium fir bark with 1 qt/lit of fine charcoal, 2 qt/lit fine fir bark, 1 qt/lit of perlite, and 1 qt/lit of New Zealand sphagnum or shredded rock wool.

By leaving out the sphagnum or rock wool, you produce a less water-retentive mix, one suitable for cattleyas. Increasing the sphagnum or rock wool produces a spongier mix, one suited to paphiopedilums and phalaenopsises.

For most mixes, bring the pH value up to 5.5-6.0 by adding lime. For lady's slipper orchids, raise the pH to 6.5.

It is possible to grow orchids in

ORCHID CONTAINERS

1 Upright orchids grow well in perforated clay pots. These provide good drainage — which is essential for all indoor orchids — and their weight helps to prevent top-heavy plants from toppling over.

2 Orchids with trailing flowers grow best in hanging wood-slat baskets. These can be hung from the greenhouse framework and positioned at an appropriate height for the flowers to open at eye level.

3 Pieces of tree bark or cork are ideal for mounting epiphytic orchids. The aerial roots of these plants eventually gain anchorage between the bark fissures, but must be tied in place to begin with.

ordinary pots, but these must have a good layer of crocks at the bottom to allow rapid drainage.

Special orchid pots or pans, which can be purchased from some garden centers and specialist orchid nurseries, are perforated around the sides as well as the bottom, and thus need no additional drainage material.

Wooden baskets are more suitable for hanging orchids. After the orchids are planted, hang the baskets up in the greenhouse on wires or slender chains, allowing the stems to droop downward.

Alternatively, hanging epiphytic orchids can be grown on sections of rough tree bark or cork. Sections of tree fern stems — if available — are also ideal. Bind the orchid roots to the slab of bark using fishing line or fine plastic-covered wire.

To prevent the orchid from drying out unduly until new roots develop and get a firm hold on the bark, pack some potting mix under the roots before you tie them in. Secure both the bark and its attached orchid to the greenhouse framework.

Providing support

Some orchids, such as *Cattleya* and *Dendrobium,* can be top-heavy and need support after they have been planted in their containers until they have produced strong new roots. Insert a bamboo stake at the back of each plant. This should stand as tall as the eventual height of the plant. Pass a piece of green string around two or three of the rear growths, halfway up, and tie them to the stake. Repeat this with the other growths.

Flowers that grow on tall, thin stems — such as those of some lady's slipper orchids *(Paphiopedilum)* — can be supported by means of galvanized wire. Bend the wire into a U-shape at the end, and then bend the U over at right angles. The U-shape then holds the stem upright. Support long, arching flower spikes by inserting bamboo stakes at an angle and fixing the stems to them with fine string. Do not tie the string too tightly, and loosen it as the orchid grows and it starts to constrict the stems.

Watering and feeding

Don't water orchids with very cold or hard water. In areas with

SHORTENING SINGLE-STEMMED ORCHIDS

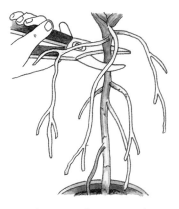

2 With pruning shears, sever the stem beneath a group of aerial roots. Remove any dead leaf bases from the severed section. Save the base of the original stem — it will produce new shoots that are suitable for propagation.

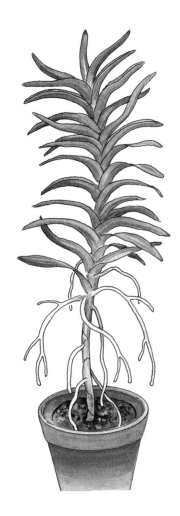

1 The slender, upright stems of *Vanda* orchids eventually become too tall and must be shortened by half to prevent collapse. Line a 5-6 in (13-15 cm) pot with crocks, and add a 1 in (2.5 cm) layer of orchid potting mix.

3 Twirl the severed uppermost section into the pot so that the roots coil around the inside. Fill the pot with more potting mix, tamping it down gently with a dibble and making sure no pockets of air remain. Water the plant well.

very hard tap water, the best source of irrigation may be rainwater. You can run a downspout from the outdoors into a barrel in the greenhouse. Keep the barrel covered as an open barrel can attract mosquitoes and plant disease spores. Rainwater can also be brought in from outdoors but allow it to warm up before applying it to warmth-loving orchids.

If rainwater in your area is scarce, polluted, or highly acidic, use tap water, preferably after it has been boiled (to reduce the chlorine content) and cooled.

Whenever the potting mix has become reasonably dry, water it thoroughly until it is saturated. If you keep the humidity in your greenhouse at a sufficient level,

watering once a week is adequate.

To water hanging plants, take them down and immerse them in a bowl of water until bubbles stop rising from the potting mix.

After orchids have been in the same potting mix for over a year, feed them with a liquid fertilizer such as fish emulsion about once every 2 weeks during the growing season (late spring to late summer). Remember to water the plants first, as fertilizer can damage roots if it is applied to them when they are dry.

The resting period

Many orchids require a resting period, usually from late summer to midfall. During this time they may lose their leaves, so that

REJUVENATING OLD PSEUDOBULBS

1 Many orchids can be propagated successfully from the old pseudobulbs known as back bulbs. In fall, or when a plant needs repotting, gently knock it out of its pot or basket.

2 Using a sharp knife, carefully cut off the largest back bulbs, trying not to sever any of their roots. Leave at least four pseudobulbs — either old or new — on the parent plant.

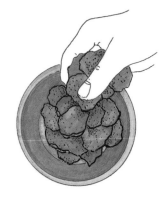

3 Back bulbs with few roots should be rooted before potting up. Put a layer of crocks or gravel in the bottom of a 3 in (7.5 cm) pot, and fill with moist orchid potting mix.

4 Cushion the base of the back bulb in potting mix, and stand it in the pot. Fill in with more potting mix, and insert a label with the name of the plant — nonflowering orchids are easily confused.

5 Stand the pot in a propagation box lined with moist sand, preferably with a bottom heat of 61°–66°F (16°–19°C). Put the propagator in a shaded, warm part of the greenhouse.

6 When shoots begin to grow from the base of the back bulb, remove it from the propagator and stand it on the greenhouse benches — still in its pot. Pot on within a year.

only the pseudobulbs remain.

When the leaves have fallen, or when the pseudobulbs have grown stout and healthy, move the plant to a shelf in better light and in a cooler part of the greenhouse. Reduce the humidity in the greenhouse to a minimum.

During this resting period, orchids with pseudobulbs need no water unless the potting mix dries out completely; if this happens, then drench it thoroughly. Orchids without pseudobulbs need occasional watering. When growth begins again, return the plant to its normal spot and resume watering.

Propagation
Some upright, slender-stemmed orchids, such as vandas, eventually become too tall and floppy for the greenhouse and should be cut down and left to grow on.

These orchids have aerial roots growing out of the stem. Every year the roots develop laterals, which begin to grow green points. When the laterals start to grow in the spring, the plant can be cut up and repotted.

The most common method of propagating orchids that grow from pseudobulbs is by division of the pseudobulbs, making sure each division contains three bulbs. Alternatively, separate and pot up the back bulbs. These are the old pseudobulbs that have lost their leaves and are found behind the new leafy bulbs.

Remove back bulbs in fall, at the end of the resting period, or when an overlarge plant is being divided and repotted in summer.

A PESTICIDE BATH

To cure scale insect, spider mite, and thrip infestations on orchid leaves — which cause yellow or brown mottling and weaken the growth — invert the entire plant and dip it in a bowl of spray-strength permethrin. Wear rubber gloves to protect your hands.

ORCHID PORTRAITS

**Exquisite orchids are remarkably tolerant,
flourishing in a greenhouse or under fluorescent lights;
some will even grow on a windowsill.**

The orchid family contains hundreds of genera and thousands of species from the world over. In addition, there are many man-made cultivars and hybrids. But not all orchids make ideal greenhouse plants for the beginner; the following pages describe the easiest and most rewarding types.

Orchids are perennials with often unusual flowers. Almost half are terrestrial (they grow on the ground), but others are epiphytic (they live on tree branches or on rocks). Without damaging the host, the epiphytes obtain food from air and rainwater and from humus in bark crevices by means of special roots. These orchids are the easiest to grow.

Most epiphytic orchids consist of a horizontal rhizome from which grow upright and usually swollen bulbous stems called pseudobulbs. Fleshy aerial roots may grow from the stems. The leaves are strap- or lance-shaped and are carried singly or in rigid tufts or fans.

Terrestrial orchids have either a tuft of fleshy roots at the base or underground tubers. Their tufted leaves are usually strap-shaped and floppier than those of epiphytic orchids; they are pale yellow or dark green, sometimes spotted with maroon.

Orchid flowers are composed of three sepals and three petals. The third petal is shaped into a lip.

General care

Orchids vary in their needs, but some general rules apply; the following points should be observed, unless stated otherwise.

❑ Grow terrestrial orchids in ordinary pots, but preferably grow epiphytes in specially perforated orchid pots or wooden baskets, or grow them directly on a piece of wood bark or tree trunk. Tie the plants on with monofilament fishing line.

❑ Use a potting mix specified for orchids; orchid nurseries carry preformulated products.

❑ Monitor the temperature. The preferred range depends on a plant's place of origin. Cool types (mountain species) do best in night temperatures of 45°-55°F (7°-13°C); intermediate types (species from upland plateaus) need a night range of 55°-65°F (13°-18°C); warm types (which originated in tropical lowlands) prefer 65°-70°F (18°-21°C). All benefit from a daytime temperature increase of 5°-10°F (3°-6°C).

❑ Ventilate well; this is essential, especially at high temperatures.

❑ Shade the greenhouse during the summer, ideally with wood-slat or plastic blinds.

❑ Maintain high humidity, especially during summer. Spray orchids with water at least once a day, and dampen the floor and benches in the greenhouse. Stand pots on bowls of moist pebbles.

❑ Keep orchids moist during the growing season, from midspring to early fall. However, let the potting mix dry out between waterings to avoid root rot.

❑ Follow specific advice on feeding — some orchids are sensitive to fertilizers. Newly potted orchids need no fertilizers, because the potting mix contains enough nutrients for one season.

❑ Allow a period of rest after flowering, a time when plants may lose their leaves. Stop watering and reduce the humidity.

◀ **Exotic orchids** Epiphytic orchids revel in the controlled atmosphere of a greenhouse. The magnificent blooms last for weeks, both on the plants and as cut flowers for the house.

Brassia verrucosa
Spider orchid

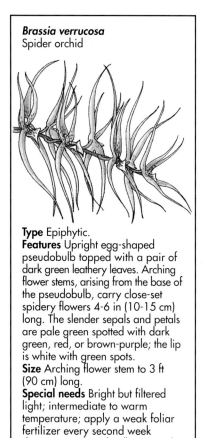

Type Epiphytic.
Features Upright egg-shaped pseudobulb topped with a pair of dark green leathery leaves. Arching flower stems, arising from the base of the pseudobulb, carry close-set spidery flowers 4-6 in (10-15 cm) long. The slender sepals and petals are pale green spotted with dark green, red, or brown-purple; the lip is white with green spots.
Size Arching flower stem to 3 ft (90 cm) long.
Special needs Bright but filtered light; intermediate to warm temperature; apply a weak foliar fertilizer every second week during active growth; allow 3-week rest period after flowering.

x Brassolaeliocattleya
(Trigeneric orchid)

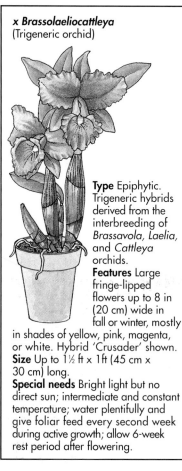

Type Epiphytic. Trigeneric hybrids derived from the interbreeding of *Brassavola, Laelia,* and *Cattleya* orchids.
Features Large fringe-lipped flowers up to 8 in (20 cm) wide in fall or winter, mostly in shades of yellow, pink, magenta, or white. Hybrid 'Crusader' shown.
Size Up to 1½ ft x 1ft (45 cm x 30 cm) long.
Special needs Bright light but no direct sun; intermediate and constant temperature; water plentifully and give foliar feed every second week during active growth; allow 6-week rest period after flowering.

Cattleya
Cattleya

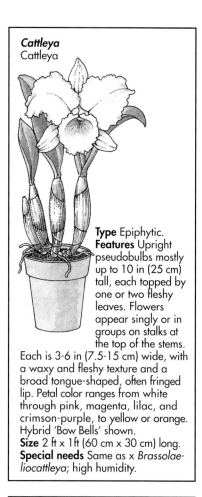

Type Epiphytic.
Features Upright pseudobulbs mostly up to 10 in (25 cm) tall, each topped by one or two fleshy leaves. Flowers appear singly or in groups on stalks at the top of the stems. Each is 3-6 in (7.5-15 cm) wide, with a waxy and fleshy texture and a broad tongue-shaped, often fringed lip. Petal color ranges from white through pink, magenta, lilac, and crimson-purple, to yellow or orange. Hybrid 'Bow Bells' shown.
Size 2 ft x 1ft (60 cm x 30 cm) long.
Special needs Same as x *Brassolaeliocattleya*; high humidity.

Coelogyne
Coelogyne

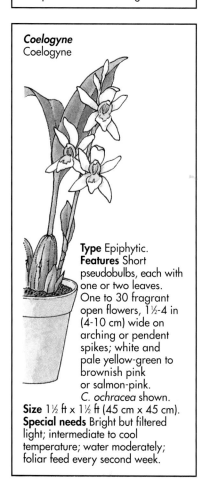

Type Epiphytic.
Features Short pseudobulbs, each with one or two leaves. One to 30 fragrant open flowers, 1½-4 in (4-10 cm) wide on arching or pendent spikes; white and pale yellow-green to brownish pink or salmon-pink. *C. ochracea* shown.
Size 1½ ft x 1½ ft (45 cm x 45 cm).
Special needs Bright but filtered light; intermediate to cool temperature; water moderately; foliar feed every second week.

Cymbidium
Cymbidium

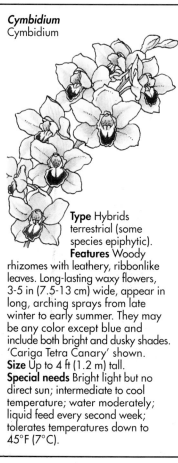

Type Hybrids terrestrial (some species epiphytic).
Features Woody rhizomes with leathery, ribbonlike leaves. Long-lasting waxy flowers, 3-5 in (7.5-13 cm) wide, appear in long, arching sprays from late winter to early summer. They may be any color except blue and include both bright and dusky shades. 'Cariga Tetra Canary' shown.
Size Up to 4 ft (1.2 m) tall.
Special needs Bright light but no direct sun; intermediate to cool temperature; water moderately; liquid feed every second week; tolerates temperatures down to 45°F (7°C).

Dendrobium
Dendrobium

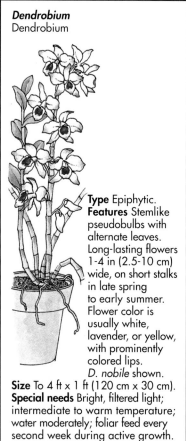

Type Epiphytic.
Features Stemlike pseudobulbs with alternate leaves. Long-lasting flowers 1-4 in (2.5-10 cm) wide, on short stalks in late spring to early summer. Flower color is usually white, lavender, or yellow, with prominently colored lips. *D. nobile* shown.
Size To 4 ft x 1 ft (120 cm x 30 cm).
Special needs Bright, filtered light; intermediate to warm temperature; water moderately; foliar feed every second week during active growth.

Laelia
Laelia

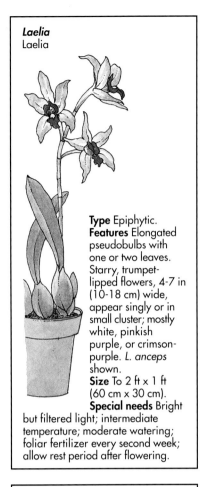

Type Epiphytic.
Features Elongated pseudobulbs with one or two leaves. Starry, trumpet-lipped flowers, 4-7 in (10-18 cm) wide, appear singly or in small cluster; mostly white, pinkish purple, or crimson-purple. *L. anceps* shown.
Size To 2 ft x 1 ft (60 cm x 30 cm).
Special needs Bright but filtered light; intermediate temperature; moderate watering; foliar fertilizer every second week; allow rest period after flowering.

Laeliocattleya
Laeliocattleya

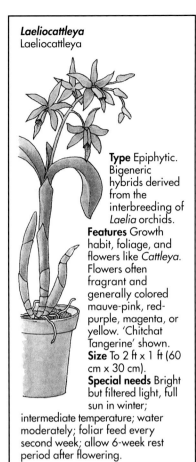

Type Epiphytic. Bigeneric hybrids derived from the interbreeding of *Laelia* orchids.
Features Growth habit, foliage, and flowers like *Cattleya*. Flowers often fragrant and generally colored mauve-pink, red-purple, magenta, or yellow. 'Chitchat Tangerine' shown.
Size To 2 ft x 1 ft (60 cm x 30 cm).
Special needs Bright but filtered light, full sun in winter; intermediate temperature; water moderately; foliar feed every second week; allow 6-week rest period after flowering.

Lycaste
Lycaste

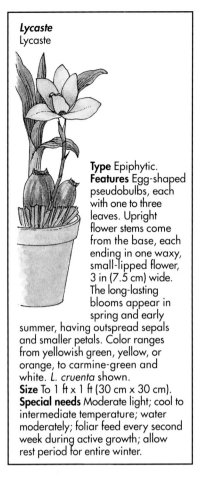

Type Epiphytic.
Features Egg-shaped pseudobulbs, each with one to three leaves. Upright flower stems come from the base, each ending in one waxy, small-lipped flower, 3 in (7.5 cm) wide. The long-lasting blooms appear in spring and early summer, having outspread sepals and smaller petals. Color ranges from yellowish green, yellow, or orange, to carmine-green and white. *L. cruenta* shown.
Size To 1 ft x 1 ft (30 cm x 30 cm).
Special needs Moderate light; cool to intermediate temperature; water moderately; foliar feed every second week during active growth; allow rest period for entire winter.

Miltonia
Pansy orchid

Type Epiphytic.
Features Egg-shaped pseudo-bulbs, each with one to three leaves; upright stalks carry one to ten large, almost flat, pansylike flowers, each 2-4 in (5-10 cm) wide; variously colored, usually with a dark blotch. 'Peach Blossom' shown.
Size To 20 in x 12 in (50 cm x 30 cm).
Special needs Moderate light; high humidity; intermediate to cool temperature; water moderately all year; foliar feed every second week; no rest period.

x Odontioda
Odontioda

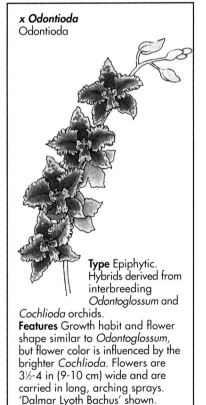

Type Epiphytic. Hybrids derived from interbreeding *Odontoglossum* and *Cochlioda* orchids.
Features Growth habit and flower shape similar to *Odontoglossum*, but flower color is influenced by the brighter *Cochlioda*. Flowers are 3½-4 in (9-10 cm) wide and are carried in long, arching sprays. 'Dalmar Lyoth Bachus' shown.
Size To 2 ft x 1½ ft (60 cm x 45 cm).
Special needs Same as for *Odonto-glossum*, but cooler temperature.

Odontoglossum
Tiger orchid

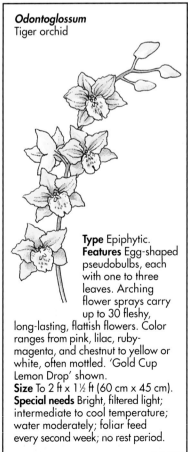

Type Epiphytic.
Features Egg-shaped pseudobulbs, each with one to three leaves. Arching flower sprays carry up to 30 fleshy, long-lasting, flattish flowers. Color ranges from pink, lilac, ruby-magenta, and chestnut to yellow or white, often mottled. 'Gold Cup Lemon Drop' shown.
Size To 2 ft x 1½ ft (60 cm x 45 cm).
Special needs Bright, filtered light; intermediate to cool temperature; water moderately; foliar feed every second week; no rest period.

Oncidium
Dancing-lady orchid

Type Epiphytic.
Features Egg-shaped pseudobulbs with two leaves. Upright or arching stems carry small blooms in succession. Color ranges from red and pink through shades of brown, to green, yellow, or white. Flower may have petallike wings at its center and a crested lip. *O. papilio* shown.
Size To 4 ft (1.2 m) tall.
Special needs Bright light; intermediate temperature; water sparingly; foliar feed every second week; allow rest period for entire winter.

Paphiopedilum
Lady's slipper orchid

Type Terrestrial.
Features Stemless with short leaves growing from the rhizome. Upright flower stalk topped with one long-lasting flower any time of year, depending on type. The bloom is 2-3½ in (5-9 cm) wide with a waxy sheen. The uppermost sepal is usually in a contrasting color to the petals, and the lip is pouched. 'Winston Churchill' shown.
Size 6-12 in (15-30 cm) tall.
Special needs Moderate light; warm, intermediate, or cool temperature, depending on species; high humidity; water moderately; foliar feed every second week.

Phalaenopsis
Moth orchid

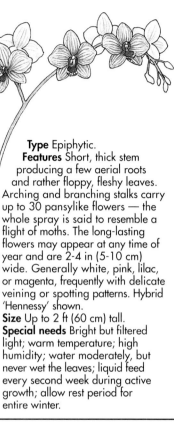

Type Epiphytic.
Features Short, thick stem producing a few aerial roots and rather floppy, fleshy leaves. Arching and branching stalks carry up to 30 pansylike flowers — the whole spray is said to resemble a flight of moths. The long-lasting flowers may appear at any time of year and are 2-4 in (5-10 cm) wide. Generally white, pink, lilac, or magenta, frequently with delicate veining or spotting patterns. Hybrid 'Hennessy' shown.
Size Up to 2 ft (60 cm) tall.
Special needs Bright but filtered light; warm temperature; high humidity; water moderately, but never wet the leaves; liquid feed every second week during active growth; allow rest period for entire winter.

Pleione formosana
Pleione

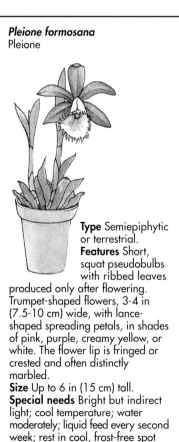

Type Semiepiphytic or terrestrial.
Features Short, squat pseudobulbs with ribbed leaves produced only after flowering. Trumpet-shaped flowers, 3-4 in (7.5-10 cm) wide, with lance-shaped spreading petals, in shades of pink, purple, creamy yellow, or white. The flower lip is fringed or crested and often distinctly marbled.
Size Up to 6 in (15 cm) tall.
Special needs Bright but indirect light; cool temperature; water moderately; liquid feed every second week; rest in cool, frost-free spot during dormant winter period.

Vanda
Vanda

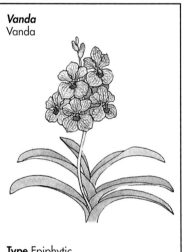

Type Epiphytic.
Features Single stem with fleshy aerial roots and leaves in two ranks — no pseudobulb. Upright or pendent stalks carry several flowers, 3-5 in (7.5-13 cm) wide, with equal-size sepals and petals, in shades of purple, blue, pink, or cream, frequently with netted markings. 'Rothschildiana' shown.
Size 1-2 ft (30-60 cm) high, or taller.
Special needs Bright but filtered light; warm to intermediate temperature; water plentifully during active growth; allow rest period for entire winter.

x *Vuylstekeara*
Vuylstekeara

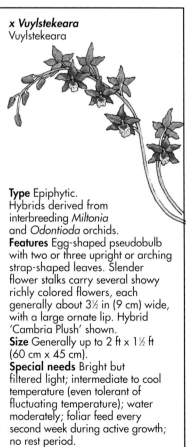

Type Epiphytic. Hybrids derived from interbreeding *Miltonia* and *Odontioda* orchids.
Features Egg-shaped pseudobulb with two or three upright or arching strap-shaped leaves. Slender flower stalks carry several showy richly colored flowers, each generally about 3½ in (9 cm) wide, with a large ornate lip. Hybrid 'Cambria Plush' shown.
Size Generally up to 2 ft x 1½ ft (60 cm x 45 cm).
Special needs Bright but filtered light; intermediate to cool temperature (even tolerant of fluctuating temperature); water moderately; foliar feed every second week during active growth; no rest period.

CONSERVATORY MANAGEMENT

As living quarters for both people and plants, a conservatory or "plant room" demands a different style of management.

Unlike a greenhouse, a conservatory — which may also be called a plant room or sun porch — is an integral part of the house. Because it is an indoor garden as well as a living space, this room must be suitable for plants yet comfortable and convenient for people. As a result, creating a balanced environment involves some compromise.

For example, hygiene becomes more than a matter of pest and disease control, and though the plants might benefit, you cannot wield the hose as freely. Whereas watering, spraying, and damping down can be a relatively haphazard process in a purely functional greenhouse, you must take more care in a conservatory laid with decorative flooring and furnished with upholstered chairs.

Display systems

If you choose only single-level staging (benches and shelves) for displaying plants, the room will look like a greenhouse. While this system makes good use of space and available sunlight, it limits the scope for decorative arrangements and the plants will be too high to be appreciated from a low, seated viewpoint.

If you choose to use aluminum or wooden staging, opt for a multilevel tiered design, which will provide surfaces for displaying all types of plants in the most imaginative way possible.

▼ **Conservatory accessories**
Bamboo plant stands and screens, together with planting bed edgings of tree bark, create a natural frame for a veritable jungle of luxuriant foliage and trailing plants.

A conservatory is a luxury and, as such, should be put to the maximum use. Don't just grow bushy and compact potted plants of the type popularly grown indoors. Try tall climbers, cascading trailers, spreading ground covers, luxuriant foliage, exotic flowers, even unusual edible fruits and vegetables, such as lemons and limes, kiwi or passion fruits, or perhaps chili peppers. Remember that to successfully grow a range of plants such as these you will need a variety of containers and support systems.

As in a greenhouse, one of the best places to grow climbers, tall perennial plants, and food crops is in a floor-level bed or border. However, because conservatory foundations are typically more substantial, and the floor is made of a solid expanse of concrete or wood, a bed must be specially constructed. It can be sunk in the floor with drainage pipes leading to the outside, or it can be designed as a raised bed with brick, concrete, or wood retaining walls.

Alternatively, grow tall plants and climbers in tubs or other large containers placed on the floor. Smaller plants can be grown individually in conventional pots or interplanted with larger ones.

There are many ways of displaying pots besides standing them on benches or on the floor. Special pot holders can be bought or made to support standard-size pots on a wall, post, or vertical glazing bar. If you don't want water to drain onto the floor, use plastic pots and clip-on saucers.

Plant stands made of bamboo, metal, or plastic are decorative and functional, capable of taking four or more plants. Many are portable, so you can change the display arrangement frequently.

Hanging baskets and wall-mounted troughs also make use of space without cluttering the floor area. They are ideal for arching and trailing species, especially those that have pendent flowers, which are best viewed from below. These are available with clip-on or built-in drip trays.

Climate control

Maintaining a temperature comfortable for plants and people is a major consideration in a conservatory. Indeed, heating or cooling is the most expensive operating cost. In the extreme North, you

DISPLAYING PLANTS

1 Wall-mounted pot holders, such as this spring-loaded metal device, which grips the rim of an ordinary plastic pot, allow you to secure plants to any vertical surface — even a glazing bar.

2 Planter poles, adjustable to various ceiling heights, or free-standing plant stands give height to a conservatory or sunroom and are ideal for displaying arching or trailing plants.

3 Hanging baskets are particularly suitable for growing flowers that are best viewed from below, such as trailing fuchsias. Buy the plastic type with clip-on or built-in drip trays if the floor isn't waterproof.

4 Tiered and staggered shelves give depth and height to your display. Plants that need maximum light can be put on the top shelves and those that prefer shade can go on the lower tiers.

WATERING SYSTEMS

1 All plants must be watered and some should be mist-sprayed regularly. A long-spouted watering can and a hand sprayer are therefore essential. An ordinary humidifier may also be beneficial.

2 Ordinary garden sprayers or a bucket of water and a "trombone" sprayer can be useful in watering hanging baskets or plant containers set up above your reach. Keep sprayer pressure low, and open the nozzle all the way to avoid washing out soil.

3 Set plants on trays filled with pebbles and water (small pots must rest above the water). Drainage water from the pots is soaked up. It later evaporates to increase humidity.

4 Mist-spray nozzles — available from drip-irrigation suppliers — can be positioned between groups of plants that require extra humidity or regular damping down.

5 Drip-irrigation nozzles inserted in each pot, linked to a network of hoses, include valves for regulating water flow. A timer makes the system self-regulating.

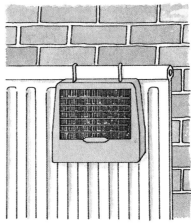

6 Water-filled containers set or hung on radiators act as passive humidifiers. Such inexpensive devices can enhance plant growth and reduce the need for watering. Be sure to keep them filled with water.

may find it too costly to heat this space through the coldest months, especially if it has been created by enclosing a sun porch. Fortunately, you will find that such a room, with its wooden or masonry walls, retains far more heat from the sun than an all-glass greenhouse of equivalent size. Conservatory walls will absorb and store this natural heat, rereleasing it through the chillier nighttime hours. This, plus the heat that escapes from the heated portion of the house, will often be sufficient to overwinter semi-hardy plants such as camellias.

By installing extra radiators from the domestic central heating system, or some other form of independent heating, you greatly increase your choice of plants and make the conservatory an all-year live-in extension to your home. Consult an expert before doing this, however, because your gas or oil burner may not be able to heat the additional space, and you may want to regulate the heat with a separate thermostat.

Of course, you can let heat into a conservatory by leaving the door open to the rest of the house. This may keep the frost out over cold nights, but it is likely to create drafts that are harmful to your plants.

In the South, the crucial concern may be cooling the room in summertime. Shading it with deciduous trees is beneficial; not only do the trees block the sun, but they actually cool the air 10°F (6°C) or more in their immediate vicinity. In wintertime, such trees drop their leaves to expose the conservatory to the full strength of the sun.

Even with a canopy of trees, a conservatory in a hot-weather region will also need some sort of cooling system. Sometimes the central air conditioning can be extended to cool the conservatory, but you may find it more economical to install a separate room-size air conditioner that cools the room only when you are using it.

Shading

To reduce cooling costs, owners of southern conservatories will also want to install shading blinds on the windows. If set outside, these deflect sunshine before it enters the room and thus help prevent overheating. Shading also protects plants from sunburn, and thus is a necessity in the North as well. High humidity can alleviate the scorching effect of high temperatures, but keeping the room both hot and moist will make it uncomfortable for people.

There are many types of blinds to choose from. Ideally, they should be adjustable, to regulate the amount of light passing through them, and they should be capable of being raised and lowered. Reeded or slatted types, whether made from natural wood or artificial materials, are best.

Fabric roller blinds can be used, but because they can only be raised or lowered, the quantity of shading they provide is not adjustable. However, they do serve as heat insulators during the night.

If you grow a lot of climbing or tall plants near the glass, it is much more convenient to put the blinds on the outside of the room, where they can be adjusted with ease. Be sure to choose weatherproof materials and secure them well, especially in exposed areas.

Ventilation and humidity

Most conservatories get too hot in summer and too cold in winter, conditions that influence both the humidity level and the condensation rate. Be sure the structure has enough windows that open or ventilators, so that in summer the excessively hot air can be continually replaced by cooler air from outside.

In winter, ventilation is just as important for eliminating stagnant, humid air, a common cause of both fungal rot disease and excessive condensation. It may be well worth the initial expense to install extra vents.

The humidity level required in a conservatory depends largely on the type of plant you are growing. In general, high humidity is advantageous when the air temperature is high. Hot, dry air is fatal to most plants and encourages serious pests such as spider mites. Tropical plants require the highest humidity, whereas cacti and other arid-region plants prefer drier air.

The frequency and quantity of watering are the main regulators of humidity. You can increase the level of humidity in a greenhouse simply by hosing down the floor and shelves. However, in a furnished conservatory where this is

not possible, provide localized humidity around each plant by standing its pot on a saucer filled with gravel or pebbles and water. Make sure the pot sits above, not in, the water.

Where shelves or benches are used, spread a layer of gravel or pebbles across the entire surface. Prevent water damage to wooden structures by lining these with plastic sheeting or galvanized metal trays. This layer can be kept moist either by watering with a hose or can, or by a drip-irrigation system. Alternatively, try capillary matting beds.

Plants that demand a higher humidity than is desirable for the rest of the conservatory can be accommodated by installing a mist-irrigation system. The nozzles can be adjusted to spread a fine spray of water over just the right plants and, if connected to some sort of automatic controller, will not overwater. However, because installing a system of this sort involves tapping into the household water supply, it should be done by a licensed plumber.

Lighting

Some form of lighting is desirable in a conservatory so that it can be used at night. Ordinary house-

▲ **Multilevel shelving** Rot-resistant wooden shelves and benches erected along a wood-frame conservatory are ideal for displaying a variety of potted plants. A rich green carpet of mind-your-own-business *(Soleirolia soleirolii)* hides the edge of the bench and makes a superb foil for the bright flowers of kalanchoe, hibiscus, and Indian shot *(Canna)*.

hold units with tungsten-filament bulbs provide all the light necessary for normal activity, but be careful where you position them.

Spotlights get very hot and can scorch plants if they are too close. However, if they are mounted on tracks, they can be redirected with ease, a useful feature in a conservatory where plant displays and seating positions are frequently changed.

Make sure that unprotected lamps are far from any watering devices. For safety reasons, it is best to choose waterproof light fixtures of the type normally rated for outdoor use. Fluorescent lighting is also suitable, but again make sure the tubes are enclosed in a plastic casing.

Wall-mounted coach lights and colored flood lamps give a garden feel to the conservatory and can create a party atmosphere.

USING GARDEN FRAMES

**Cold frames are indispensable. They provide
a place to ripen vegetables out of season, harden off bedding
plants, root cuttings, and overwinter stock plants.**

A garden frame is a low, generally oblong box designed for a variety of purposes. It is mainly associated with raising or protecting plants, similar to a greenhouse but on a smaller scale. The frame invariably has a sloping roof to allow rainwater to run off and has a glazed lid to allow sunlight to reach inside. The sides may be glazed or solid.

Traditionally, a frame has no artificial heating: the soil and air temperature are increased by warmth from the sun alone — the "greenhouse effect." It is there-fore known as a cold frame. However, with the increasing availability of easy-to-install electric heating cables, garden frames need not be cold and can serve as a small extension to, or replacement for, a heated greenhouse. In most gardens a frame is an invaluable tool.

Types of frame
Three main types of frame are in use in gardens.
Wooden frames that are fitted with glass lids (known as lights) and with solid sides are the most efficient for heat conservation.

Until recent years, most frames were built from wood and glass. Nowadays, however, very few suppliers offer ready-made frames of these expensive and hard-to-ship materials, so if you do choose wood, you may have to build your own frame, buying materials from a lumberyard.

▼ **Twin-light cold frame** Invaluable for the intermediate stage between greenhouse and the open garden, a cold frame should be easily accessible, with lights that prop open.

HARDENING OFF ANNUALS

1 Seedlings that have been raised indoors or in a greenhouse must be acclimatized gradually to outdoor temperatures. Put them in the frame 2 to 4 weeks before planting out.

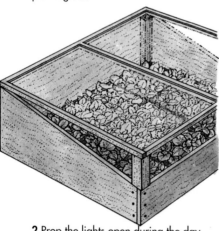

2 Prop the lights open during the day for the first week — provided it is not too cold or windy — but close them at night. During the second week, leave the lights partially open at night.

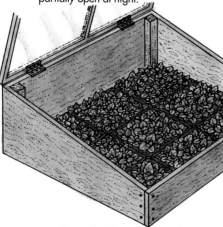

3 At the end of the second week open the lights fully at all times unless it is very windy. Water the plants as necessary — they may dry out quickly. Plant out about a week later.

Cedar, cypress, and redwood are the best woods for this purpose, since their resins provide good resistance to decay and wood-boring insects. Alternatively, use exterior-quality (marine) plywood and apply a wood preservative to the structure.

Because the standard glass sash dimensions are 3 ft × 6 ft (90 cm × 180 cm), frames have traditionally been built 3 ft (90 cm) wide and some multiple of 6 ft (180 cm) long, usually with an internal height of 1-2 ft (30-60 cm). However, if you intend to glaze the frame with plastic, you may build it to any dimensions, except that the distance from front to back should never exceed your reach — you must always work from outside the frame.

The glass lights can be designed to slide on runners or hinge from the back wall or the sides to provide ventilation and give access to the plants. The walls of a wooden frame can be built with bricks or cinder blocks, though it is difficult to fit these to the required sloping side edges.

A well-constructed wooden frame should last for many years. However, lumber requires some routine care and attention to prolong its life. One way to protect a wooden frame from rot is by setting it on a footing of concrete or bricks laid dry.

Aluminum frames need no routine maintenance and are lightweight, making them easy to move from one part of the garden to another if necessary. For those gardeners with little carpentry skill, aluminum frames sold in kit form are a good choice.

These frames can be fitted with glass or clear-plastic (rigid acrylic) lights. Glass lets the maximum sunlight pass through it, whereas plastic filters out a small amount of sunlight, though this is not generally a problem. Plastic does not shatter easily, so it is safer to use than glass where children play in the garden. But plastic can be scratched easily, and damaged panes are difficult to keep clean, because algae build up on the roughened surface.

Most aluminum frames have glazed sides, making them ideal for growing plants that demand a lot of light, such as melons. But they are less efficient than wooden frames at keeping the heat in during cold weather. They have a very modern, architectural look and may appear out of place in an old-fashioned garden.

Iron or steel frames that have been galvanized are similar in construction to aluminum types. Years ago, they would have been sturdy and heavy, but modern types use more slender structural members to minimize the price of iron and steel. For this reason, modern galvanized frames may be even less sturdy than those made of aluminum.

Positioning the frame
For general purposes, position the frame in a sunny, south-facing spot sheltered from cold winds. If you already have a greenhouse with solid side walls, position the frame against it so that some of the heat escaping from the greenhouse will help to heat the frame during the winter months.

If you intend to use the frame mainly for rooting cuttings, choose a lightly shaded position. However, cuttings can be rooted successfully in a sunny frame provided some form of temporary shading is used during the hottest sunshine — shading paint or shade cloth, for instance.

A nonslip path around the frame will improve ease of access and reduce the risk of accidents — especially if you have to lean over to reach plants in the center or at the back of the frame.

Using a cold frame
There are two main ways of growing plants in a frame — whether it is unheated or heated. You can grow them directly in the soil in the base of the frame or grow them in containers. The first method is best for plants that will spend their entire life in the frame, while the second is appropriate for shorter-stay plants.

Raising seeds An unheated cold frame can be used to raise seeds of all plants that would normally be sown directly in the garden, such as many half-hardy annual and hardy biennial bedding plants and hardy perennials — even shrubs and trees. Cold-frame protection means that the seeds can be sown a few weeks earlier than in the open, so that young plants have more time to develop before being planted out.

Seeds are best sown in pots or flats of a commercial seed-starting mix and set out on a bed of gravel in the frame to provide good drainage. Water them regularly — the seed-starting mix will dry out quickly in warm weather.

Hardening off Another valuable function of a cold frame is to harden off greenhouse-raised plants before planting them outdoors — young plants must be acclimatized gradually to the lower outdoor temperature. By adjusting the ventilation in the frame, the day and night temperature can be modified over the course of several days or weeks.

Growing vegetables In a cold frame, you can grow earlier crops than in the open and keep plants producing into early winter. Cold-tolerant crops such as lettuce and spinach are common choices for cold frames. Gardeners in northern regions also use cold frames to raise long-season crops such as cucumbers and melons, which might not otherwise fruit successfully in their region. Typically the seeds are germinated indoors and then transplanted out into the soil inside the frame.

Prepare the cold-frame soil some weeks before planting by digging in well-rotted manure or compost at the rate of a bucketful

▼Aluminum frames Virtually maintenance free, aluminum frames are durable and easy to move around if needed. They allow plenty of light to penetrate, but they retain heat less effectively than wood-structured frames.

▲ Plastic tunnels Frames of metal tubing or PVC pipe may be covered with plastic and set down over a garden bed to create an impromptu frame. They may extend the growing season by a couple of weeks in both spring and fall.

per sq yd/m. Just before planting, rake into the top a general fertilizer at 3 oz (75 g) per sq yd/m.

Grow on the vegetables in the frame, ventilating it as needed during the day. Close the lights at night until the plants are fully established. In early summer remove the lights or hinge them open during the day and night.

Shrub cuttings These can be rooted successfully in a shaded cold frame — softwood cuttings in early summer; semihardwood cuttings in midsummer to late summer. Insert them directly into the soil in the bottom of the frame or into pots of a clean rooting medium.

Overwintering tender plants In all but the most northerly regions, a cold frame provides enough protection to overwinter slightly tender plants such as border chrysanthemums.

Cut back the plants after flowering, lift them, and box the root clumps and crowns in potting soil. Place the boxes in the cold frame. To reduce fungal infections, ventilate whenever the temperature rises above freezing.

Forcing bulbs Instead of storing your freshly potted hyacinths, narcissi, and tulips in a shed or cellar, try starting them off in a cold frame — the cooler conditions promote sturdier growth. Plant the bulbs in pots or bowls, and bury them under a 6 in (15 cm) layer of soil. Eight weeks later they can be uncovered and brought indoors for flowering.

Using a heated frame

By providing supplementary heat you can expand the use of a garden frame considerably — it then becomes a mini hothouse. Electric soil-warming cables laid under the surface of the soil in the bottom of the frame will hasten early vegetable crops. Be sure to follow the manufacturer's directions carefully when installing the cables.

Prewarm the soil for early crops — such as carrots, lettuces, spring onions, and radishes — and ornamental plants by switching on the heating 2 days before you sow. Hardy species can be sown as early as midwinter to late winter in a heated frame; or late winter to early spring for halfhardy types. Set the thermostat at around 64°F (18°C) for most vegetable crops.

Ventilate the heated frame during mild days. On cold nights cover the frame lights with burlap, sheets of newspaper, or some other insulating material anchored with bricks — soil heating won't be able to compensate for extremes of weather. Open the lights progressively during the day as the weather warms up, but close them again at night and during spells of windy weather.

When all danger of frost is over, remove the lights or open them fully and switch off the heating.

As with chrysanthemums, the more tender rootstocks of fuchsias and pelargoniums can be overwintered in a frame provided it is heated. In early fall cut down the plants and lift them from the ground. Transfer them to boxes of potting soil, and stand them in the bottom of the frame.

USING A COLD FRAME

1 A plunge bed helps to reduce drying out and maintain an even soil temperature for germinating seeds of alpines, shrubs, and trees. Spread a 4-6 in (10-15 cm) layer of sand in a solid-sided frame — if it is a wooden frame, line the sides with a waterproof plastic membrane. Bury the pots of seeds up to their rims in the sand.

2 Semihardwood and hardwood shrub cuttings can be rooted directly in prepared soil in the bottom of a cold frame or inserted in pots or flats of potting soil. They require no extra heating. To reduce the risk of disease, those rooted in unsterilized garden soil should be taken with a heel of older wood at the base.

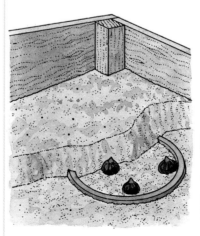

3 Bulbs for early indoor flowering can be started off in a cold frame. Pot them in bowls of well-drained potting soil. Bury each bowl to its rim in a plunge bed of soil, and then cover it with 6 in (15 cm) of soil. Ventilate the frame slightly. Eight weeks later, uncover the bowls and bring them indoors to a cool room. Flower buds will soon appear.

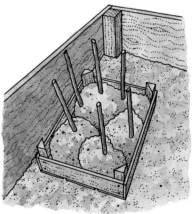

4 Lifted clumps of frost-tender perennials, such as chrysanthemums, can be stored during the winter months in a cold frame. Dust the dormant clumps with sulfur to prevent mildew, place them in boxes, and cover with potting soil. Water sparingly. Ventilate the frame slightly. Take cuttings as new shoots emerge in spring.

Pest and weed control

Gardens are attractive places — not only to people but also to wildlife. And soil that is hospitable to desirable garden plants is also attractive to weeds. Beds filled with lush growth seem to invite insect pests and weeds to settle in. If you don't control the numbers of such invaders, you'll soon find your garden entirely overrun.

A generation ago, the accepted method of pest control was regular applications of chemicals. Although there is still a role for chemical pesticides and herbicides in the garden, today's gardeners recognize that overuse of such chemicals can wreak environmental havoc, deplete the soil, and may even cause unintended harm to desirable plants.

By gardening more skillfully, you can control pests with a method known as integrated pest management (IPM). This method is based on the premise that a modest level of pests and weeds is not necessarily harmful and that any control measures should be carefully targeted to minimize interference with nature. To use IPM techniques, you must be able to identify pests accurately (the portraits on the following pages will help) and to recognize acceptable levels of infestation. The presence of a few aphids, for instance, may actually be desirable, because they attract insect predators such as ladybugs, which keep a wide variety of insect pests in check. When pest populations do multiply to unacceptable levels, IPM may prescribe a change in cultural routines to make the garden inhospitable to the pest.

IPM does not rule out the use of chemical controls. But when it calls for the use of a pesticide, it makes sure that the application coincides with the most vulnerable period in the pests' life cycle. This method does require more knowledge and skill than the traditional techniques most gardeners are familiar with. But its rewards are multiple: healthy plants, a chemical-free garden, and far less time spent with sprayer, spreader, and duster.

Beautiful and helpful Beneficial insects such as this butterfly help to pollinate garden flowers.

MANAGING GARDEN PESTS

**Identifying pests and understanding
their habits are the first steps in successful
integrated pest management.**

Integrated pest management sounds technical, but in fact it is a simple approach to pest control. The method is called "integrated" because it combines several strategies to achieve its goal. The old-fashioned system of pest control relied wholly on regular applications of toxic chemicals — whether or not there was evidence of infestation. In IPM, chemical pesticides are just one of many tools; they are not applied unless there is a clear need and then usually as a last resort.

The "management" part of the name represents a basic shift in approaching pest control. In the past, a regular schedule of spraying was used to eliminate a problem insect or weed entirely. Those gardeners who practice IPM realize that total eradication is rarely possible and may not even be necessary — there's no harm, for instance, in a few whiteflies if they don't affect the garden's beauty or fruitfulness. In fact, IPM theory suggests that a small population of the pest should be allowed to remain as food for the beneficial predators that are natural checks on pest infestations.

Beneficial insects

An important first step in any program of pest management or control is the recognition that not all uninvited plants or insects are bad. Some insects, such as ladybugs and lacewings, are actually beneficial, because they feed on some plant-eating insects. Similarly, the clover that pops up in your lawn has the valuable ability to absorb nitrogen directly from the atmosphere and so serves as a natural fertilizer for adjacent turf.

Eliminating beneficial species such as these only makes extra work for the gardener — if you kill insect predators or useful weeds, you will most likely inherit their jobs. To avoid this mistake, you must first learn to identify common weeds and insects accurately and develop some knowledge of their habits.

The following pages feature many common garden pests. In addition, local nurseries are usually glad to share their knowledge of common local pests. Also, most states have cooperative extension services with offices in every county (they are usually listed in the blue pages of your telephone book); these services are an expert source of assistance in weed and pest identification.

Obviously, appearance is the key to pest identification, but it is also important to note the circumstances in which you found the insect or weed. Most insects are selective about the plants on which they will feed. You will not find a tomato hornworm, for example, feeding on cabbage — the green caterpillar you find there is more likely to be an imported cabbageworm that feeds on all members of the cabbage family, including broccoli, brussels sprouts, cauliflower, collards, and kale. Some weeds prefer shady spots, others prefer sunny ones; there are weeds of wet soils and

◄ **"Good" bugs** Though harmless to plants and wildlife, applications of beneficial nematodes can control beetle grubs, cutworms, and a variety of other soil-dwelling pests.

CONTROLLING JAPANESE BEETLES

1 An early clue to the severity of a Japanese beetle infestation is the density of the grubs (the larval stage) in a lawn. In midspring, cut and overturn a 1-ft-sq (30-cm-sq) section of turf; more than 10 grubs here would be excessive.

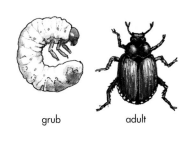

grub   adult

2 Accurate identification is key because other beetles also produce grubs. Those of the Japanese beetle are grayish white, ¾-1 in (2-2.5 cm) long, with brown heads and a V-shaped row of spines on the underside of the last body segment.

3 Beneficial nematodes can eliminate grubs if applied when grubs are active (spring or fall). Water the lawn well and activate nematodes according to product label; apply to turf with garden sprayer in early morning or late afternoon.

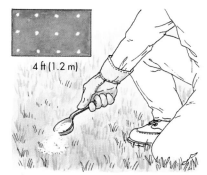

4 ft (1.2 m)

4 For long-term control, introduce milky spore disease to the lawn. Apply 1 tsp (5 ml) of powder to every 4 ft (1.2 m) of lawn in spring or fall. The disease will take effect over the following few years.

weeds of dry ones. Weather can also play a role in pest identification. Some fungal diseases — the anthracnose that often attacks sycamore and plane trees, for example — emerge during cool, wet weather, while others — such as powdery mildew of roses — flourish during warm, humid periods. Noting details of this kind will make pest identification both easier and more accurate.

Monitoring Checking the garden for the appearance of pests must be a regular part of your gardening routine. For weeds, this will involve nothing more than a quick survey of the areas you wish to keep weed free. Monitoring for insect pests and plant diseases is more involved.

Begin by selecting a number of sample specimens of the plants you wish to protect; then check these individual plants in detail, scanning from top to bottom and examining the undersides as well as the tops of the leaves for evidence of insect infestation, and inspecting the plant thoroughly.

Look for soil-borne pests by digging into the ground; to find Japanese beetle grubs in the lawn, for example, you must cut out a square of turf and count the grubs feeding on the grass roots.

Of course, any plants that are showing obvious signs of distress — yellowing, wilting, or damage to the foliage and stems — should be checked too.

Identifying problems early allows the gardener to take action promptly, when small measures are still effective. If, for example, you find a small infestation of aphids in the vegetable garden, you can wash them off the plants in a minute or two with a strong jet of water from the hose. A few weeks later, however, the population may have increased to such an extent that stronger and more time-consuming remedies are necessary. Eliminating perennial weeds such as field horsetails while they are still seedlings takes only a pass with the scuffle hoe; wait a few weeks and their deep, tenacious roots must be dug out individually.

Levels of tolerance After diagnosing an infestation, the next step is to determine whether the pest is sufficiently numerous to require treatment.

The degree of tolerance varies with the species of plant and the pest. The appearance of even a single leafhopper on a China aster, for example, calls for immediate and vigorous remedies, because this insect spreads aster yellows, an incurable and fatal disease. On the other hand, a few hornworms on your tomatoes probably deserve no treatment at all. They will devour a few leaves, but they will also serve as incubators for the eggs of parasitic braconid wasps. If allowed to hatch, the eggs will produce a swarm of predators that serve to keep the hornworm population in check naturally.

You may not care about minor attacks on foliage, and feel that the pest causing this slight damage does not deserve any sort of control. But you will certainly resent any pest that disfigures your flowers' blossoms, and will probably want to take action against the culprits.

In deciding whether to take action, keep in mind the progress of the pest. If you note an insect or weed increasing rapidly from day to day and spreading quickly throughout a planting, that is a clue there is an epidemic in the making. A prompt response is in order. If, however, a pest remains constant in numbers and the damage it does continues to be minor, then it's probably as well to let nature take its course.

Strategies for control
The best type of pest management is prevention, and that depends on good planning during the design of your garden. When purchasing plants try to select cultivars that are naturally resistant to disease. Some modern apple hybrids — 'Liberty' and 'Freedom,' for example — have been bred specifically for resistance to the common fungal diseases apple scab and cedar-apple rust. Mail-order catalogs of flower

and vegetable seeds customarily note which cultivars are pest and disease resistant — for instance, if you see the letters "VFN" following the name of a tomato you'll know that it is resistant to the attacks of verticillium and fusarium wilts and nematodes. That will mean not only a bigger crop but a more wholesome one.

Read the plant descriptions on seed packets to note which particular plants are likely to remain pest free. And, once again, nurseries and cooperative extension and agricultural services are useful sources of information.

You can also design for pest resistance by emphasizing diversity in your planting. Setting out large blocks of identical plants increases the size of the pests' target and makes it easy for them to spread from plant to plant. Intermingling plants of different species makes it harder for pests to find their preferred host and less likely that once they do they will spread to neighbors.

Rotating crops in the vegetable garden, moving a given plant such as lettuce to a new part of the plot every year, also helps to prevent pests from building established populations. Keeping the garden free of weeds and plant debris deprives pests of hiding and breeding spots.

Cultural controls Changing your cultural routines may make the garden less attractive to a pest. Reducing lawn irrigation in July and August, for example, makes it far more difficult for adult Japanese beetles to lay their eggs there and thus reduces the number of grubs that will infest the turf. Forking over garden beds in late fall exposes overwintering insect eggs and larva to frost, reducing their numbers.

The most effective cultural step you can take against weeds is to change your pattern of watering. Weeds produce seeds in huge quantities and spread them as widely as possible. As a result, a single acre of cultivated land usually contains about 10 million weed seeds in the top layer of soil. Broadcasting water all over with sprinklers creates ideal conditions for the germination of this host of invaders. In contrast, drip irrigation delivers water to the root zone of each plant, leaving the soil surface and most of the scattered weed seeds dry.

Physical barriers Denying access to pests is another effective and low-impact strategy. Conventional mulches isolate existing populations of weed seeds from sunlight and so help block their germination; a thick mulch also helps keep new seeds from reaching the soil. Mulches are even more effective if combined with "geotextiles" — spun or woven fabrics made of plastic. Spread the textile over the soil between rows of vegetables or the individual plants of a shrubbery border, and pin it in place with wire staples; then hide it under a layer of a more attractive organic mulch. Because it is porous, the textile allows the passage of air and water down to plant roots, but the weave is sufficiently fine to block the upward growth of weed seedlings.

Biological controls IPM stresses encouraging natural predators — the insects, other animals, and microorganisms that naturally prey on plant eaters — to move into your garden.

Insect-eating birds can significantly reduce pests. Provide such birds with havens for nesting and roosting, such as a small tree set at the edge of the lawn and underplanted with shrubs, vines, and flowers. By including fruit-bearing bushes and trees such as crab apples or hollies in your planting, you provide the birds with wintertime food and encourage them to stay year-round.

The most effective insect predators, however, are other insects — ladybugs, lacewings, braconid wasps, and others — that feed on harmful insects and can multiply rapidly to meet the challenge of a pest epidemic. Many of these predators can be purchased by mail order, but unfortunately most imports fly away as soon as released.

A more effective strategy is to maintain populations of the plants that beneficial insects need as sources of nectar or pollen. Herbs of the mint family, such as lemon balm, pennyroyal, or thyme, and plants of the carrot family — dill and parsley, for example, or wild carrot ("Queen Anne's lace") — are all attractive to desirable predacious insects. Abstaining from the use of non-selective and persistent chemical insecticides will also help ensure that predator levels in your garden remain high.

Pest parasites provide yet an-

CONTROLLING GYPSY MOTHS

1 Overwintering eggs attached to tree trunks, fences, or other shady places give rise to the new year's caterpillars. In late winter, scrape these egg masses off into a can of bleach.

2 In spring, spray survivors with Bt (*Bacillus thuringiensis*). This natural bacterium, which is harmless to other animals, must be applied to caterpillars less than ½ in (12 mm) long.

3 Use twine to tie strips of burlap 1-1½ ft (30-45 cm) wide around the trunk. Let the top hang down to make daytime hideaways for caterpillars. Lift the flap daily to pick pests by hand.

other form of biological control, and it is possible to thoroughly infect a yard or garden with these desirable microorganisms. Milky spore disease — a type of bacterium that infects and kills Japanese beetle grubs — is available in powdered form through mail-order distributors. Spread it over the lawn when the grubs are active (spring or fall). Once established in the soil, milky spore controls grubs effectively for many years.

Another type of useful microorganism is the bacterium known as Bt *(Bacillus thuringiensis)*. This is available as a concentrate that can be mixed with water. Spray Bt on plants afflicted with a variety of insect larvae: cabbage loopers and cabbageworms, fruit worms, corn borers, and gypsy moth caterpillars, among others. Bt must be applied when the larvae are actively feeding, and the appropriate strain (there are several) must be used for each pest. The advantage of this microorganism is that it affects only the pest and does not harm predators or other forms of wildlife.

Nematodes — tiny soil-borne parasitic worms — are among the gardener's most troublesome pests in areas where they are abundant. Those that parasitize plants may cause swelling and stunting of roots, stems, leaves, and flowers. There are a number of nematodes, however, that feed on soil-borne insect pests such as beetle grubs and termites. These "beneficial" nematodes are also available through mail order. Apply them as a spray for spot treatment of epidemics. Though relatively expensive, they provide quick and effective relief and do not harm other forms of wildlife.

Traps Using traps may be the only effective way to combat four-legged pests such as moles, gophers, and woodchucks. Mail-order companies sell traps that do not harm the pest, but allow you to release it far from your garden.

A variety of homemade or commercially produced devices can provide inexpensive and nontoxic control of insect pests. Squares of plywood painted bright yellow and then coated with specially formulated horticultural adhesive or SAE90 motor oil will capture substantial numbers of whiteflies, fungus gnats, and imported cabbageworm moths. For nearly

complete control of apple maggots, hang sticky-coated red spheres (which may be made from old croquet balls) in apple trees (one sphere per dwarf tree, up to six for a standard tree).

Often traps do not completely control pests, but are valuable nonetheless because they alert you to the presence of new and unwelcome insects and animals.

Chemical controls These are the integrated pest manager's last resort, but their application may be necessary when other strategies prove insufficient.

In general, try to avoid the use of "broad-spectrum" pesticides, chemical blends that kill nearly any insect they touch. By killing beneficial insects and predators, such controls may ultimately exacerbate the infestation they are meant to cure. Pesticides that are targeted to kill only the pest are preferable. IPM also stresses the use of nonpersistent pesticides, which break down soon after application and so do not build up in the garden food chain.

Insecticidal soaps, for example, kill insects only on direct contact with them, but will not harm most plants. Refined "horticultural" oils are another relatively nontoxic pesticide. When mixed with water and sprayed on plants, these oils suffocate the eggs and immature stages of many insects as well as killing adults. More toxic to pests than to beneficial insects, they break down within a matter of days. Horticultural oils are available in two grades, a so-called dormant oil, which is applied during the dormant season when temperatures are above 40°F (5°C), and "summer oils," which may be applied during the growing season when the temperature does not exceed 85°F (29°C). Summer oils provide effective control of aphids, spider mites, scales, psyllas, mealybugs, and some caterpillars.

When using pesticides, timing is important. Many are effective only against certain stages of the pest's development — Bt, for example, is ineffective against gypsy moths more than ½ in (12 mm) long. Preemergent herbicides work only if applied just before weed seeds begin germination, usually in early spring, and insecticidal or fungicidal sprays are always more effective if applied while an infestation is still small.

CONTROLLING WEEDS

1 Weed seeds may lie dormant for years, germinating only when exposed to surface light. Turn over beds in midfall, and let frost kill the seedlings that emerge. Turn again 10 days before spring planting and hoe to kill another generation of weeds.

2 Spread a plastic geotextile over soil between crop rows and shrubs. This material permits downward passage of water, air, and nutrients but blocks upward growth of weeds. An additional cover of mulch ensures even better control.

3 Perennial weeds may defy mulches and soil cultivation. Hand-digging with a Cape Cod weeder or asparagus knife is the most effective control for individual plants; large populations may require chemical herbicides.

IDENTIFYING WEEDS

**If you can recognize some of the more
persistent and troublesome weeds in the garden,
you're halfway to eradicating them.**

A weed is simply any plant growing where it's not wanted. Native wildflowers and grasses are generally regarded as weeds whenever they appear among cultivated plants, though some gardeners may actively encourage them in a "wild" garden or meadow. The most troublesome weeds, however, are generally not native plants but species introduced from other lands. In the move to this continent, these weeds left their natural predators behind and, without any natural checks, multiplied rapidly.

Some commonly cultivated plants become weeds when they sprout in the wrong locations. Blackberries, for example, are welcome in the fruit garden, but not in the flower border. Even attractive plants may be weeds when they grow too vigorously for their allocated site — snow-in-summer *(Cerastium tomentosum)* is a charming rock garden plant, but will quickly smother its neighbors if left untrimmed.

Weeds are a problem when they compete with ornamental plants or food crops, reducing the available nutrients, light, water, and space, and interfering with the garden's visual appeal. They may even harbor pests and diseases.

Certain weeds can be an indicator of soil type — for example, sheep sorrel or mosses on acid soils, common yarrow and cinquefoils on sandy soils, mouse-ear chickweed and wild carrot ("Queen Anne's lace") on alkaline soils. But the most troublesome and common weeds, such as dandelions and quack grass, are found on all types of soil.

Annual weeds live for just a year. They produce seeds that lie dormant over winter, then germinate in spring or summer. Some even produce two or three generations a year — in fact, the main problem gardeners have with annual weeds is their capacity for shedding seeds. One of the worst, pigweed or lamb's-quarters, produces about 3,000 seeds on an average plant. Another annual, chickweed, has seeds that may remain alive, buried in the soil, for more than 25 years and then germinate when brought to the surface by cultivation. These annual seeds may be spread around the garden in mud on your shoes, by wind, on animals' fur, in bird droppings, or in composts.

Perennial weeds are often the most difficult to get rid of. Many multiply by creeping stems, either above or below ground, as well as by seed. New plants are also produced from tiny pieces of roots or underground stems, which are severed during digging or hoeing. When turned over with the soil, they remain unnoticed until vigorous, well-rooted shoots spring up everywhere.

Docks and dandelions are able to withstand longer periods of drought than most cultivated plants, as their long tap roots penetrate the soil deeply. Some plants, such as bindweed, may send roots down as deep as 10 ft (3 m), but others have relatively shallow rooting systems.

◄ **Troublesome weeds** With their deep or spreading roots, perennial weeds and wild grasses often grow better than cultivated plants. They usurp space, nutrients, water, and light.

Annual bluegrass
(Poa annua)

seedling

Height × spread 2-12 × 12 in (5-30 × 30 cm).
Leaves Bright green, ribbon-like, often wrinkled, in tufts or on creeping stems.
Flowers Greenish to buff, in triangular upright spikes, ½-3 in (1-8 cm) tall; spring to summer.
Other features Continually reseeds itself. Annual.

Annual sow thistle
(Sonchus oleraceus)

seedling

Height × spread 4-40 × 4-8 in (10-100 × 10-20 cm).
Leaves Dull blue-green, variable in shape with lobed and serrated edges.
Flowers Pale yellow, somewhat dandelionlike, ½-1 in (1-2.5 cm) wide in small clusters; summer through fall.
Other features Fluffy seed heads. Annual.

Bitter dock
(Rumex obtusifolius)

seedling

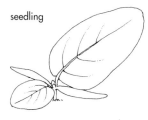

Height × spread 20-48 × 24 in (50-120 × 60 cm).
Leaves Large, wavy, broad, coarse-textured, with hairy underside, to 10 in (25 cm) long.
Flowers Green to reddish; tiny but in large, branched spikes; summer to fall.
Other features Seedlings often crimson. Resistant to most weed killers. Perennial.

Common chickweed
(Stellaria media)

seedling

Height × spread 2-14 × 8-16 in (5-35 × 20-40 cm).
Leaves Bright green, oval, ⅛-¾ in (3-20 mm) long, hairy at base.
Flowers Tiny, white; year-round in mild regions.
Other features Sprawls along the ground, but can scramble up through other plants. Annual.

114

Catchweed bedstraw
(Galium aparine)

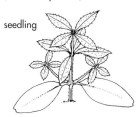

seedling

Height × spread 6-40 × 6-40 in (15-100 × 15-100 cm).
Leaves Green, "sticky," narrow, ½-2 in (1-5 cm) long.
Flowers Insignificant.
Other features Scrambling habit; can smother others, clinging by hooks on stems and leaves. Fruits are bristly, globular burrs that stick to clothing and fur. Annual.

Quack grass
(Agropyron repens)

seedling

Height 12-40 in (30-100 cm).
Leaves Dull green, slender blades forming large tufts.
Flowers Upright buff-green spikes; spring to fall.
Other features Rhizomes spread vigorously, often breaking during cultivation and producing new plants. Perennial.

Creeping buttercup
(Ranunculus repens)

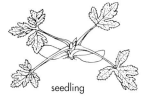

seedling

Height × spread Up to 12 × 20 in (30 × 50 cm).
Leaves Divided into three lobes, coarse-toothed, hairy, covered with pale spots.
Flowers Bright yellow, cup-shaped, about ½ in (1 cm) wide; spring and summer.
Other features Spreads by stout runners. Common in heavy, damp soil. Perennial.

Cinquefoil
(Potentilla spp.)

seedling

Height × spread Prostrate. Spreads to 40 in (1 m).
Leaves Divided into five finely serrated leaflets.
Flowers Yellow, strawberry-like, to ⅝-1 in (1.5-2.5 cm) wide; midspring to midfall.
Other features Creeping stems root at leaf joints. Several species: some annual, others perennial.

Canada thistle
(Cirsium arvense)

seedling

Height × spread 1-4 × 1½ ft (30-120 × 45 cm).
Leaves Dark green, long, narrow, wavy, with triangular teeth and prickly spines.
Flowers Pale purple, fading to white; heads ⅝-1 in (1.5-2.5 cm); summer to midfall.
Other features Creeping roots. Resistant to most weed killers. Perennial.

Dandelion
(Taraxacum officinale)

seedling

Height × spread 2-14 × 14 in (5-35 × 35 cm).
Leaves Dark green, glossy, lobed with toothed edges.
Flowers Yellow, 1½-2 in (3.5-5 cm) wide; spring to late summer; open in sun.
Other features Fluffy, globular seed heads — seeds dispersed by wind. Deep, tough roots. Perennial.

Lamb's-quarters (pigweed, goosefoot)
(Chenopodium album)

seedling

Height × spread Up to 3 × 1 ft (90 × 30 cm).
Leaves Gray-green with a whitish coating, mostly lance-shaped, lower ones broader and toothed, 3 in (8 cm) long.
Flowers Tiny, greenish, in upright spikes; early summer to midfall.
Other features Thousands of fatty, edible seeds. Annual.

Field bindweed
(Convolvulus arvensis)

seedling

Height × spread 3-10 × 10 ft (1-3 × 3 m).
Leaves Arrow-shaped, mid-green, 1-2 in (2.5-5 cm) long.
Flowers Pink and white striped, funnel-shaped, up to 1¼ in (3 cm) wide, long stalks; late spring through summer.
Other features Deep roots that fragment easily. Twining stems. Perennial.

Field speedwell
(Veronica persica)

seedling

Height × spread Up to 12 × 16 in (30 × 40 cm).
Leaves Pale green, oval, toothed, ½-1¼ in (1-3 cm) long.
Flowers Bright blue, often paler or white in the center, ⅜ in (8 mm) wide; spring to late summer.
Other features Stems hairy and spreading. Annual.

Field woodrush
(Luzula campestris)

seedling

Height × spread 8-16 × 8 in (20-40 × 20 cm).
Leaves Hairy, light green grasslike tussocks.
Flowers Close, brownish-green spikes; yellow anthers; early to late spring.
Other features Creeping rootstock; also spreads freely by seed. Perennial.

Goutweed
(Aegopodium podagraria)

seedling

Height × spread 12-44 × 36 in (30-110 × 90 cm).
Leaves Divided into sprays of three, each toothed, 2-4 in (5-10 cm) long.
Flowers Umbrellalike heads up to 2½ in (6 cm) with tiny white flowers; early summer to midsummer.
Other features Oval fruits, ridged, ⅛ in (4 mm) long. Hard to control. Perennial.

Groundsel
(Senecio vulgaris)

seedling

Height × spread 3-18 × 8 in (8-45 × 20 cm).
Leaves Dark green, long and fairly narrow, irregularly lobed and toothed.
Flowers Rich yellow, ⅛ in (4 mm) wide, like tiny thistles in shape; spring through fall.
Other features Germinates whenever weather is mild. Succulent stems. Fluffy fruits. Annual.

117

Field horsetail
(Equisetum arvense)

seedling

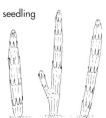

Height × spread Up to 2 × 3 ft (60 × 90 cm).
Leaves Evergreen, fernlike. Jointed stems; whorls of scalelike sheaths at stem joints.
Flowers Nonflowering; spores in terminal heads in spring.
Other features Deep creeping rootstock. Perennial.

Knotweed (goosegrass)
(Polygonum aviculare)

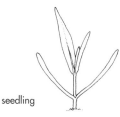

seedling

Height × spread Creeping, to 5 ft (150 cm).
Leaves Lance-shaped; silver sheath around stalk base.
Flowers Small, pink and white, in clusters at base of leaves; summer to fall.
Other features
Germinates mainly in early spring. Branching stems trail or scramble. Annual.

Wood sorrel
(Oxalis spp.)

seedling

Height × spread 1 × 1 ft (30 × 30 cm).
Leaves Trefoil, pale green.
Flowers Yellow clusters; late spring to midfall.
Other features Reproduces by seed; some species also by bulblets. Invasive perennial.

Lady's thumb
(Polygonum persicaria)

seedling

Height × spread 1 × 2 ft (30 × 60 cm).
Leaves Lance-shaped, dark green, often with purple blotches, on branching stems.
Flowers Dense pink or whitish spikes; early summer to midfall.
Other features Annual. Self-seeds freely. Common in damp soils.

Pineapple weed
(Matricaria matricarioides)

seedling

Height × spread 4-16 × 10 in (10-40 × 25 cm).
Leaves Finely divided, feathery, strongly aromatic, pineapple-scented when bruised.
Flowers Yellow-green, ¼-⅜ in (5-8 mm) wide; spring to summer.
Other features Particularly common along paths and hard-packed ground. Annual.

Purple dead nettle
(Lamium purpureum)

seedling

Height × spread 6-12 × 6 in (15-30 × 15 cm).
Leaves Oval, edges serrated, often tinged purple, up to 2 in (5 cm) long.
Flowers Pinkish purple, hooded, about ½ in (1 cm) long, in rings at upper leaf joints; spring to midsummer.
Other features Hairy stems, square in cross section. Annual.

Fireweed
(Epilobium/Chamaenerion angustifolium)

seedling

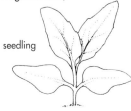

Height × spread Up to 80 × 12 in (200 × 30 cm).
Leaves Dark green, narrow; reddish veins; wavy edges.
Flowers Rose-purple, 1-1¼ in (2.5-3 cm) wide, in a tall spire; summer.
Other features Slender pods release white fluffy seeds in fall. Common on newly cleared land. Perennial.

Shepherd's purse
(Capsella bursa-pastoris)

seedling

Height × spread 4-24 × 10 in (10-60 × 25 cm).
Leaves Gray-green, long and narrow, variably toothed or lobed along the edges, all in a ground-level rosette.
Flowers Tiny, white, in a tall upright spike; spring to fall.
Other features Small purse-shaped seedpods. Can carry clubroot disease. Annual.

Stinging nettle
(Urtica dioica)

seedling

Height × **spread** 1-4 × 1 ft (30-120 × 30 cm).
Leaves Deep green, toothed, hairy, 1½-3 in (4-8 cm) long.
Flowers Yellow-green tassels, 4 in (10 cm) long; summer to early fall.
Other features Gives painful stings. Very tough yellow roots. Perennial.

Sun spurge
(Euphorbia helioscopia)

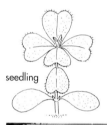

seedling

Height × **spread** Up to 20 × 8 in (50 × 20 cm).
Leaves Oval and finely toothed, pale green.
Flowers Yellow-green bracts in broad clusters; summer to midfall.
Other features Various euphorbias common throughout U.S. Milky saps may irritate human skin.

Elodea
(Elodea canadensis)

Height × **spread**
Submerged, wide-spreading oxygenator.
Leaves Dark green and lance-shaped, in groups of three.
Flowers Scarce, minute, purple-tinged white; summer to early fall.
Other features Spreads by water-borne seed. Perennial.

Duckweed
(Lemna minor)

Height × **spread** Prostrate, indefinite spread.
Leaves Tiny, modified, pale green. No roots or stems.
Flowers Minute and rarely seen; summer.
Other features Covers water surface with floating leaf carpet. Common annual.

CONTROLLING WEEDS

Lift out perennial weeds when digging beds and attack annual weeds with a hoe. Use chemicals only in extreme cases.

Weeds must be controlled in the garden for a number of important reasons. Obviously, they are unsightly, especially among flower beds and borders, but they also threaten the health and vigor of cultivated plants. During hot spells they compete for valuable water, and throughout the year, they tap nutrients and shade adjacent plants. Many weeds also harbor pests and diseases, which can easily spread to ornamental plants and food crops.

The old saying "1 year of seeding means 7 years of weeding" is very apt. Both annual and perennial weeds, if left uncontrolled, shed seeds, which germinate when conditions suit — particularly when they are brought to the surface by soil cultivation. Many even flourish during cold weather, when other plants lie dormant.

Never allow weeds to flower and produce seed, even though some, such as the cinquefoil, chickory, and bindweed, may be attractive in their own right. You can avoid a long-term war on weeds only by acting promptly whenever seedling weeds appear.

Learn to distinguish between weed seedlings and cultivated seedlings. Sowing in orderly rows, especially in the vegetable garden, makes this task easier.

Manual weeding

The thought of weeding by hand can be daunting, but if you tackle it promptly and don't let weeds take over the garden, this can be a relatively painless task. Old-fashioned hand-weeding is still the most effective and safest deterrent against perennial weeds.

Individual weeds can be pulled up directly by hand. This technique is best where a few large weeds have grown up between ornamental or crop plants, since, with care, the neighboring plants are not disturbed. Wear gloves for protection, especially when dealing with stinging nettles or thistles. Grasp the main stem as close to the soil as possible, then pull gently but firmly — if the weed resists, loosen the root with an asparagus knife so that the whole may be removed intact. Removing the entire root is important, since many perennial weeds can regrow from any severed sections left in the soil.

For dealing with more widespread weeds, a hoe — either a general gardening hoe or a scuffle hoe — and a small border fork are needed. A hand fork, trowel, and onion hoe may also be useful. Use an onion hoe, a short-handled version of the general gardening hoe, where plants are growing close together — in seedbeds and rock gardens, for example. Drawing the hoe toward you, cut off the weeds at soil level with a chopping action. Be careful not to damage the tops of young ornamental plants.

Use a scuffle hoe for general surface hoeing or between crop rows, working with a skimming action back and forth through the soil to sever weeds and remove their roots. A border fork should be used only to loosen those weeds that are deeply rooted

◀ **Annual weeds** Left unchecked, rampant weeds like purple dead nettles can quickly swamp bedding plants. Apart from their unsightliness, these weeds can encourage fungal diseases by excluding air and light.

USING A HOE

1 A scuffle hoe has a forward-pointing cutting edge — use with a skimming action to slice small weeds.

2 A general gardening hoe has a backward-slanting blade — use with a chopping action to cut down larger weeds at soil level.

around the base of a plant — remove those by hand to avoid disturbing the soil around the roots of ornamental plants.

Sometimes perennial weeds such as Bermuda and quack grass become entangled with the roots of ornamental plants. The only manual solution is to dig up both, separate them by hand, and replant the ornamentals.

Collect weeds to make sure they don't root again. They can be put on the compost heap unless they bear seed heads, in which case they should be disposed of as trash.

Choosing herbicides

Herbicides — chemical weed killers — take much of the physical effort out of weeding, but they need careful handling and application. Some gardeners prefer not to use them for ecological reasons, but they can be very effective against difficult weeds. There are several types of herbicide, classified by their mode of action.

The chemicals referred to below are the active ingredient, not the brand name — read the contents label on herbicides carefully if you are unsure.

Selective foliage types kill only certain plants, leaving others unharmed. They are commonly used on lawns — for example 2,4-D, which selects all broad-leaved

weeds among narrow-leaved grasses. Here, the selective action relies on most of the herbicide running off the narrow, channeled grass leaves, but wetting the broader weed leaves.

Nonselective foliage types kill most plants they touch. Some have a contact action, killing only the parts above ground that are directly touched by the chemical — for instance, potassium salts of fatty acids. Other herbicides are translocated — absorbed into the plant's circulatory system — and kill the entire plant, even the roots and bulbs. Among these is glyphosate, which takes several weeks to act thoroughly but is very effective. Some nonselective types can be applied selectively by spraying or painting them onto individual plants. Wick-type applicators, in which the herbicide is drawn down from a reservoir through a wick and then wiped on the weed, are especially effective.

Soil-applied residual types, such as DCPA, remain active in the soil for some time and are taken up by the roots of weeds. They are effective against existing weeds and subsequent germinating weed seeds — acting as weed preventers. Residual types are useful for clearing land that won't be used for several months.

Some soil-applied herbicides have a selective action when used in low concentrations and a nonselective action at higher doses; follow the manufacturer's instructions carefully.

Total herbicides, such as prometon or triclopyr, are used for clearing scrubland. Because they can remain active in the soil for a year or more, do not use them among ornamentals or food crops, or on land that will soon be planted with food crops, ornamentals, or lawn grasses. Test soil before replanting by scattering radish seed — this crop germinates in a few days and by its success or failure will reveal if the soil is free of total herbicides.

Applying herbicides

Herbicides may be sold as liquids that require dilution, as dry granules for direct application, or as wettable powders or soluble granules. They are applied by watering can, sprayer, or lawn-fertilizer spreader or sprinkled over the soil. Check the manufacturer's instructions for application.

Weeds near a pond
These weeds pose a special problem. Never spray a herbicide close to the edge, since it could drift into the water and kill water plants and animals.

Avoid soil-applied chemicals with a residual action — especially near an unlined pond — as they can leach into the water. Instead, weed by hand or use a paint-on contact type.

Where foliage types are suitable for sprayer application, this is the most effective method, giving an even coating of fine droplets that do not run off the leaves. Choose a calm day, when the spray won't drift to ornamental or food plants. Spray systematically to avoid overdosing some and undertreating others.

You can make an effective guard against spray drift for a pressurized sprayer. Cut the tube off an old plastic funnel so that the funnel will fit snugly over the tip of the spray nozzle. Fasten it in place with a hose clamp. When spraying herbicides do not pump up the sprayer as much as you would for an insecticide or fungicide — lower pressure produces larger droplets and less drift.

When applying liquid herbicides to bare or open ground, use a watering can. To keep the application as uniform as possible, cover the area systematically and at a constant speed.

Granular herbicides need careful application. First calculate the total area to be treated, and weigh out the appropriate total quantity of the chemical. When applying such herbicides to lawns, use a fertilizer spreader — the herbicide package may specify the correct aperture for the spreader, but if not, keep the aperture small and apply in several coats to achieve an even dispersal. When applying granular herbicides to a flower bed, square off the area into small segments and treat one segment at a time.

Where individual weeds are growing too closely among garden plants for any kind of herbicide treatment to be practical, a paint-on formulation of glyphosate can be used. This is also effective against isolated weeds in lawns.

Whichever type of herbicide you use, it is important while mixing and applying it to wear rubber gloves and any other protective gear recommended on the product label. If any herbicide contacts your skin or eyes, wash it off immediately and check the manufacturer's recommendations for accidental contact.

Weed suppressors

Systematic and continuous hand-weeding, or the use of preventive herbicides as recommended here, will keep your garden clear of most weeds. However, there are

HOW HERBICIDES WORK

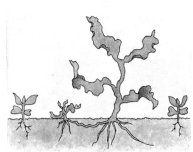

1 Contact herbicides are absorbed into leaves and stems, quickly killing tissue directly under the surface. But any part not wetted, including roots, may survive — the poison doesn't travel throughout the plant.

2 Systemic herbicides are absorbed into the plant's circulation, killing the entire weed, including roots and suckers, even if only part is wetted.

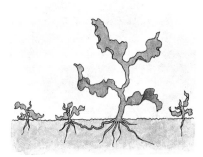

3 Soil-acting herbicides are also absorbed into the weed's circulation, but via the roots. They, too, kill the entire plant. In addition, they remain active in the soil, killing any weed seeds that germinate later.

HERBICIDE DO'S & DON'TS

- ❏ Do follow manufacturer's instructions regarding application method, dilution, and dosage.
- ❏ Do keep out of reach of children — regard all herbicides as toxic.
- ❏ Do keep pets and other animals away from treated areas.
- ❏ Do mix up only as much liquid chemical as you need — don't store diluted solutions.
- ❏ Don't apply chemicals to flowering plants — you may also kill pollinating insects such as bees.

- ❏ Don't mix up solutions more potent than recommended — you may scorch and kill some leaves and in so doing prevent systemic types from reaching and killing the root system.
- ❏ Don't get chemicals on your skin or eyes — if you do, wash off immediately. Always wash your hands thoroughly after use.
- ❏ Don't allow spray to drift onto wanted plants — keep nozzles close to the ground and pressure low. Don't spray on a windy day.

HERBICIDE APPLICATORS

1 Watering can — prevents drift, but gives less uniform application.

2 Pressurized sprayer with a fine spray drift guard — applies fine droplets.

3 Ready-mixed herbicide applicators — liquid gun *(above)* and paint-on types *(below)*.

SPECIAL WEED PROBLEMS

Weeds in paths, drives, and patios are perhaps the easiest to deal with, since they are not growing among decorative plants. Douse them with boiling water, or slice them off with an old knife or Cape Cod weeder. Perennial weeds with deep tap roots are best pulled out by hand or with the aid of an asparagus knife.

Herbicides provide the longest-lasting cure. Choose nonselective or total foliage-applied herbicides, such as prometron, triclopyr, glyphosate, and potassium salts of fatty acids.

Ready-mixed herbicides for use on paths and paving usually contain a foliage-acting chemical that kills existing weeds, and a residual soil-acting chemical for preventing subsequent weed germination. Most of these herbicides are effective for several months and may even persist for a year or more.

Mosses, algae, and lichens are a nuisance on paving and steps, often making the surface slippery in wet weather. Glyphosate or a spray containing a strong solution of chlorine bleach and water provides effective control. Glyphosate can be purchased already diluted in a hand-held gun-type spray canister, making spot treatment of a dangerous patch of moss very simple.

Weeds in flower beds are more of a challenge to remove. In established beds it's often difficult to use herbicides. There are no chemicals that can select the weeds from wanted plants. Unlike the typical weed problem in a lawn, where the wanted grass has narrow leaves in contrast to the broad leaves of the weeds, here most weeds and ornamentals have broad leaves.

Nonselective herbicides can, however, be applied selectively by painting them on with a brush or special spot-treatment applicator. Glyphosate is ideal for painting on individual weeds. Applications of persistent preemergent herbicides, such as trifluralin, will stop all seeds from germination, thus preventing regrowth of weeds after removal. Obviously these cannot be used where you plan to start flowers from seed.

Hand-weeding is the most effective method in a flower bed, either using a hoe or pulling out individual weeds, but be careful not to uproot or disturb the cultivated plants.

Weeds among roses and shrubs can be treated with S-ethyl dipropylthiocarbamate. Use it around rosebushes, shrubs, and ornamental trees, but be careful to keep this chemical away from young, green bark.

DCPA can be applied well before spring growth starts if the plants have been established for at least 2 years. Hoeing is easy, but you can accidentally damage roots and induce suckering in roses.

Weeds in lawns can to some extent be controlled through regular mowing. Isolated weeds should be removed by hand, with an asparagus knife, a small hand fork, or a spot herbicide. Selective herbicides can be applied from late spring until early fall. They are often sold as combined formulations with lawn fertilizers. Adding lime (if soil is acidic) and aeration are effective treatments for moss.

Where bulbs are naturalized in grass, do not apply herbicide until the bulb foliage has died down. Do not use chemicals on newly seeded or sodded lawns; hand-weed only for the first 6 months after seeding or sodding.

Weeds among fruit crops can be treated in the same way as those among rosebushes and shrubs. S-ethyl dipropylthiocarbamate — which has a contact action — can be applied around fruit trees and small-fruit bushes. DCPA can be used around apple and pear trees and small-fruit bushes, but not around blackberries or other cane fruits. Use it well before growth starts in the spring, but only if plantings are at least 2 years old.

Do not use herbicides among strawberries. Hand-weeding is the only safe method of removal.

Weeds among vegetable crops must be eradicated, as they compete strongly with these food crops for nutrients, water, and light, significantly reducing the vegetable yield.

Regularly hoe lightly between all vegetable rows to get rid of as many germinating annual weeds as possible. Choose a hot day, so that uprooted weeds will wither before they can reroot in the loose soil. Where weeds are growing in crop rows, hand-weed carefully.

Brush and rank growth in neglected areas can be treated with liquid herbicides containing triclopyr and 2, 4-D. These chemicals are unsuitable for clearing a site just before planting as both leave residues in the soil.

Glyphosate applied from midsummer onward will kill or strongly check most perennial weeds. It takes 3 to 4 weeks to be fully effective. The site can then be cleared and planted or sown at once.

other, almost labor-saving techniques that can solve the problem before it arises. Prevention is always better than a cure.

Ground-cover plants are ideal for covering every inch of soil in shrub and mixed borders. They spread rapidly into a dense carpet of foliage and roots and thus deprive emerging weed seedlings of light and space. Some form flowering carpets, such as the shade-loving 'London Pride' *(Saxifraga × urbium),* lungwort *(Pulmonaria* species), the red-flowered dead nettles *(Lamium maculatum),* and the almost-invasive evergreen, blue- or white-flowered periwinkles *(Vinca* species).

Better in sun, but equally good, are the evergreen, blue-flowered and bronze-leaved bugles *(Ajuga reptans),* the blue catmints *(Nepeta × faassenii)* with their gray-green foliage, and the semi-evergreen *Viola labradorica.*

Low-growing shrubs give excellent ground cover over large areas. Good examples are the evergreen euonymuses such as *Euonymus fortunei* 'Coloratas' and 'Emerald 'n Gold.' Prostrate junipers *(Juniperus horizontalis),* the evergreen Californian lilac *(Ceanothus thyrsiflorus repens),* and the hummocky rock rose *(Helianthemum*

hybrids) are other good choices. In smaller gardens, ericas spread their lush foliage. Particularly valuable is the winter-flowering *Erica carnea,* which, unlike other heathers, tolerates alkaline soil.

Ivies smother the ground in almost any situation, providing a year-round rich green cover.

▲ **Black plastic** Spread in spring when the ground has warmed up, this cover helps to suppress weed growth and conserve soil moisture. It is particularly effective for thirsty crops such as Swiss chard, with its handsome ruby-red stalks.

Mulch covers

Another effective preventive measure is to cover the bare soil around desirable plants with a layer of mulch. You can use straw, plastic film, roofing felt, or synthetic geotextiles in the vegetable and fruit garden. Among ornamental plants, organic mulches are visually more pleasing and are also good soil conditioners. Shredded hardwood leaves or well-rotted horse manure can be spread in a layer 2-3 in (5-7.5 cm) deep over the soil — though these materials may themselves harbor weed seeds.

Bark nuggets and shredded bark make a decorative and long-lasting mulch that withstands winds and keeps soil from being splashed onto nearby plant foliage by rain and irrigation. Composted bark is finer in texture and particularly suitable for acid-loving plants.

Small pebbles, crushed rock, and gravel look natural around alpine plants in the rock garden and in raised beds. They keep plant crowns dry and rot free in winter. They also act as a good obstacle to slugs and snails.

◄ **There are many commonly available types of mulch.**
Organic types:
cocoa bean shells *(top left);* coarse and fine bark *(far right).*
Stone types:
(from top) finely screened grit, small pebbles, gravel, colored and white crushed rock, washed pebbles.

HERBICIDES FOR ALL SITUATIONS

LOCATION	TYPES OF WEED	CHEMICAL TREATMENT	COMMENTS
Uncultivated areas, waste ground	All types, including grass weeds, woody weeds	Prometron Triclopyr Potassium salts of fatty acids	Persists 1 year. Persists 4 to 6 weeks. Apply early in the season.
	Woody weeds, ivy, sucker growths from old tree stumps	Triclopyr	Apply when target is in leaf; persists 4 to 6 weeks.
	Perennial weeds, including grasses	Glyphosate	Apply from midsummer on; works in 3 to 4 weeks; no persistence.
Paths and drives	Algae, moss	Potassium salts of fatty acids, zinc, and copper	Apply at any time of year; apply zinc and copper when wet or as liquid solution; effective in 2 to 4 weeks.
	Liverworts	Potassium salts of fatty acids	Apply at any time of year.
	All types, including germinating weed seeds, established annuals and perennials	Imazapyr and oxyfluorfen	Apply early spring; these herbicides control germinating weed seedlings for several months.
	Smartweed	Glyphosate	Apply from midsummer on; fully effective in 3 to 4 weeks; nonpersistent.
Lawns	Clovers, crabgrass, and other creeping weeds	MCPP; 2,4-D; calcium acid; methearsonate	Apply as weed seedlings begin growth in spring.
	Daisies and other rosette-type weeds	2,4-D mixtures	
	Most weeds of both preceding types	Calcium acid; methane arsenate (CAMA); 2,4-D; MCPP	
	Quack grass	Glyphosate	Spot-treat in spring; hand-digging also effective.
	Moss	Zinc and copper, potassium salts of fatty acids	Apply zinc and copper when turf is wet or as liquid solution; fertilization and improving drainage and aeration of lawn also effective.
New lawns	Annual weeds	None	Avoid herbicides for the first 6 months after germination of grass.
Tree and shrub borders	Annual and perennial weeds	DCPA	Preemergent — apply to ground around shrubs after transplanting.
	Established perennials	Glyphosate	Paint on individual weeds from early summer onward.
	Quack and most other grassy weeds	S-ethyl dipropylthiocarbamate	Apply in spring or fall as weed seeds germinate.
Roses	Germinating weeds	Trifluralin	Apply early spring; persists for several months; not for use on lawns.
	Grassy weeds	S-ethyl dipropylthiocarbamate	Apply when weed seeds are germinating.
Bulbs in borders	Established annuals and perennials	Fluazifop-butyl	Apply at any time of year.
Herbaceous borders	Established perennials	Glyphosate	Paint on persistent weeds from midsummer onward.
	Grassy weeds	S-ethyl dipropylthiocarbamate	Apply when weed seeds are germinating.
Fruit	Established annuals	Potassium salts of fatty acids	Apply early in growing season.
	Germinating weeds	DCPA	Apply early in growing season.
	Grassy weeds	Potassium salts of fatty acids	Apply early in growing season.
Vegetables	Germinating weeds	None	Hand-weed or hoe; apply mulch.
Pools, new	Green algae and blanket weeds	Commercial algicides	No safe chemical control; establish a balance of water plants and fish.

Problems in the flower garden

The flower gardener's foes include a number of insect pests as well as various disorders and diseases (which may be encouraged by unchecked weed growth). The following pages describe the range of troubles that can afflict ornamental plants, from herbaceous perennials and bulbs to shrubs and trees. Don't be discouraged — although together they present a formidable picture, only a few of these problems are likely to be found in any one garden.

The best defense is to ensure that plants are well cared for. Plants that are developing well are generally healthy and able to withstand pest attacks. Plants weakened by such sap-sucking pests as aphids and whiteflies are more likely to succumb to disease. Keep a constant eye on all plants to check whether leaves, stems, or flowers look in any way sickly, distorted, or discolored. If you keep weeds down and scrupulously remove garden debris, you will deprive common pests of their favorite hiding places. You can also discourage infestations by avoiding certain troublesome plants — honeysuckle and nasturtiums, for example, attract aphids in large numbers, and certain rose cultivars are especially prone to mildew and black spot.

A range of pesticides and fungicides can be sprayed or dusted on infested plants once you have identified the cause of any symptoms. Make sure you use only approved chemical controls, and avoid repeatedly using a particular insecticide, since pests may become resistant to the chemical as a result.

Viridiflora tulips The beautiful "broken" colors of some tulips may be caused by natural mutation — or by a viral disease.

BULB PESTS AND DISEASES

**Bulbs from reputable sources are
usually healthy, but poor garden hygiene can
encourage pests and diseases.**

Garden plants grown from bulbs, corms, tubers, and rhizomes are not especially vulnerable to pests and diseases. It's important, however, to be aware of the symptoms and causes of a number of problems, so that you can take early measures to eradicate them or avoid trouble altogether. Always start with healthy stock — buy dormant bulbs from a reputable supplier — and give them appropriate growing conditions. Never plant a sun-loving species in shade or one that likes well-drained soil in a damp corner — it won't grow vigorously and will be more vulnerable to attack.

To get the right conditions, you need to prepare the ground. If the soil is heavy, work in plenty of sharp builder's sand to improve drainage. At the same time dig out all perennial weeds.

Fungal rots cause most problems — they attack the leaves and underground parts. Tulip fire, for instance, can cause considerable losses, spreading rapidly in wet weather from one bulb to others close by — especially if the bulbs are crowded. Other bulbs, lilies in particular, are susceptible to basal rot, which leads to plant collapse. Stored bulbs are particularly vulnerable to fungal diseases, so check them carefully and often.

Viruses can be damaging, although individual plants may take a long time to succumb. Sucking insects, such as aphids, are mainly responsible for transmitting viruses from one plant to another; keep these pests in check, even when their direct damage seems minor.

Inevitably, the food supply so neatly packaged in a bulb, corm, or tuber is attractive to pests such as mice, nematodes, and insect grubs. Leaves and flowers are less frequent targets, although thrips can disfigure gladioli and birds mutilate crocus blooms.

Bulbs may also be affected by disorders from other sources. Blindness, for example, is a disorder of narcissi and tulips (especially those grown in containers), in which the flower bud actually ceases to develop. The causes are quite varied — pest and disease attack may be responsible, and perhaps waterlogged soil, very dry conditions, nutrient deficiency, or exposure of the bulbs to high temperatures after lifting for storage over the summer.

Secondary diseases may also infect bulbs that have already succumbed to pest or disease damage. Bacterial soft rot, for example, usually invades cut or bruised tissues. Preventive measures are more effective than cures — maintain a balanced soil nutrient content, avoid waterlogging, eliminate wound-forming pests and diseases, and handle bulbs carefully.

Chemical treatment
Pesticides and other chemicals for disease control can be expensive, and you may prefer not to use them for ecological reasons. The chemical names referred to in the subsequent pages are the active ingredients, not the brand names of each product. Read the contents label of each package carefully, and meticulously follow the manufacturers' instructions.

If you decide to adopt a wait-and-see policy to bulb pests and diseases, be vigilant and take quick action to limit any damage if you see a problem developing. Always destroy diseased bulbs and preferably dispose of them off-site. Never put them on the compost pile, as they can spread the disease that they harbor even in the hottest compost.

◄ **Bulbs and tubers** Firm, dry, and with visible growth buds, these bulbs and corms are in prime condition. They include crocus corms; narcissus, tulip, lily, and hyacinth bulbs; and the fleshy roots of the foxtail lily *(Eremurus)*. Store in cool, dry conditions until planting time.

BASAL ROT

Plants affected Crocuses, lilies, and narcissi.

Symptoms Roots and corm bases show dark strands from the base, or brown rot spreading through the inner scales.

Danger period All year, including in storage.

Treatment Destroy rotten bulbs. Dip newly lifted bulbs in a solution of thiophanate-methyl. In early stages, cut out affected roots and scales of lily bulbs.

BULB SCALE MITES

Plants affected Amaryllises and narcissi.

Symptoms Deformed leaves and stems, especially on forced plants. Damaged tissue often covered with russet-brown scars.

Danger period Midwinter to midspring.

Treatment Destroy severely damaged plants. No chemical treatment available. Expose bulbs for forcing to frost for 2 to 3 nights a week before planting.

CUCUMBER MOSAIC

Plants affected Dahlias and gladioli.

Symptoms In dahlias, leaves become mottled with pale green bands along midribs and larger veins; in gladioli, flower colors are broken.

Danger period All season.

Treatment Destroy affected plants. Plant early in the season, and control aphids and leafhoppers (which transmit the disease) with a mulch of aluminum foil or by spraying with malathion.

DRY ROT

Plants affected Gladioli and related plants such as acidantheras, crocuses, and freesias.

Symptoms Top growth turns yellow, then brown, and finally topples over, as a result of decay of leaf sheaths. Affected leaves are covered with tiny black clusters. Many small dark lesions also develop on corms, which eventually merge to form larger black areas; finally, corms shrivel completely and die.

Danger period Top growth affected during growing season; corms affected in storage.

Treatment Remove and destroy affected corms as soon as first symptoms appear. Dip corms in thiophanate-methyl solution before storing or replanting them. Plant corms in a fresh site each year — the fungus that causes dry rot is soil borne. Improved soil cultivation helps to prevent spread of the disease.

GLADIOLUS THRIPS

Plants affected Gladioli and related species, such as acidantheras.

Symptoms Fine silvery flecks on petals and foliage; in severe cases, flowers discolor completely and may die.

Danger period Early summer to early fall.

Treatment Spray infected plants with insecticidal soap, neem, acephate, or carbaryl. Dip corms in thiophanate-methyl solution before storing.

GRAY BULB ROT

Plants affected Hyacinths and tulips; also sometimes crocuses, fritillaries, gladioli, irises, and narcissi.

Symptoms Dry gray rot at the bulb neck, soon developing into large areas of black fungal clusters, which cause the bulb to disintegrate. Emergence of plants in an infected bed is patchy; those that do appear are usually stunted and discolored, and they eventually die.

Danger period Soon after bulbs are planted.

Treatment Remove and destroy debris from diseased plants, and replace surrounding soil with sterilized soil. No chemical treatment available to home gardeners. Grow bulbs on a different site each year.

HARD ROT

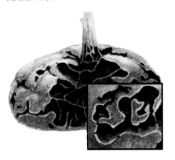

Plants affected Acidantheras and gladioli.
Symptoms Brown spots on leaves, which develop small black fungi. Black-brown sunken spots on corms; may become hard and shriveled.
Danger period Infection in summer; symptoms may appear during storage.
Treatment Dip corms in a solution of thiophanate-methyl before storing. Destroy affected corms.

NARCISSUS BULB FLIES

Plants affected Narcissi, as well as amaryllises and snowdrops.
Symptoms Leaves deformed, narrow, and yellow; no flowers. Bulbs rotten; yellowish-white larvae inside.
Danger period Late spring to early summer; symptoms usually spotted too late at planting time.
Treatment Destroy soft bulbs at planting time. Cultivate soil around plants in early summer — preventing flies from entering the soil to lay eggs.

RHIZOME ROT

Plants affected Rhizomatous irises.
Symptoms Soft, yellow acrid-smelling rot at the growing point; leaf fan collapses at ground level.
Danger period All year; most prevalent in wet weather.
Treatment Improve soil drainage. Control slugs and other pests. Cut out rotting parts. No effective chemical treatment known; destroy seriously affected plants.

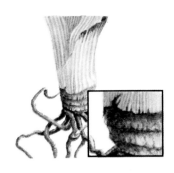

SCAB (NECK ROT, STEM ROT)

Plants affected Gladiolus species and cultivars.
Symptoms Red-brown specks form near base of leaves, enlarging into dark brown spots. Stems may decay and keel over at ground level in wet weather. Pale yellow, water-soaked circular lesions appear on corms.
Danger period Infection occurs during summer, but symptoms may not be noticed until corms are lifted for storage.
Treatment Destroy affected corms. Dip remaining healthy corms in a solution of thiophanate-methyl. Grow corms in a fresh site each year to prevent recurrence of the disease.

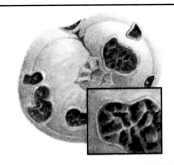

SLUGS AND SNAILS

Plants affected Acidantheras, alliums, alstroemerias, chionodoxas, daffodils and narcissi, dahlias, hyacinths, irises, lilies, puschkinias, and tulips.
Symptoms Irregular holes eaten in leaves, stems, buds, and flowers; sometimes also in bulbs and roots. Telltale slime tracks on damaged plants and surrounding soil.
Danger period Mainly warm and humid spells during spring and fall.
Slugs and snails generally feed during night.
Treatment Handpick individual slugs and snails in early morning. Cultivate soil thoroughly, and remove accumulations of decaying plant material. Avoid heavy dressings of organic mulches. Scatter slug baits around susceptible plants. A broad ring composed of diatomaceous earth, wood ashes, or crushed seashells around each plant provides some protection.

SMOLDER

Plants affected Narcissi.
Symptoms Leaves rot; covered with gray velvety mold. Bulbs decay.
Danger period During storage; foliage symptoms appear in spring.
Treatment Store cool and dry. Keep beds free of weeds to ensure good air circulation. Destroy affected plants and bulbs immediately.

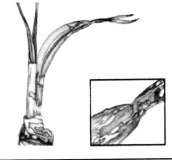

STEM AND BULB NEMATODES (RING DISEASE)

Plants affected Narcissi; sometimes hyacinths, irises, scillas, snowdrops, and tulips.
Symptoms Leaves stunted, deformed, bent, and yellowish, turning brown. Pull infested leaves between fingers to feel small lumps of yellowish tissue. Scales inside infested bulbs appear in dark circles, not normal white.
Danger period Growing plants mainly affected in spring; dormant bulbs show symptoms in late summer and fall.
Treatment Remove and discard diseased plants and surrounding soil. Avoid rich, wet soil with a high humus content. Do not replant susceptible bulbs in affected area for 3 years. No effective chemical treatment is available.

TULIP BULB APHIDS

Plants affected Crocuses, freesias, gladioli, irises, and tulips.
Symptoms Pale brown or green aphids infest stored bulbs; also damage growth after planting.
Danger period Winter to spring.
Treatment Dip bulbs before planting in 1 oz (30 ml) diazinon mixed with 3 gal (4 l) of water; spray infestations on plants with malathion or neem.

TULIP FIRE

Plants affected Tulips.
Symptoms Young shoots are stunted and rot above ground, becoming covered with gray velvety mold. Small brown spots appear on flower petals, later becoming covered in mold. Bulbs rot and bear small black fungal growths.
Danger period Bulbs affected shortly before or after planting; flowers and shoots in spring.
Treatment Remove garden debris. Carefully inspect bulbs before planting, removing outer husks to check for diseased spots beneath. Remove plants as soon as infection is observed, taking care not to leave any part of infected bulb in the soil. Do not plant where disease has occurred unless soil has been replaced.

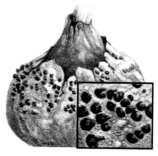

OTHER PESTS AND DISEASES

A number of other pests, diseases, and disorders may occasionally affect bulbs, corms, and tubers.

Bacterial soft rot Quite common among bulbs, both those in the garden and in storage. Invades tissues already damaged.
   Watery lesions appear around a wound and enlarge quickly to form bad-smelling slimy patches, or the tissues may disintegrate. Growing leaves may be affected, as may stored bulbs.
   Chemical control rarely succeeds, though small infections may be cut out of the bulbs, which should then be dusted with Bordeaux mixture powder. Eliminate wound-forming pests, and do not plant bulbs or rhizomes too deeply. Remove and destroy infected material.

Botrytis (gray mold) Common on flowers and buds, and may be associated with stem and leaf rots. Grayish mold covers the affected surface — it spreads rapidly by air currents. Avoid overcrowding bulbs; don't plant in damp, shady sites; deadhead frequently; and spray affected plants with benomyl or thiophanate-methyl fungicide.

Crane fly larvae (leatherjackets) These larvae cause symptoms similar to those of cutworms, mainly in spring. Hoe diazinon + chlorpyrifos into the soil to protect plants. Cultivate soil thoroughly before planting.

Cutworms Noctuid moth caterpillars, which cut through stems at ground level, cause wilting and top-growth death. Hoe weeds regularly, as they attract egg-laying adults. Dig over soil in winter to expose caterpillars to predators. Treat surrounding soil with diazinon + chlorpyrifos or carbaryl.

Iris leaf spot Affects irises and members of the iris family, forming yellow-edged brown spots in spring, which later enlarge into oval patches with a gray central mold and a reddish edge (on bulbous irises the blotches don't have the distinct edging and are grayer). Outbreaks are worse in wet seasons. Rake and destroy old foliage in fall or early spring. Spray with chlorothalonil, mancozeb, or thiophanate-methyl.

Mice Eat almost anything, but juicy bulbs are favorites, both in storage and in the open ground. Set traps in storage buildings. Animal-repellent dusts applied at planting time may deter mice.

Powdery mildew Forms a white coating on leaves and stems, especially on begonias. Plants may droop and leaves turn yellow. Avoid crowding plants, and when plants are not wet, remove and destroy affected parts. Apply sulfur or thiophanate-methyl if needed.

Smut A fungal disease that forms sooty black patches. Some types spread through the plant's veins, reproducing in the roots or bulbs. Destroy infected plants, and replant on a new site.

Swift moth caterpillars Similar to cutworms, but live below ground.

BED AND BORDER PESTS

Annual, biennial, and perennial plants are vulnerable to many pests and diseases, but the attacks are rarely fatal.

Border and bedding plants are mostly quite fast growing, with soft, relatively succulent leaves and stems. This often makes them particularly attractive to sap-sucking, chewing, and biting pests such as aphids, caterpillars, slugs, and snails.

Fungal and bacterial diseases are also able to infest the soft tissues of annuals and perennials more easily than the woody stems of shrubs and trees.

The following pages will help you to recognize and control these pests and diseases. Although they present a formidable picture when listed all together, only a small number are likely to attack a single plant or garden.

Watch all your plants to see whether the leaves, stems, or flowers are in any way unhealthy. Distorted or discolored tissues, for example, are sure signs of a problem. Practice good garden hygiene at all times, weeding, mulching, and feeding regularly. Remember that vigorously growing plants are better able to withstand disease attacks.

Plants that have been regularly troubled by pests or diseases in the past should be protected against recurrence. Regularly hoe or fork over affected soils.

When using chemical pesticides to protect plants or destroy pests and diseases, always spray in calm, windless weather. Spray drift can contaminate nearby food crops. Don't spray or dust plants when they are in flower, since you may also kill valuable pollinating insects, such as bees. Never spray in hot weather — some chemicals injure foliage at high temperatures.

▼ **Slug and snail damage** Moist, shady conditions are preferred by hostas — as well as slugs and snails, which can reduce leaves to skeletons. Slime trails betray their presence.

APHIDS

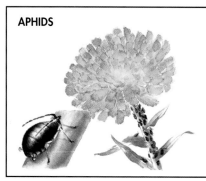

Plants affected Almost all cultivated plants.
Symptoms Small, mostly wingless plump insects cluster in large numbers on tips of young shoots and below flower buds. Several types may appear, colored green, gray, brown, or black. They excrete a sticky honeydew on foliage below, and this may nourish a secondary infection of black sooty mold. Aphids multiply rapidly, sucking plant sap and thus distorting and stunting shoots.
Danger period Spring and summer.
Treatment A strong spray of water can knock pests off plants, and insecticidal soaps are often adequate treatment for limited infestations. For major infestations apply horticultural oil or spray with malathion, acephate, neem, or resmethrin if plant is indicated on pesticide label.

PLANT BUGS

Plants affected Mainly asters, chrysanthemums, dahlias, fuchsias, pelargoniums, salvias, sunflowers, and zinnias.
Symptoms Drooping flowers and leaves; irregular bronze spotting on foliage.
Danger period Late spring to late summer.
Treatment Kill weeds that harbor pests; spray with insecticidal soap, malathion, acephate, or carbaryl.

CLUBROOT

Plants affected Stocks, wallflowers, and other members of the cabbage family.
Symptoms Roots become swollen and distorted. Plants become weak and turn yellow.
Danger period Growing season.
Treatment Apply hydrated lime to raise soil pH to 7.5. Do not plant susceptible plants where disease has attacked previous crops. Dip roots in thiophanate-methyl solution before planting seedlings.

EARWIGS

Plants affected Chrysanthemums, dahlias, delphiniums, dusty millers, pansies, violas, and zinnias.
Symptoms Irregular, tattered holes in leaves and petals.
Danger period Late spring to midfall.
Treatment Trap earwigs in shallow containers baited with fish oil, then destroy pests. Surround plants with barriers of diatomaceous earth, wood ashes, or crushed seashells.

ROOT ROT

Plants affected Bedding plants.
Symptoms Stem bases, which may be discolored, rot; roots usually die.
Danger period Growing season.
Treatment Rotate bedding plants from year to year. Improve soil drainage. Remove and destroy infected plants and surrounding soil. Water seedlings with copper oxychloride before planting out.

SPITTLEBUGS

Plants affected Campanulas, chrysanthemums, goldenrods, lavenders, perennial asters, phlox, rudbeckias, and many others.
Symptoms Frothy masses of "spittle" covering small green insects nestled in leaf axils.
Danger period Summer.
Treatment Rarely a serious problem. Wash off with strong jet of water from a hose, or spray with insecticidal soap.

BOTRYTIS (GRAY MOLD)

Plants affected All plants.
Symptoms Gray velvety mold on rotting leaves and flowers, especially in greenhouses or in sheltered sites.
Danger period Growing season.
Treatment Destroy infected plants. Don't overcrowd plants in damp, shady sites. Spray with benomyl (except food crops), mancozeb, or thiophanate-methyl.

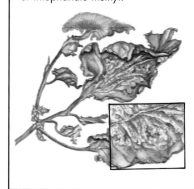

CROWN GALL

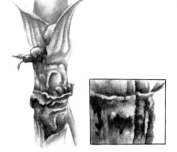

Plants affected Many types, but particularly carnations, chrysanthemums, pelargoniums, and sweet peas.
Symptoms Abortive, often flattened shoots with thickened, distorted leaves develop at ground level.
Danger period During propagation and throughout growing season.
Treatment Destroy infected plants. Don't grow susceptible plants on the same site again.

CHRYSANTHEMUM PETAL BLIGHT

Plants affected Chrysanthemums; sometimes cornflowers.
Symptoms Dark water-soaked spots or blotches spread on petals until flowers rot.
Danger period At flowering time, particularly in hot, wet summers.
Treatment Control is not easy. Cut off and dispose of affected flowers. Avoid high humidity when growing in a greenhouse; ventilate well.

PETUNIA STEM ROT

Plants affected Petunias; also zinnias.
Symptoms Plants wilt, often as they are about to flower. Stem bases may be discolored.
Danger period Growing season.
Treatment Remove and destroy affected plants and those in 1½-ft (45-cm) radius; then sterilize tools in bleach solution and wash hands with soap. Rotate bedding plants so that susceptible species are grown on a fresh site every year.

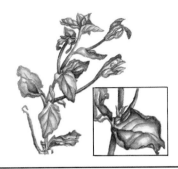

POWDERY MILDEW

Plants affected Forget-me-nots, goldenrods, and New York asters.
Symptoms Floury white coating mainly on leaves and shoots.
Danger period Growing season.
Treatment Avoid crowding plants. When plants are dry, remove and destroy affected parts. Remove all garden debris, and apply sulfur or thiophanate-methyl as needed.

RUST

Plants affected Many types, but especially hollyhocks, pelargoniums, and snapdragons.
Symptoms Brown, orange, or yellow powdery masses of spores develop on leaves and stems.
Danger period Growing season.
Treatment Pick and destroy all diseased leaves. Apply sulfur or chlorothalonil. Destroy diseased shoots at the end of the season.

SLUGS AND SNAILS

Plants affected Delphiniums, hostas, primroses, rudbeckias, sweet peas, violets, and many other plants.
Symptoms Irregular holes eaten in leaves and flowers. Slime tracks.
Danger period Growing season.
Treatment Avoid dressings of mulch, compost, or manure. Scatter slug baits around susceptible plants, or ring with diatomaceous earth, wood ashes, or crushed seashells.

STEM ROT

Plants affected Carnations, godetias, lobelias, and pelargoniums.
Symptoms Rotting of stems, but no obvious fungal growth visible. The same fungus may cause basal rot of carnation cuttings taken from diseased plants.
   Blackleg disease also causes rotting of pelargonium cuttings at the stem base, causing them to collapse. Affected tissues are soft and black.
Danger period Growing season; blackleg soon after taking cuttings.
Treatment Where possible, cut out and destroy affected parts; spray with Bordeaux mixture, ferbam, or captan, except on pelargoniums, for which no chemical treatment is available. Destroy badly affected plants. Maintain good hygiene during propagation.

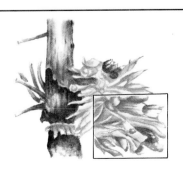

SWIFT MOTHS

Plants affected Various herbaceous perennials.
Symptoms Off-white caterpillars of the swift moth, which live in the soil and feed on the roots. See also Cutworms, below.
Danger period All year.
Treatment Weed control and cultivation reduce the risk of attack. Protect susceptible plants by working diazinon + chlorpyrifos into the soil.

LEAF-ROLLING CATERPILLARS

Plants affected Many herbaceous plants, especially chrysanthemums, heleniums, and phlox.
Symptoms Caterpillars eat irregular small holes in leaves and bind them with silk webbing.
Danger period Late spring to summer.
Treatment Handpick and destroy caterpillars. Apply biological controls; for serious infestations spray with carbaryl.

VIRUSES

Plants affected Many types of plants, but particularly chrysanthemums, pelargoniums, violas, and wallflowers.
Symptoms Leaves crinkled, small, and sometimes irregularly shaped. Flowers distorted, or colors broken — white streaks or stripes in a lighter or darker shade. May not affect vigor.
Danger period Growing season.
Treatment Dig up and destroy.

WHITEFLIES

Plants affected Mainly indoor and greenhouse plants, but often appear on container-grown plants on a deck or porch, especially fuchsias.
Symptoms White-winged flies like tiny moths on leaf undersides — often flying off when disturbed. Tiny white scalelike nymphs may also be present. No obvious damage to leaves, but pests weaken the plants by sucking sap from tissues.
Danger period Late spring to early fall; all year indoors or in a heated greenhouse.
Treatment Releases of predacious insects effective for greenhouse plants. Outdoors, catch adults with yellow sticky traps or vacuum from leaves. Spray with insecticidal soap or neem; with pyrethrin or resmethrin for severe infestations.

OTHER PESTS AND DISEASES

Birds, especially house sparrows, may damage flowers, buds, and leaves, usually in search of seeds. Their favorite targets are low-growing, bushy, continuously flowering plants such as marigolds. Deadhead flowers to prevent seed production. Keep seedbeds moist to deter dust bathing of birds. Crisscrossing newly seeded areas with black threads discourages foraging birds.

Chafer grubs are C-shaped whitish grubs, each with three pairs of legs and a brown head. They eat the roots of many annuals and herbaceous perennials, causing top growth to wilt and die. Biological controls may be effective. Work diazinon + chlorpyrifos into the soil around the roots.

Cutworms are fat grayish-brown caterpillars living in the soil. They eat through young shoots at soil level and are most troublesome in light soils in dry summers. Plants fall over and die. Control weeds that encourage cutworms. Cultivate soil in winter to expose cutworms — birds then eat them. Protect young plants as for chafer grubs. Biological controls are available.

Damping-off is a common disease of young seedlings, especially in greenhouses. Seedlings fall over and die. Avoid overcrowding by sowing thinly. Use sterilized seed-starting mix for sowing indoors. Don't overwater, and keep plants well ventilated. Apply copper sulfates or copper oxychloride. Remove dead seedlings immediately when they collapse.

Leatherjackets (crane fly larvae) are legless grayish-brown pests of newly cultivated soil. They feed on roots and stems. Young plants are damaged in spring, but attacks may occur through-out the growing season. Plants turn yellow, wilt, and die. Protect plants by working diazinon + chlorpyrifos into the soil. Hoe soil regularly, and improve drainage — birds eat grubs that are brought to the surface.

Sclerotinia is a disease that can affect all types of herbaceous plants, but it is most common on sunflowers (*Helianthus*). A brown wettish rot forms at the base of stems, often with a mass of white mold. Plants wilt and lower leaves turn yellow; stems may fall over. Control weeds that may harbor the disease, do not crowd plants, and destroy those affected.

Spider mites are a serious pest of houseplants, but they also infest outdoor bedding perennials in summer. Leaves of infested plants are faintly speckled, eventually discoloring, wilting, and dying. As mites swarm over the plant, very fine webbing is visible. Use biological controls (*see* page 86), or spray forcibly with water. Spray with insecticidal soap, horticultural oil, or malthion.

WATER PLANT PROBLEMS

**Aquatic plants — in a pool or bog —
are susceptible to a few destructive pests and diseases,
the control of which demands special care.**

Most water plants are perennials and, as such, share some of the pest and disease problems associated with their terrestrial cousins. Indeed, the marginal aquatic types — those which grow in wet soil at the edge of the water with most of their foliage above the water surface — suffer from the same troubles as border perennials.

There are two main difficulties in overcoming water plant pests and diseases — access to the plants for hand control is often impossible or at best precarious, and chemical control is usually inadvisable, especially if there are fish or other animals in the pool. Most chemical pesticides are poisonous to fish.

To add to the problem, the foliage of many water plants is damaged by chemical pesticides, so even if you don't have any fish you shouldn't spray water plants

with chemicals. In many cases, pest infestations can be controlled with forceful jets from a hose to dislodge insect larvae and eggs, especially if the pool is stocked with hungry fish.

In general, the most effective way of dealing with serious outbreaks of pests and diseases is to cut off and destroy all the affected stems, leaves, and flowers. You may have to crawl across the water on a bridge of sturdy boards or wade to get to the plants. However, you should never wade in any pool that is lined only with PVC, butyl rubber, or fiberglass — you may unintentionally puncture or crack it.

When you are using boards for access across a fiberglass pool, always rest the boards' ends on bricks or cinder blocks set outside the pool; otherwise your weight may cause the pool's rigid lining to crack.

Fish and other livestock can do much toward eliminating water pests, as well as adding to the tranquil charm of the pool. They eat the larvae and grubs of pests such as caddis flies and water-lily beetles, together with other undesirable water dwellers like mosquito larvae.

Fish, however, also have their predators, notably raccoons and herons. Small pools can be protected with a fine wire-mesh covering. Herons, which usually feed from a standing position in the water, can be deterred by stretching plastic-covered wires along the inside edges of the pool.

▼ **Water-lily beetle** In early summer water-lily beetles and brown china mark moths migrate from poolside vegetation to lay clusters of eggs on water-lily leaves. They hatch into larvae and caterpillars that feed voraciously on flowers and foliage.

BROWN CHINA MARK MOTHS

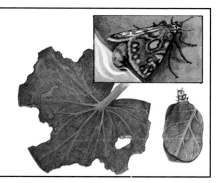

Plants affected Floating aquatic plants, especially water lilies.
Symptoms Small brown and white moths lay eggs on floating leaves. These hatch into small caterpillars, which chew oval segments out of the leaves and use them to build protective cases around themselves. At first, the cases are attached to the undersides of the leaves, but as the caterpillars grow and build larger cases, they float on the water. Caterpillars feed on leaves, cutting unsightly holes.
Danger period Eggs laid in midsummer to late summer; caterpillars begin eating leaves 2 weeks later.
Treatment Remove cases by hand. Cut off and destroy the leaves of badly infested plants to promote new growth.

CADDIS FLIES

Plants affected Any aquatic or floating plants.
Symptoms Mothlike insects lay jellylike trails of eggs in the water. Some larvae build protective cases around themselves and feed on water plants. Damage is rarely severe.
Danger period Summer.
Treatment Remove by hand, and destroy any larva cases.

WATER-LILY APHIDS

Plants affected Water lilies and poolside plants.
Symptoms Colonies of grayish-black aphids disfigure leaves and flowers.
Danger period Growing season.
Treatment Knock aphids into the water by squirting with a garden hose — fish then eat them. Or drown them by submerging leaves for several hours under weighted netting or cloth.

WATER-LILY BEETLES

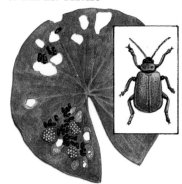

Plants affected Mainly water lilies.
Symptoms Small dark brown beetles, ¼ in (6 mm) long, lay eggs on the leaves. These hatch into leaf-eating, yellow-bellied, brownish-black larvae.
Danger period Early to late summer.
Treatment As for water-lily aphids.

OTHER POOL TROUBLES

Leaf miners, the grubs of certain midges, tunnel through the inner tissues of water plant leaves, leaving translucent trails and causing disfigurement and loss of vigor. In severe cases, the leaves can be reduced to skeletons.

Fish eat these grubs and generally keep them under control, but if you don't have any fish in the pool, pick off by hand and destroy infested leaves. False leaf-mining midges do not tunnel into the leaf tissues, but eat serpentine lines over leaf surfaces, giving the same effect.

Leaf spot disease may affect water lilies, causing dark blotches on the leaves, which eventually rot and disintegrate. This disease occurs mainly in very humid summers.

If you don't have any fish or other livestock, spray the foliage with Bordeaux mixture. Otherwise, pick off by hand and destroy affected leaves, preferably disposing of them off-site.

Another type of leaf spot disease — which should be treated in the same manner — causes brown dried-out patches on the leaves. Seriously infected leaves eventually crumble away, and the disease spreads rapidly. In severe cases the whole stock has to be replaced.

Pond snails are not pests, unless they occur in plague proportions — small numbers actually do good by eating decaying leaves, fish droppings, and algae, which dirty the pond.

Fish eat snail eggs and generally keep them under control. Scoop out excess populations of snails using a small fishing net.

Root rot is a fungal disease that sometimes affects water lilies. Leaves and flower stalks become black, and rot spreads down to the roots, which turn slimy, usually with an unpleasant smell. Destroy affected leaves, or pull up the entire plant in severe cases.

Slugs and land snails are attracted by the constantly moist environment. They devour the succulent young leaves and stems of many bog plants and marginal aquatics growing around the edges of a pool. They eat ragged holes and leave slime trails.

The only really effective method of control is to scatter slug pellets around susceptible plants, or to spray the ground with a slug and snail egg killer. Avoid dropping bait in the pond, especially if there are fish in it; keep pets away from treated areas.

Frogs are generally beneficial, helping to control the insect population, but they may attack small and weak ornamental fish.

ROSE PESTS AND DISEASES

Roses suffer from their fair share of pests and diseases, but few pose a real threat. With routine control, serious problems can be avoided.

As with all garden plants, the surest way to keep rose pest and disease attacks to a minimum is to maintain the best cultural conditions possible. Vigorous plants that are actively growing are invariably better able to cope with minor physical damage to foliage than already sickly plants.

There are a few problems, however, that nearly every rose grower will experience. Black spot, mildew, rust, and aphids are, sadly, synonymous with growing roses, but they should not deter you. Most healthy plants will tolerate at least minor outbreaks without undue loss of bloom.

Certain problems, such as black spot, may be more serious in one region than another. Black spot tends to be most serious in cool, rainy regions, for instance, while rust is a serious affliction mainly on the Pacific Coast.

Powdery mildew is the most common disease in California and the Southwest and second only to black spot in importance elsewhere. Like other fungal diseases, it is virtually impossible to eradicate, though it can be controlled through regular sprays of sulfur, benomyl, or other recommended fungicides. If fungal diseases are particularly troublesome in your area, consider cultivating roses that have shown a natural resistance such as 'Bonica,' 'Fragrant Cloud,' 'Queen Elizabeth,' 'Tiffany,' and 'Tropicana.'

Above all, watch out for early signs of attack and take measures to eliminate pests and diseases before they become entrenched.

Fungicides work best when sprayed evenly over both upper and lower leaf surfaces, thus producing a protective barrier against infection. When actively growing, new shoots should be protected at 2-week intervals, especially against mildew — fungicides are much more effective as preventive measures than as cures. Begin spraying as soon as active growth is under way in late spring. Also spray after heavy rain, when the protection may have been washed away.

Insecticides, in contrast, should be applied only when an insect infestation has been observed and has not responded to gentler methods of control. If you do use a chemical pesticide, follow the manufacturer's instructions for rate and frequency of application. Avoid continuous use of one chemical or formula — some pests and diseases can develop resistance quite quickly.

There are some "broad-spectrum" pesticides, mixtures of different chemicals that offer control of a wide variety of pests and diseases with the same application. These seem to offer convenience, but in the long run may worsen problems, since they kill insect predators as well as pests and so leave your rosebushes without natural defenders.

It is better to use other chemicals that control specific pests and diseases, either by direct surface contact or by systemic action. Suitable types are recommended under each of the problems on the following pages — the names of the chemicals refer to the active ingredient specified in the manufacturer's ingredients, which are listed on the label of the bottle or packet, not to brand names.

◄ **Black spot** This virulent rose disease can cause the loss of most leaves, especially on heavily pruned hybrid tea roses. It overwinters on fallen leaves — rake them up and destroy them.

APHIDS

Symptoms Small, mostly wingless plump insects cluster in large numbers on tips of young shoots and buds. There are several types — green, pinkish, orange, or black. They excrete a sticky honeydew onto the foliage below the attack. Black sooty mold is a common secondary infection on the sticky leaves. Aphids multiply rapidly, sucking sap and thus distorting and stunting the rose shoots.
Danger period Mainly spring and early summer, but may persist through the growing season.
Treatment If infestation is observed while still small, aphids may generally be controlled by spraying plants with a strong jet of water several times a day for 2 to 3 days to knock insects off bushes. Spray persistent infestations with horticultural oil or insecticidal soap. Severe infestations may be sprayed with malathion, acephate, or neem according to label directions.

BLACK SPOT

Symptoms Distinct black blotches on leaves, surrounded by yellow halos. Leaves fall prematurely. Shoots, and often the entire plant, are weakened by severe attacks.
Danger period From late spring on.
Treatment Remove and dispose of affected foliage and plant parts, including fallen leaves, off-site. For serious outbreaks, apply mancozeb, benomyl, copper hydroxide, lime sulfur, or chlorothalonil according to label instructions.

CANKER

Symptoms Brown, cracked, and sunken patches on stems, often with a corky edge and tiny black spots. The patches eventually encircle the stem, causing dieback and death.
Danger period All year.
Treatment Cut out and destroy diseased wood. Fungus attacks through wounds to bark and stem. Keep insects and mites under control as these pests spread the disease.

JAPANESE BEETLES

Symptoms Leaf tissue eaten between veins, giving foliage a lacy appearance; young foliage preferred. Beetles attack buds and blossoms as well.
Danger period Early to late summer.
Treatment Handpicking or beneficial nematodes control slight infestations; apply milky spore to lawn for long-term reduction. For severe infestations, spray weekly with carbaryl or rotenone.

CATERPILLARS

Symptoms Irregular, often quite large holes cut in leaves.
Danger period Midspring to late spring onward.
Treatment Remove and kill isolated caterpillars by hand. (They are most active, and therefore visible, in the evening.) Spray more serious infestations with carbaryl or pyrethrum according to label instructions.

CHAFER BEETLES

Symptoms Adult beetles eat flowers, often devouring the entire side of a bloom; they also eat irregular holes in leaves. Large, fat grubs of the chafer beetle attack roots, and may sometimes kill the whole rose. But this is an infrequent rose pest.
Danger period Adults: midsummer. Grubs: all year.
Treatment Adults: remove by hand or spray with carbaryl or methoxychlor; avoid spraying on flowers when bees are present. Grubs: treat soil with chlorpyrifos.

DIEBACK

Symptoms Shoots wither and die from the top downward. No specific cause — bad planting, black spot, canker, mildew, frost damage, mineral deficiency, and waterlogging may all be responsible in part.
Danger period Spring to fall.
Treatment Cut off dead shoots to healthy wood, and spray with foliar feed. Fertilize in spring, not fall.

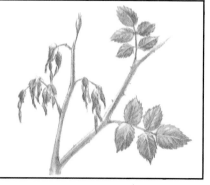

MOSAIC VIRUS

Symptoms Yellow mottling spreading from midrib; may create ring, oak-leaf, or watermark patterns. Dwarfing of bush and gradual loss of vigor.
Danger period Growing season.
Treatment Dig up and destroy infected bushes. Disease is spread during propagation, so the best defense is to buy from a reputable nursery source that offers only disease-free stock.

LEAF-CUTTER BEES

Symptoms Neat semicircular pieces cut from leaf edges. May weaken growth; disfigure plants.
Danger period Midsummer to late summer.
Treatment Destroy nests if found (in soil, rotting wood, or brickwork). No effective chemical control. Never spray when in bloom — you will also kill pollinating insects.

LEAF-ROLLING CATERPILLARS

Symptoms Leaves rolled downward or upward by pale green grubs. Plants disfigured and weakened.
Danger period Spring to summer.
Treatment Remove affected leaves and destroy. Handpick and destroy grubs. Spray severe infestations with insecticidal soap, malathion, or methoxychlor.

LEAFHOPPERS

Symptoms Coarse white flecks on leaves. More serious in warm spots, where leaf fall and loss of vigor may result.
Danger period Early summer to midfall.
Treatment Spray with acephate, carbaryl, or malathion according to label instructions.

POWDERY MILDEW

Symptoms Leaves, shoots, and flower buds covered with a white powdery coating; growth distorted.
Danger period Spring to fall.
Treatment Space plants properly to ensure good air circulation. Prune affected parts; rake up and destroy fallen leaves. Spray with sulfur, triforine, or thiophanate-methyl according to label instructions.

ROSE ANTHRACNOSE

Symptoms Small, irregular purplish dots on leaves. Distinct from black spot in that the spots are smaller and do not have a yellow edge.
Danger period Midspring to fall.
Treatment Remove and destroy affected parts; rake up fallen leaves and destroy them. Spray with sulfur just as leaves emerge, during growing season, with benomyl combined with a spreader-sticker.

SPIDER MITES

Symptoms Minute yellowish-green mites — like tiny spiders — suck sap by piercing leaf undersides and spin fine webs. In severe cases the webbing shows as a whitish halo at the edges of leaves, but the most obvious symptom is a bronze discoloration of upper leaf surfaces. Leaves may eventually turn yellow and fall prematurely.

Danger period Late spring to fall, especially in hot, dry weather.
Treatment Spray with a hard stream of water early in the morning for several days. If problem persists, spray with insecticidal soap or horticultural oil, treating undersides of leaves as well as upper sides. For severe infestations, apply acephate or malathion. Biological control can be effective in greenhouses.

ROSE SLUGS

Symptoms Holes eaten partly through leaf tissues, leaving transparent "windows" of dried material. Damaged areas turn brown, appearing scorched. Pale yellowish-green grubs may be seen.
Danger period Early summer to early fall.
Treatment Spray with insecticidal soap, acephate, or carbaryl.

RUST

Symptoms Swellings on stems, stalks, or leaf undersides burst to reveal masses of orange powdery spores.
Danger period Mainly from midsummer onward.
Treatment Cut out and destroy affected shoots. Occasional applications of sulfur, mancozeb, or triforine according to label instructions should provide control.

THRIPS

Symptoms Flower petals blackened at the edges; also mottled or streaked with lighter color. Flowers may darken and rot. Leaves show silvery flecking.
Danger period Early summer to early fall, especially in hot, dry weather.
Treatment Biological controls available. Spray severe infestations with insecticidal soap, neem, or rotenone.

TORTRIX MOTHS

Symptoms Tortrix, or leaf-rolling, caterpillars spin characteristic silken webs. These are used to draw together the edges of leaves, forming a protective cover, inside of which they can feed in safety. Irregular small holes are eaten in the leaves and flower buds. When disturbed, tortrix caterpillars wriggle backward, often dropping from the rose on a fine strand of silk.

Danger period Caterpillars cause most damage in late spring to early summer.
Treatment Isolated attacks are best dealt with by hand — pick off and squeeze together rolled-up leaves to crush the larvae and pupae. Chemical control may be difficult, but spraying thoroughly with pyrethrin may be effective.

OTHER PESTS AND DISEASES

Ants loosen soil around roses, especially in sandy areas, and can cause wilting or even plant death. Dust or spray with chlorpyrifos or silica gel + pyrethrin.
Crown galls are large brown knobbly swellings on the stem close to ground level. They can be left untreated — the effects are not serious. If you wish, cut out and destroy unsightly galls.
Curled rose sawfly maggots — gray-green with yellowish-brown heads — at first eat away leaf undersides in summer, leaving the top surface intact, but later eat irregular holes through leaves. They eventually bore into pithy stems or pruning cuts to pupate. Cut off and burn affected stems. Spray or dust with pyrethrin.
Honey fungus causes the sudden death of affected plants. White fan-shaped sheets of fungal growth are found beneath the bark of roots and stems at ground level in fall. They are up to 6 in (15 cm) wide and usually

yellowish brown. Black shoelacelike strands may be found in the soil and on rose roots. Dig up and destroy affected plants and all roots.
Mossy rose gall produces red or green mosslike galls on leaves and around stems from late summer to early fall (turning brown in winter). Inside live tiny wasp larvae. Can be left untreated, or cut off and destroyed.
Rose scale may infest stems, weakening and disfiguring growth. Scales are grayish-white, flat protective disks over tiny insects. If possible, scrape off minor infestations with fingernail. Or apply horticultural oil to stems according to label instructions.
Spittlebugs cause little damage, but their nymphs suck sap and may cause wilting or distortion. They engulf themselves in a white frothy "spittle" around a stem or stalk. Spray with water from the garden hose or insecticidal soap, using high pressure

to penetrate the froth. Rub out minor infestations between finger and thumb.

DEFICIENCIES
Correct these by fertilizing.
Iron deficiency: yellowing between veins; young leaves worst.
Magnesium deficiency: pale leaf centers brown or dead along midvein.
Manganese deficiency: yellowing between leaf veins — striped.
Nitrogen deficiency: poor, stunted growth and small, pale leaves, sometimes with red spots.
Phosphate deficiency: new leaves dark, small, and purplish below.
Potash deficiency: poor-quality, small blooms; brown-edged leaves.

DISORDERS
Blindness: shoots fail to develop flower buds. Prune shoot to half its length.
Waterlogging: leaves yellow — first in veins, then in rest of leaf. Improve drainage or replant.

SHRUB PROBLEMS

**With good cultivation, most shrubs will be
trouble free, but learn to identify pests and diseases so that
you can take remedial measures when necessary.**

All shrubs are woody-stemmed plants, generally with a well-branched, bushy habit, though the term includes many climbing or sprawling plants. They may be deciduous or evergreen, but all live for many years on the same site. As such, they often present a rather tough and undesirable source of food for potential disease organisms and pests — especially those that feed by biting into the plant tissues to suck sap. If a pest or disease does take hold, however, the problem can persist for many years unless measures are adopted in the early stages to eradicate it.

The young shoots of all shrubs lack protective wood and are soft and inviting to biting pests, so make regular visual checks of all shrubs in spring and early summer. Turn leaves to reveal pests that hide on the undersides. Distorted or discolored foliage and shoots invariably indicate trouble — though some harmless viruses may be responsible for attractive distortions of plants such as the twisted branches and crimped leaves of the corkscrew hazel *(Corylus avellana* 'Contorta') and the flattened and recurved stems of the Japanese willow *(Salix udensis* 'Sekka').

When buying shrubs from a nursery, remember that these plants will provide a permanent feature in the garden, so it is worth paying a little extra to ensure you get good-quality stock — vigorous compact plants are far more immune to pest and disease attack when planted out.

Prepare the planting site, supplying adequate organic matter and fertilizers to encourage strong, healthy growth. Water shrubs regularly until well established. Control all weed growth, and remove debris in which many pests will breed. Prune all damaged or dead branches back to strong and healthy wood to discourage the spread of fungal diseases; also cut out weak and crossing stems.

Encourage wildlife in the garden — some birds and beneficial insects are good friends, helping to control pests ranging from caterpillars to aphids and scale insects.

If some branches of a shrub are attacked by pests or diseases, the simplest and most effective cure is to cut the infested material back to healthy wood and destroy or dispose of the prunings. Never put infested material on a compost pile. However, if complete removal of branches will disfigure the shrub, chemical treatment may be the only answer.

The following pages will help you to identify the major pests, diseases, and disorders of garden shrubs and offer advice on the selection of a treatment. The chemical names listed here refer to the active ingredients, not the brand names. Carefully follow the manufacturer's recommendations for application method, dilution rate, and use — and, of course, all safety instructions.

◄ **Sap suckers** Aphids are troublesome pests of many shrubs, infesting soft young shoots, such as those of mock orange *(Philadelphus coronarius* 'Aureus'). They also excrete a sticky honeydew on the foliage near the infestation, and this in turn invites fungal diseases, further weakening the shrub.

ADELGIDS

Plants affected Firs, hemlocks, larches, pines, spruces, and others.
Symptoms Colonies of small, dark aphidlike insects partially covered by tufts of white woolly wax infest undersides of leaves and leaf axils. Some adelgids cause galls.
Danger period Spring to late summer.
Treatment Spray thoroughly with horticultural oil, insecticidal soap, or malathion in early spring; repeat three weeks later.

APHIDS

Plants affected Many shrubs; mainly young, soft growth.
Symptoms Colonies of small, plump black, green, or pinkish bugs; sticky honeydew excreted on leaves, can cause secondary black fungus.
Danger period Spring to summer.
Treatment Spray with strong jet of water several times daily for 2 to 3 days. For more severe infestations, spray with insecticidal soap, horticultural oil, malathion, neem, or acephate.

PLANT BUGS

Plants affected Buddleias, caryopterides, forsythias, hydrangeas, roses, and others.
Symptoms Drooping flowers and leaves on terminal shoots; irregular bronze spotting of foliage.
Danger period Late spring to late summer.
Treatment Good general garden hygiene and weed control may reduce plant bug infestation. Spray with insecticidal soap, malathion, acephate, or carbaryl.

CHLOROSIS

Plants affected Many shrubs, especially ceanothuses, hydrangeas, and acid lovers in lime soils.
Symptoms Yellowing between veins on young leaves.
Danger period Growing season.
Treatment Work sulfur into surrounding soil to lower the pH. Mulch with pine needles or other acidic leaves.

CORAL SPOT

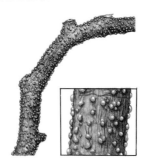

Plants affected Many shrubs, especially currants, figs, magnolias, and maples.
Symptoms Dieback of branches caused by coral-red, spore-filled pustules on dead wood.
Danger period All year.
Treatment Cut out dead shoots to well below the disease, and destroy.

FIRE BLIGHT

Plants affected Cotoneasters, hawthorns, pyracanthas, quinces, and stranvaesias.
Symptoms Shoots die back, leaves turn brown and wither, and cankers develop at base.
Danger period Flowering time.
Treatment Cut out diseased wood (only when foliage is not wet) to 2 ft (60 cm) below affected tissues. Disinfect pruning tools after use.

SPITTLEBUGS

Plants affected Blackberries and raspberries, forsythias, hypericums, lavenders, pines, roses, and many other ornamental shrubs.
Symptoms Frothy masses of "spittle" covering small yellowish-green insects about ¼ in (6 mm) long. Young shoots may eventually become distorted or wither, but damage is rarely severe, though infested shoots are unattractive.
Danger period Early summer to midsummer.
Treatment Wash off "spittle" with a powerful jet of water from a garden hose. This may be enough to dislodge the insects, but you can also spray with insecticidal soap or malathion — use a powerful spray to penetrate the protective froth.

HONEY FUNGUS

Plants affected Almost all woody plants, especially those growing near old, decaying tree stumps.
Symptoms Sudden death of shrubs. White fan-shaped growths of fungus beneath root and trunk bark at soil level. Brown-black rootlike structures may be found in the soil around the roots. Honey-colored toadstools may appear at the base of a dying shrub.
Danger period All year; toadstools usually appear from midsummer to early winter.
Treatment The only effective cure is to dig up and destroy the entire plant. Even the surrounding soil should be excavated and removed. Do not replant shrubs or trees on the same site for at least a year. Grow only resistant shrubs.

LEAF MINERS

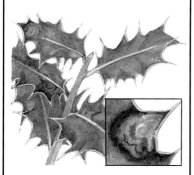

Plants affected Holly, honeysuckle, lilac, privet, and others.
Symptoms Small larvae tunnel within the leaves, creating blistered patches. Leaves may also be rolled.
Danger period Late spring to summer.
Treatment Cut off and destroy affected leaves, or spray with malathion, neem, or acephate.

LEOPARD MOTHS

Plants affected Cherries, cotoneasters, lilacs, maples, rhododendrons, and shrubby willows.
Symptoms Branches tunneled by caterpillars, causing wilting of leaves.
Danger period All year.
Treatment Kill the caterpillars by pushing a piece of wire into the tunnels. Seal holes with putty. Destroy severely infested branches.

POWDERY MILDEW

Plants affected Euonymuses, lilacs, and many other shrubs.
Symptoms A white floury coating on leaves and shoots, and sometimes on flowers.
Danger period Growing season.
Treatment Space plants properly to ensure good air circulation. Cut out severely affected shoots in fall; rake up and destroy fallen leaves, branches, and fruit. Spray with sulfur, triforine, or benomyl.

SPIDER MITES

Plants affected Hydrangeas, roses, wisterias, and others.
Symptoms Older leaves turn a bronzed yellow color, dry out, and eventually die.
Danger period Late spring to early fall.
Treatment Spray with hard stream of water early in day for several days. For severe infestations, spray with insecticidal soap, horticultural oil, acephate, or malathion.

RUST

Plants affected Barberries, box, mahonias, rhododendrons, roses, and some other shrubs.
Symptoms Brown spots appear on the foliage.
Danger period All year.
Treatment Dust plants with sulfur to prevent infection and prevent mild infections from spreading. Remove and destroy seriously affected parts. Spray severe infections with mancozeb or triforine.

SCALE INSECTS

Plants affected Azaleas, camellias, ceanothuses, cotoneasters, and many other shrubs.
Symptoms Colonies of brown, yellow, or white scales on stems or leaves of older shoots.
Danger period All year.
Treatment Control in early spring with dormant-grade horticultural oil. Control in crawler stage with acephate.

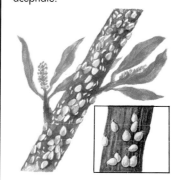

SILVER LEAF

Plants affected Lilacs, *Prunus,* and certain other shrubs.
Symptoms Some leaves become silvered. When a cut cross section of an affected branch is moistened, a brown or purple stain appears.
Danger period Fall to spring.
Treatment Cut out branches to 6 in (15 cm) below where the stain in the wood stops. Treat cuts with Bordeaux mixture.

THRIPS

Plants affected Honeysuckle, lilac, privet, and other shrubs.
Symptoms Leaves finely mottled with a general silvery brown appearance.
Danger period Early summer to early fall, especially during hot, dry weather.
Treatment Spray with neem, malathion, carbaryl, or diazinon when the symptoms are first seen.

LEAF-ROLLING CATERPILLARS

Plants affected Many shrubs and other garden plants.
Symptoms Irregular small holes eaten in leaves, which are drawn together with silk webbing to form a tight cylinder.
Danger period Late spring and early summer.
Treatment Handpicking and biological controls effective for minor infestations. Spray heavy infestations with carbaryl.

VINE WEEVILS

Plants affected Camellias, clematises, euonymuses, rhododendrons, wisterias, yews, and some other shrubs.
Symptoms Small irregular notches eaten out of leaf edges at night by adults. Legless white larvae feed on roots, checking growth and sometimes causing sudden wilting and collapse of shoots and leaves, especially on small container-grown shrubs.
Danger period Spring and summer.
Treatment Remove accumulations of leaves and plant debris, where the weevils rest by day; spray affected plants and soil beneath with acephate at dusk in late spring and early summer. Apply beneficial nematodes to soil to control larvae.

OTHER TROUBLES

Birds strip dormant flower buds of certain shrubs in late winter and early spring. Forsythia, lilac, viburnum, and wisteria may be badly damaged. Blackbirds and thrushes devour the berries of many shrubs in fall and winter. Large birds such as pigeons may cause physical damage to delicate branches. Various bird-scaring devices may be used, though most are unattractive in the ornamental garden and may not be effective. In general, birds' benefits outweigh any damage.
Boxwood psyllids feed only on box (*Buxus*). Tiny yellowish or green nymphs (young insects) suck sap from shoot tips in spring, causing stunted growth with cabbagelike cupped leaves. Sticky honeydew is also excreted. Spray with acephate before leaves become cupped in midspring. Spray with insecticidal soap at first sign of infestation by adults.
Caterpillars of various moths eat the leaves of certain shrubs, making large irregular-shaped holes. Handpicking and biological controls such as Bt are effective against mild infestations; spray severe infestations with neem or carbaryl.
Dieback is a disorder that causes foliage to turn brown and die, starting at the branch tips and working downward. Prune individually damaged branches back to healthy wood. Keep remaining plants vigorous by applying a general fertilizer and mulching in spring and giving a foliar feed in summer.
Phytophthora root rot affects camellias, heathers, junipers, maples, rhododendrons, and other shrubs. Leaves are abnormally small, yellow, or sparse over all or part of the crown in broad-leaved shrubs; gray then turning brown in conifers and heathers. Partial dieback is followed by death of shrubs. A reddish-brown triangular patch shows beneath bark at ground level. Destroy affected plants and apply metalaxyl soil drench or replace the soil well beyond the full depth and spread of the roots. Replant with less susceptible shrubs.
Scab affects pyracanthas from spring to fall, showing as blackish-brown spots on leaves, which may then fall prematurely. Fruits become covered with scabby spots, turn black, and shrivel. The fungus overwinters as small scabby patches on the twigs. Rake up and destroy fallen leaves, and cut out infested shoots in fall. Plant the more resistant species *Pyracantha fortuneana*. Spray any affected plants with chlorothalonil or Bordeaux mixture.
Woolly aphids produce woody swellings and tufts of white "wool" on stems and branches of cotoneasters and pyracanthas from early summer to early fall. Spray with insecticidal soap, horticultural oil, or neem at the first sign of infestation.

TREE PROBLEMS

Trees are sturdy and don't succumb readily to pests or diseases, but if problems do occur remedial measures are essential.

Trees are woody plants with a permanent above-ground framework. Their living tissues are protected by a coarse layer of bark, which, if damaged, can allow parasites and diseases to enter.

For this reason it is important to trim away any damaged wood as soon as possible, leaving a clean surface that heals quickly. The tree forms its own protective layer within such a wound — the practice of dressing with a "protective" substance actually enhances the likelihood of infection.

A few serious diseases — honey fungus and fire blight, for example — can infect structural wood despite the tree's built-in defenses. These are long-term diseases that are carried over many years and spread from tree to tree. Early diagnosis is vital if you want to save the trees.

Because dead or rotting wood is weaker than healthy wood, infected trees look unsightly and

are potentially dangerous, as they can topple over in high winds.

Leaves and soft young stems are susceptible to attack from sucking and biting insects and to fungal diseases. However, because of the sheer size of a mature tree, such infestations have to be widespread to do major damage. Young trees, however, can be set back permanently.

Horticultural oil sprays are based on a mixture of refined petroleum and water; they are applied to trees during dormancy to kill overwintering insects (but only when temperatures are above 45°F/ 7°C), and during the growing season to control the active forms of many pests such as aphids and spider mites.

Look out for curling or eaten leaves, sticky deposits, abnormal discolorations, or growths and other unusual features on your trees; then follow the advice on the following pages.

PHYSICAL PROTECTION

In rural and suburban areas trees are frequently plagued by rabbits and squirrels. If the garden is unfenced, deer can also be a problem in many regions.

Rabbit damage to young trees — chewed bark — can be eliminated by wrapping the base of the trunk with a spiral-shaped plastic tree guard.

However, tree guards are not effective against squirrels or deer, since these pests can reach the branches to chew bark, buds, and leaves. The best protection against deer is to build a strong fence all around the garden.

Squirrels cannot be controlled effectively by physical barriers because they are agile climbers. They can, however, be removed from a garden by live-trapping the pests and then releasing them in some distant spot.

▼ **Honey fungus** (*Armillaria mellea*)
This disease can infect all woody plants, causing death of the limbs or even of the entire tree. It occurs mainly in areas that have many broad-leaved trees. Honey-colored toadstools around the base of a tree are the obvious signs, but the main damage is done by the brown-black rodlike structures that are found in the soil around the roots.

UNUSUAL GROWTHS

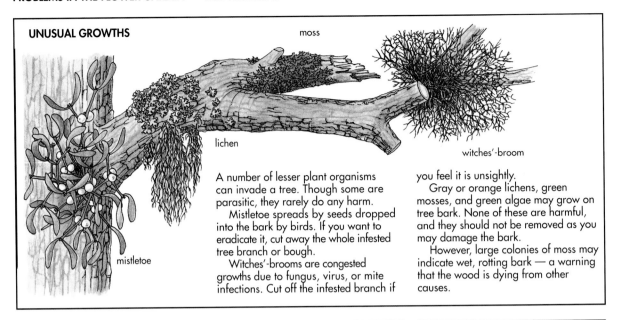

moss

lichen

witches'-broom

mistletoe

A number of lesser plant organisms can invade a tree. Though some are parasitic, they rarely do any harm.

Mistletoe spreads by seeds dropped into the bark by birds. If you want to eradicate it, cut away the whole infested tree branch or bough.

Witches'-brooms are congested growths due to fungus, virus, or mite infections. Cut off the infested branch if you feel it is unsightly.

Gray or orange lichens, green mosses, and green algae may grow on tree bark. None of these are harmful, and they should not be removed as you may damage the bark.

However, large colonies of moss may indicate wet, rotting bark — a warning that the wood is dying from other causes.

ADELGIDS

Trees affected Firs, hemlocks, larches, pines, spruces, and other conifers.
Symptoms Colonies of small, dark aphidlike insects covered by tufts of white woolly wax infest undersides of leaves and leaf axils.
Danger period Spring to late summer.
Treatment Spray entire tree thoroughly with insecticidal soap, horticultural oil, or malathion in early spring; repeat 3 weeks later.

BARK SPLITTING

Trees affected Many types, including fruit trees.
Symptoms Bark splits and the cracks open up.
Danger period All year.
Treatment Using a disinfected pruning knife, cut out any dead wood, and trim away all loose bark. If the tree is then fed, mulched, and watered well, the wound should heal naturally; don't paint with any wound substance.

CANKER

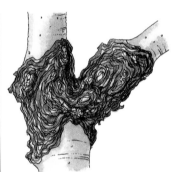

Trees affected Ashes, beeches, crab apples, mountain ashes, and poplars.
Symptoms Oval cankers on the trunk and branches; bark shrinks in rings until inner tissues exposed.
Danger period All year.
Treatment Cut out and destroy infected spurs or small branches. On larger branches and trunks, pare away diseased material and destroy it. Fertilize the tree.

CATERPILLARS

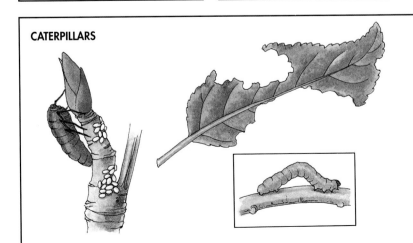

Trees affected Broad-leaved trees.
Symptoms Young leaves and buds eaten by green, yellow-green, or brown "looper" caterpillars, leaving ragged holes and edges.
Danger period Eggs laid in winter and early spring; leaves eaten during spring and early summer.
Treatment Wrap a grease band around the trunk in midfall to prevent the wingless female moths from climbing up the trunk to lay their eggs. Or spray small trees with neem, malathion, or pyrethrin as soon as buds open in spring.

CORAL SPOT

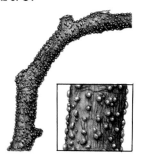

Trees affected Birches, magnolias, maples, and many others.
Symptoms Dieback of branches caused by coral-red spore-filled pustules on dead wood.
Danger period All year.
Treatment Cut out dead branches or boughs to well below the diseased area, and destroy.

FIRE BLIGHT

Trees affected Cotoneasters, crab apples, hawthorns, mountain ashes, pears, and other members of the rose family.
Symptoms Branches die back (particularly flowering spurs). Leaves turn brown and wither; cankers develop at their bases.
Danger period Flowering time.
Treatment If disease occurred the previous year, spray with fixed copper during bloom. Cut out and destroy all affected wood.

GALL MITES

Trees affected Mainly elms, lindens, maples, and sycamores.
Symptoms Mites feed on leaves, thus producing small reddish or green growths. These disfigure, but mites cause no real damage.
Danger period Spring onward.
Treatment Spray with horticultural oil + ethion in early spring to midspring; insecticidal soap in midspring to late spring.

GALL WASPS

Trees affected Oaks.
Symptoms Many different galls resembling peas or buttons growing out of leaves; other galls occur on shoots, catkins, and acorns — sometimes singly, often numerous. Growth is response to tissue attack by tiny wasp larvae.
Danger period Growing season.
Treatment Horticultural oil during dormancy will kill some wasps overwintering on branches.

HONEY FUNGUS

Trees affected Most species.
Symptoms Sudden death. White fan-shaped fungus growth beneath bark of roots and trunk at soil level. Toadstools at base.
Danger period All year.
Treatment No cure. Cut down and destroy the tree, including roots and surrounding soil. Do not replant trees or shrubs on the same site for at least a year. Grow resistant types.

RUST

Trees affected Ashes, birches, hawthorns, hemlocks, pines, willows, and others.
Symptoms Brown, orange, or yellow powdery masses develop on leaves and stems. Leaves may turn yellow in severe cases.
Danger period Summer.
Treatment Pick off and destroy diseased leaves. Encourage vigor by good cultural treatment. Apply sulfur or spray with mancozeb, triforine, or thiram.

SCAB

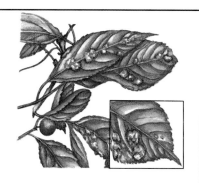

Trees affected Apples, crab apples, magnolias, pears, willows, and others.
Symptoms Olive-green blotches of fungal growth on leaves, which then fall prematurely. Small blisterlike pimples develop on young shoots, later burst the bark, and then show as ringlike cracks or scabs. Open lesions are prone to secondary infection by canker. Dark corky scabs appear on fruits.

Danger period All year.
Treatment Cut out cracked and scabby shoots. Pick off and destroy affected leaves. Spray with captan, benomyl, sulfur, lime sulfur, Bordeaux mixture, or mancozeb. For choice of product, timing, and frequency of sprays, consult directions on product labels.

SILVER LEAF

Trees affected Crab apples, pears, plums, and other *Prunus* species.
Symptoms Some leaves become silvered. When a cross section of an affected branch is moistened, a brown or purple stain appears. A flat purple fungus eventually develops on dead wood.
Danger period Early fall to late spring.
Treatment Cut out branches to 6 in (15 cm) below the point where the stain in the wood stops. Treat cuts with Bordeaux mixture.

TAR SPOT

Trees affected Maples and sycamores.
Symptoms Yellow patches on the upper surfaces of the leaves develop into large black blotches, often with a yellowish halo. Other types of leaf spot on maples show as red-brown to yellowish lesions.
Danger periods Growing season.
Treatment Sweep up and destroy all fallen leaves in fall. Tar spot is not usually severe except on Norway maples, where treatment with mancozeb may be needed.

WOOLLY APHIDS

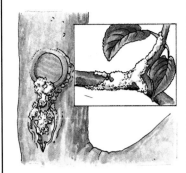

Trees affected Cotoneasters, crab apples, and pyracanthas.
Symptoms Woody swellings and tufts of white wool on trunks and branches, especially in crevices around old wounds.
Danger period Midspring to early fall.
Treatment Where possible, brush a spray-strength solution of malathion onto affected areas when the wool first appears. An alternative solution is to spray the entire plant with horticultural oil.

OTHER TROUBLES

Aphids are small, plump black, green, or pinkish bugs. Colonies of them infest leaves and young shoots, stunting, distorting, and weakening growth. They also excrete sticky honeydew, which frequently encourages a secondary infection of sooty mold. Linden trees are especially susceptible. Aphids may also transmit virus diseases, although this is rarely a problem with trees.

Spray with insecticidal soap, neem, malathion, or horticultural oil. However, do not use insecticidal soap on Japanese maples.

Birds may peck off flower buds in winter and early spring. There is no effective deterrent, but various bird-scaring devices may give some control.

Bracket fungi produce shelflike toadstools, each up to 1 ft (30 cm) wide, on trunks and branches. The spores enter through dead or damaged tissues and may cause dieback and rotting of the heartwood. Fungal growth may not appear until several months after the initial spore infection.

Cut off small diseased branches. If the fungus appears on the main trunk, employ a tree surgeon to evaluate the safety of the tree.

Leopard moth caterpillars tunnel into the branches of acers, ashes, birches, crab apples, cotoneasters, flowering cherries, hawthorns, mountain ashes, oaks, and willows, causing wilting of their leaves. Damage occurs at any time.

Kill the caterpillars by poking a piece of wire into the tunnels, then seal the holes with putty. Cut off and destroy severely infested branches.

Powdery mildew forms a white powdery coating of spores on stems and leaves. Crab apples and pears are particularly susceptible, and their shoots may become stunted and weakened.

Where possible, remove and destroy all badly infected shoots. Disinfect pruning tools between cuts. Apply sulfur as necessary, and thin branches to promote air circulation.

Scale insects attack many different garden plants, including beeches, cherries, cotoneasters, horse chestnuts, lindens, and maples. Colonies of brown, yellow, or white scales appear on older shoots at most times of year, but particularly in late spring and summer. Persistent infestations weaken the growth of the tree.

Spray with horticultural oil in early or late winter when the temperature is over 45°F (7°C). When crawlers are active in summer, spray thoroughly with insecticidal soap or acephate.

Scorch may affect beeches, maples, and some other trees in spring. Pale brown spots appear on the young leaves, which in serious cases become papery and withered.

Spread mulch and water well to ensure that the trees do not suffer from dry soil during the critical period of spring growth. Cold, drying winds may cause leaf scorch (salt used in winter highway de-icing is also responsible), so put up some form of windbreak to shield susceptible species in exposed gardens.

Spider mites often infest ornamental trees of the rose family — especially crab apples, hawthorns, peaches, and plums. Colonies of minute red mites accumulate on leaves from spring onward, causing speckling, bronze discoloration, and drying out of tissues.

Spray trees with horticultural oil before leaf growth begins, or with insecticidal soap when damage is observed.

Verticillium wilt is a disease caused by soil-borne fungi. It enters trees through young roots or through wounds, causing brown discoloration on leaves and stems. Maples are the most commonly affected trees.

Wilt diseases are difficult to eradicate, but rarely kill trees. Fertilize properly, and water during dry spells.

Problems in the kitchen garden

Pests and diseases can have devastating effects on fruits and vegetables, seriously reducing yields and in extreme cases wiping out whole crops. Some gardeners follow a regular spraying program to protect the kitchen garden, while others believe in avoiding all artificial chemicals, not only in the battle against weeds, pests, and diseases, but also as fertilizers and soil improvers. Such an organic approach to gardening relies on soil management and good cultivation techniques to maintain a natural balance between predators and parasites.

Chemical controls are quick and usually effective, but can also kill other insects, including pollinating bees and butterflies and beneficial insects such as ladybugs. With edible crops, it is particularly important to follow the manufacturer's instructions for strength of dosage and length of time between spraying and harvesting.

The most sensible approach is to use good cultivation methods in conjunction with chemical control that is applied only when absolutely necessary. A regular crop-rotation program can minimize the buildup of certain soil pests and diseases, while forking up beds in fall will expose overwintering grubs and other insects to natural predators. Many fruit cultivars are bred to be resistant to particular diseases, and some chemical formulations are environmentally sound: for example, grease bands tied around fruit tree trunks in fall trap insects as they crawl up to lay their eggs on fruit spurs, and a spray of horticultural oil will kill any that escape.

Organic gardening Untouched by chemical sprays, organically grown produce is healthy and environmentally friendly.

ORGANIC GARDENING

**Organic gardening involves a mental attitude that
views plants and their place in the garden as an ecosystem
and excludes artificial chemicals.**

Organic gardening makes use of animal manures and compost, as well as stressing the fundamentals of gardening, without any shortcuts or quick fixes. Organic gardeners aim for the total removal of chemicals from the garden scene unless they are of organic origin — that is, unless they come from plants or animals. Even then, the use of any chemical to control a pest, disease, or weed or to control or improve crop qualities may upset the natural balance.

Rather than using chemicals, you should ensure that the soil, light, moisture, and other environmental conditions are at their best, so that plants grow to their full potential. Where possible, you should grow plants that are naturally pest and disease resistant.

Many organic gardeners maintain in fact that the addition of concentrated chemically synthesized fertilizers to food crops, such as 5–10–5, can be wasteful, as much of the fertilizer's nutrient content leaches away through the soil before it is absorbed.

Some concentrated fertilizers are better than others, namely those of organic rather than mineral origin. Cottonseed meal and bonemeal are examples — they break down slowly and remain within reach of plant roots for some time.

Some unprocessed mineral products of natural origin — rock phosphate and granite meal, for example — are also used to supplement minerals that may be in the soil already but only in short supply. In the average garden, however, such mineral deficiencies are rare, and supplements, even organic ones, seldom need to be added.

Many principles of organic gardening — using manures and compost, and taking measures to deter pests and diseases rather than simply destroying them with chemicals — are familiar to most gardeners. But gardening organically involves looking at the garden as a whole. You must take into account the condition of the soil and the climate, and evaluate all factors together. You can then make decisions about the need for improving some aspects and altering others to produce the most fruitful and healthy plants.

▼ **Green manure** Long before organic gardening became fashionable, farmers plowed quick-growing green crops of rape, mustard, vetch, or annual lupine into the soil. This so-called green manure crop helps to enrich and fix the soil's nitrogen content as well as to improve its texture and structure.

WEEDS AND PESTS

1 The most organic method of weed control is removal by hand-weeding and hoeing. These control methods are effective and eliminate the need for chemical control, but are hard work.

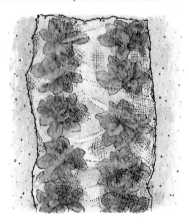

2 Floating row covers — sheets of transparent, woven, or spun plastic fibers — serve two functions in the organic vegetable plot: they protect seeds and young plants from pests and adverse weather. The soft material won't harm the foliage.

3 Organic control methods for slugs and snails include the use of beer traps: Partly fill a watertight container with beer, sink it in the soil near susceptible plants, and prop a saucer over the top. Slugs and snails, attracted by the smell, crawl inside the trap and drown in the beer.

Going organic

If your approach to gardening has always been to buy herbicides to destroy weeds, chemical insecticides to spray on aphids and other pests, and fungicides to get rid of diseases, or if you have relied on synthetic fertilizers to feed plants, it takes quite a shift in outlook to attempt gardening without these props.

Moreover, organic gardening may not be entirely successful at first. Indeed, in some gardens it may be essential to use chemicals at first in order to eliminate existing pests, diseases, and weeds. If you want to try organic gardening and have never done it before, you may prefer to ease into it gradually. In this way you can discover how to manage your own garden organically in the way that best suits it — and you.

Organic gardening affects three main areas of garden management — pest, disease, and weed control; soil treatment; and cultural practices. Companion planting, in which one plant species is thought to benefit another growing alongside, is a fourth element.

Pests, diseases, and weeds

If plants become severely or even mildly infested by a pest, the normal reaction of most gardeners is to reach for the nearest spray gun. Chemical controls are unquestionably efficient and destructive, quick and timesaving. Pests are killed rapidly by man-made chemicals, some of which are long-lasting.

Unfortunately, many chemicals also kill pollinating insects, such as bees, butterflies, moths, and syrphid flies, along with other insects that are predatory or parasitic on the very insects for which the insecticide is intended. Moreover, many garden pests and diseases — and now some weeds as well — are becoming resistant to these chemicals and to new ones as quickly as they are produced.

Chemicals are expensive; they need to be applied frequently in many cases; and they have effects not only on the soil, but also on discharges made into groundwater and hence rivers and seas. There are a variety of ways in which pest, disease, and weed problems can be overcome without the use of chemicals, and it is well worth considering them.

In a garden where no pesticides are used at all, the natural balance can operate and prevent the large and detrimental buildup of a particular insect to plague proportions — a process you can encourage through the techniques of integrated pest management (pp. 109-112). Natural pest predators can live and breed in your garden — ladybugs and their larvae, syrphid flies, and lacewing larvae all feed on aphids and a variety of other pests; ground beetles and centipedes attack small insects and slugs in the soil; and the predatory mites feed on other, herbivorous mites. There are many more examples of this natural control of insects and of larger creatures — snails are eaten by birds, for instance.

Fungal diseases can be prevented by applying the correct method of cultivation for the specific plant and taking special care with soil management. Weeds, too, can be eliminated by cultural practices such as thorough weeding with small hand tools or hoeing.

Soil treatment

It is not as easy to switch from traditional to organic methods of soil improvement as it is to introduce integrated pest management into your garden. You must know what your soil type is — remembering that it can vary appreciably in different parts of the garden. Find out whether it is acid, alkaline, or neutral; what the drainage is like; and whether it is fertile or starved of nutrients such as phosphorus.

Managing the soil organically relies heavily on the use of bulky organic composts derived from decaying animal or vegetable residues. These improve and maintain the actual structure of the soil — mixing these materials into the soil alters the way in which the separate soil particles stick together, ensuring that there is enough air for the roots to develop to their full extent and for surplus water to drain into the subsoil.

Most soils benefit from the addition of bulky organic material: rotting manures of cow, pig, or horse origin; garden compost; seaweed compost; spent mushroom compost; poultry litter; and leaf mold. Sphagnum peat and shredded bark are also organic materials, but these are not as useful as soil conditioners because they contain little food on which plants can feed.

Dig any of these organic composts into the soil, thoroughly mixing them in as you go, or use them on the surface as a mulch. Though some types may be difficult to obtain, you can make garden compost all the time, and it has the additional advantage that it makes use of most of the garden "trash" — grass clippings, leaves, soft stems, faded flowers, weeds (unless they have set seed), and kitchen scraps.

Although the bulky organic composts are primarily used for ensuring a good soil structure, they also contain plant foods and,

▶ **Straw mulch** A surface covering of straw will keep the fruits of these zucchini plants clear of the soil, while a companion edging of marigolds deters such pests as aphids.

GREEN MANURE CROPS

Green manure crops are grown for several purposes. Legume crops (clover, alfalfa, and hairy vetch) fix nitrogen in their root nodules, making it available for subsequent crops. Deep-rooted plants bring nutrients from the subsoil to the surface and encourage bacterial activity. Their green foliage, when dug in, adds humus to the soil. Root systems break up the soil, making it easier to work. Winter crops help to keep nutrients, such as nitrogen, in the soil.

Green manure crops should be cut down and turned into the soil while they are green and soft, before they flower or set seed.

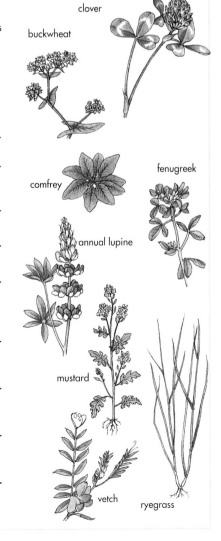

CROP	SOWING TIME	FEATURES
Buckwheat	Spring or summer	Deep roots. Flowers attract syrphid flies (which feed on aphids) and pollinating bees. Dig in before the leaves turn yellow in late summer.
Clover, crimson	Spring or fall	Good nitrogen fixer. Suppresses weeds. Dig in when the land is needed; annual.
Comfrey	Spring or fall	Grown from root divisions taken any time except midwinter to late winter. Needs a plot to itself.
Fenugreek	Late spring to midsummer	Fast-growing with strong roots. Fixes nitrogen. Seed from organic food stores usually germinates well. Dig in 10 to 12 weeks after sowing, before flowers appear.
Lupine, annual	Midspring to midsummer	Fixes nitrogen; fungi associated with its roots also help to make phosphates available to plants. Dig in before flowers open.
Mustard, white	Spring or summer	Fast-growing; useful for filling gaps in crops. Don't grow on ground infected with clubroot disease. Suppresses weeds. Dig in before the first frost.
Ryegrass	Spring to midfall	Excellent winter green manure. Strong root system helps to break up soil. Dig in as soon as seed stalks begin to develop.
Vetch	Late summer or fall	Fixes nitrogen. Suppresses weeds. Dig in during spring several weeks before planting vegetable crops.

ORGANIC COMPOSTS AND FERTILIZERS

 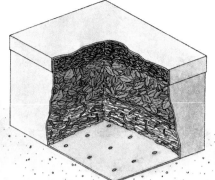 

1 Organic garden compost can be made from kitchen scraps and all kinds of garden plant waste — provided it doesn't include weed seeds or diseases. Slatted-wood bins keep the pile tidy and allow air to penetrate the compost. Cover the compost with a plastic trash bag to retain heat and moisture.

2 A worm box quickly breaks down compost. Drill air and drainage holes in a wooden box, half-fill with moist compost or soft leaves, then add food scraps at the sides. Cover tightly. Stock with worms from a fish-bait shop; cover tightly. Let worms breed for a couple of months, then start adding scraps.

3 Organic liquid fertilizer can be made from shredded comfrey leaves. Stuff a barrel or bucket full of leaves and cover tightly. Depending on the temperature, it will have fermented after about 2 weeks, at which time you can draw off the juice. Dilute the juice to about half strength before applying as a foliar feed.

in a well-maintained soil, will provide sufficient nutrients to produce strong, healthy plants.

Think of the soil as a living organism, rather than as a lifeless substance. Soil teems with life forms — some of it microscopic, all feeding, fighting, resting, and dying continuously. In the process, these organisms have a profound effect on the soil particles, gases, and moisture. Anything you do to the soil — even walking on it — will alter it.

Soil improvement

Special cultural practices play an important role in organic gardening. Mulching the soil not only improves it and keeps it moist in summer, but also keeps weeds under control. But some weeds provide food for the adult stages of insects whose larvae are predators on other insects, and a light cover of annual weeds will keep the soil cool and moist in summer. Provided the weeds are removed before they set seed, they do no great harm. Two exceptions are groundsel and chickweed, which should be pulled up while quite young; they harbor the very destructive cucumber mosaic virus, which has a wide host range.

If there is space in the vegetable or fruit garden, a good way of improving the soil is to grow a green manure crop and dig it in before it flowers. This will build up the humus content in the soil as composts do.

Rotation of vegetable crops does much to prevent the buildup of pests and diseases in the soil that results from growing crops in the same soil every year.

Pests and diseases can be avoided by growing resistant plant varieties — some modern fruit and vegetable cultivars are bred especially for this.

Companion planting

One of the best ways of preventing epidemics of pests and diseases is to grow mixtures of plants, rather than blocks of one kind — a mixed herbaceous border, for instance, will be more resistant to problems than a formal bed planted with a single species. Roses mixed with shrubs or herbaceous perennials are less likely to be plagued by aphids. Mixing rows of vegetables is another method — for example, planting lettuce between rows of sweet corn.

The theory of companion planting goes further — certain plants grown close together are believed to benefit one another, while other plants are thought to have deleterious effects. Chives are claimed to control black spot disease on roses, carrots mixed with onions ward off carrot rust fly, and hyssop attracts cabbage butterflies away from cabbages. Gladioli, on the other hand, can inhibit the growth of nearby peas and beans, and fennel has a bad effect on tomatoes. Very little will grow in the ground surrounding a black walnut tree.

Falling back on inorganics

The gardener can take a strong stand one way or the other — working solely with organic principles or using inorganic methods when needed. The latter approach will probably appeal to the majority of people, and there are, indeed, times when inorganic gardening becomes essential. On a site that has been gardened poorly or excessively and where the soil is little more than stones, sand, and debris, quick-acting mineral fertilizers must be used at least for the first few years.

Despite the most careful control, epidemics of pests or disease do occasionally occur. The best way to deal with such problems is to apply a quick and thorough blanket spray, preferably using one of the insecticides or fungicides harmless to beneficial insects. Botanical sprays such as Bt are useful for this reason, as they typically do not affect any but the target insects. Insecticidal soaps may harm beneficial insects; however, they kill only on contact and leave no toxic residue, so they are ideal for food crops.

Other naturally derived insecticides are fairly toxic to other insects and wildlife, but still valuable because they do not persist once applied. Pyrethrin, which is extracted from a type of chrysanthemum, is dangerous to insects and mammals and highly toxic to fish, but is often used on food crops because it breaks down within a day of application.

GREEN VEGETABLE PESTS

Troubles in the kitchen garden can be disastrous, disfiguring plants and reducing both crop quantity and quality.

Brassicas — including cabbages, brussels sprouts, broccoli, and cauliflower — and other green vegetables, such as beans, peas, celery, and lettuces, produce their harvestable yield above ground, and this can be damaged directly by leaf and stem pests and diseases, or indirectly by pests that attack the root system.

The following pages explain how to recognize the common pests and diseases of green vegetables and how to deal with them. Though the list may appear daunting, many of these troubles can be avoided if your soil is fed and maintained at the proper pH for these plants to grow vigorously. Skillful irrigation — giving the plants adequate water when they need it (and no more) — also helps plants resist pests. Setting trans-plants at the proper distance (resisting the urge to crowd in too many) and thinning seedlings to the proper intervals also help ensure healthy pest-resistant plants.

General garden hygiene is particularly important when growing vegetables — weeds and plant debris can harbor many pests and diseases. Always gather up fallen leaves and other organic trash and put them on the compost pile. If dead plant matter contains pests or diseases, however, dispose of it off-site.

If you apply chemical pesticides and fungicides, follow the manufacturer's instructions carefully regarding the safety interval between spraying and harvesting — many chemicals can take weeks before they disperse or become harmless to consume. Never spray vegetables that are ready for harvesting, and avoid letting spray drift when treating nearby crops.

If a particular chemical proves ineffective, try another one — the pests in one area may develop resistance to a particular substance if it is used over a long period. But do not spray crops indiscriminately, as you may destroy creatures that are beneficial. Avoid spraying crops that are in flower and alive with pollinating bees and other insects. If possible, spray on overcast, still days, in the morning or evening hours.

▼ **Caterpillar damage** Eggs of white butterflies hatch into yellow-bodied caterpillars that feed voraciously on the leaves and hearts of cabbages and cauliflowers. In severe cases, they can destroy entire plants.

ANTHRACNOSE

Crops affected Beans, cucumbers, peppers, and squashes.
Symptoms Black-brown sunken areas on the pods; brown spots on the leaves and stems. Leaves may fall prematurely.
Danger period Throughout growing season — especially in cool, wet summers.
Treatment Apply fixed copper or sulfur-based fungicide, or destroy diseased plants.

SEED-CORN MAGGOTS

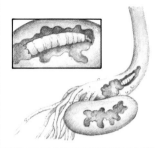

Crops affected Beans, especially pole and snap beans, and peas; certain other crops like sweet corn.
Symptoms Small white maggots tunnel into seeds, which then often fail to germinate. Emerging seedlings wilt and become distorted.
Danger period Immediately after sowing.
Treatment Pull up and destroy affected seedlings. Purchase seeds treated with insecticide, and use gloves to plant them.

BLACK BEAN APHIDS

Crops affected Asparagus, beans, carrots, corn, lettuce, and others.
Symptoms Small black aphids infest young shoots and suck sap.
Danger period Late spring to midsummer.
Treatment Wash off insects with a hard spray of water. Spray severe infestations with insecticidal soap.

CABBAGE CATERPILLARS

Crops affected Cabbages, cauliflowers, and other brassicas.
Symptoms Large ragged holes eaten in leaves by the caterpillars of imported cabbageworms, cabbage loopers, and diamond back moths. Some attack the cabbage head and some the outer leaves. Plants may be totally destroyed, leaving just a skeleton of the tougher leaf veins.
Danger period Early summer to fall.
Treatment Inspect the undersides of leaves after white butterflies have been seen; rub off and destroy any eggs. Remove and destroy caterpillars by hand. Spray with Bt, insecticidal soap, malathion, or rotenone.

CABBAGE ROOT MAGGOTS

Crops affected Brassicas.
Symptoms Fly maggots in the soil feed on the roots, causing collapse of young plants.
Danger period Immediately after transplanting.
Treatment Place mats around the base of transplants to prevent flies from laying eggs. Mix diazinon in the soil when planting.

CARROT RUST FLIES

Crops affected Celery.
Symptoms Maggots burrow into the leaves, causing brown blotches. Growth is checked; severe attacks cause complete plant death.
Danger period Early summer to fall.
Treatment Spray plants with diazinon when damage is seen, or cut off and destroy affected leaflets.

WHITEFLIES

Crops affected Brassicas.
Symptoms Small white mothlike insects take off from the undersides of leaves. These may become soiled with honeydew and sooty mold.
Danger period Late spring to early fall.
Treatment Spray with insecticidal soap, malathion, or pyrethrin according to label instructions.

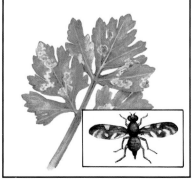

CLUBROOT

Crops affected Brassicas.
Symptoms Swollen, distorted roots; yellowing, sickly, wilting foliage.
Danger period Throughout growing season.
Treatment Improve drainage if necessary. Apply a hydrated lime to the soil to raise the pH to 7.2. Move plants to a different garden location from previous year. Destroy infected plants.

CUTWORMS

Crops affected Lettuces.
Symptoms Shoots eaten through at soil level; fat caterpillars in the soil.
Danger period Early spring and late summer.
Treatment Control weeds, which encourage cutworms. Protect lettuces with cardboard collars around each plant, or surround with diazinon baits.

FLEA BEETLES

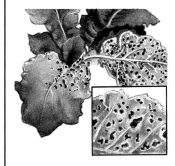

Crops affected Beans, beets, brassicas, potatoes, rutabagas, and turnip tops; also wallflowers.
Symptoms Youngest leaves pitted with very small holes; growth of seedlings stunted.
Danger period During dry, sunny spells in late spring.
Treatment Eliminate weeds and use row covers in spring, removing at onset of hot weather. Spray or dust with carbaryl or diazinon.

BOTRYTIS (GRAY MOLD)

Crops affected Beans and peas; lettuces in greenhouses.
Symptoms Gray mold on bean and pea pods or bases of lettuces.
Danger period Growing season.
Treatment Prick off and destroy diseased pods. Promote good air circulation; apply thiophanate-methyl.

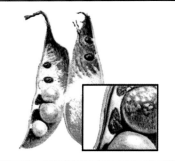

HALO BLIGHT

Crops affected Lima, scarlet runner, and snap beans.
Symptoms Brown spots surrounded by a halo on pods, leaves, or stems. Infected seeds show raised blisters.
Danger period Growing season, especially in wet weather.
Treatment Buy seeds from a good source, and rotate crops on a 3-year cycle.

LEATHERJACKETS

Crops affected Brassicas.
Symptoms Roots eaten by tough-skinned, fat, gray-brown legless grubs. Plants wilt and may die.
Danger period Spring to early summer.
Treatment Before planting, dig deeply to expose grubs to birds. Work diazinon + chlorpyrifos into the soil.

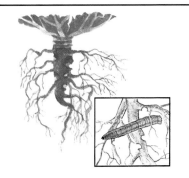

PEA LEAF WEEVILS

Crops affected Beans and peas.
Symptoms Leaf edges are eaten in a scalloped or U-shaped pattern by small beetles. Growth of young plants is retarded. Seedlings may die if the attack is severe. Pea leaf weevils can also transmit a virus disease that affects beans.
Danger period Throughout early spring to early summer.

Treatment Prepare the ground thoroughly before sowing to encourage rapid growth. Eliminate weeds. Apply biological controls as soon as symptoms are observed. Older plants are not seriously affected and generally recover without loss of yield. Clear away plant debris and coarse vegetation, which harbor overwintering weevils.

PEA MOTHS

Crops affected Peas.
Symptoms Peas inside the ripening pods are eaten and a small maggotlike caterpillar — about ¼ in (6 mm) long with a pale yellow body and a black head — is present. It eventually eats its way out and crawls to the ground.
Danger period Early summer to late summer.

Treatment If this pest is common locally, grow early- or late-maturing pea varieties, which are not in flower or pod during the critical egg-laying period. Cultivate the soil thoroughly in winter to expose the caterpillars — which overwinter in the soil in cocoons — to predatory birds and cold weather, which should destroy many of them.

PEA THRIPS

Crops affected Peas.
Symptoms Minute elongated insects feed on leaves and pods causing silver mottling and distortion of pods. Severe attacks result in stunted growth and few flowers.
Danger period Hot, dry summers.
Treatment Spray with insecticidal soap or horticultural oil as soon as symptoms appear.

ROOT APHIDS

Crops affected Beans and lettuces.
Symptoms White waxy aphids on roots. Leaves wilt and turn yellow.
Danger period Summer and fall.
Treatment Water infested plants with a spray-strength solution of pyrethrin or rotenone. Buy cultivars that are immune to root aphids.

WHIPTAIL

Crops affected Broccoli and cauliflowers, mainly in acid soils.
Symptoms Leaves ruffled, thin, and straplike — caused by deficiency of molybdenum.
Danger period Throughout growing period.
Treatment Add lime to the soil, or apply a fritted trace element product containing molybdenum.

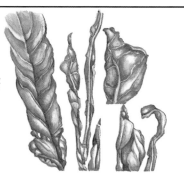

OTHER PROBLEMS

Bolting Lettuces produce tall flower-bearing stems and fail to form hearts, especially in hot weather. Avoid late transplanting and overcrowding. Keep lettuces well watered, especially at the seedling stage.

Cabbage loopers Light green caterpillars with yellowish stripes attack beans, brassicas, lettuces, parsley, radishes, and turnips, leaving large ragged holes in leaves. They may destroy seedlings. For minor infestations, handpick or treat with biological controls. For severe infestations, spray with pyrethrin.

Leaf spot Small brown or black spots, caused by various bacteria and fungi, may appear on cabbage and cauliflower leaves, which then fall prematurely. Cut off and destroy diseased leaves. Where plants are growing close together, space plants to improve air circulation.

Pigeons These birds may tear or eat brassica leaves almost completely, uproot newly transplanted brassicas, and take bean and pea seeds. Damage occurs throughout the year. Stretch netting over crops where pigeons are very troublesome. A framework of threads or strings tied with glittering foil strips may also deter them.

Rabbits These pests eat lettuces, often nibbling several plants at a time. Erect a wire-mesh fence 4-5 ft (1.2-1.5 m) high around the vegetable garden, burying 1 ft (30 cm) of the mesh below soil level to prevent rabbits from burrowing underneath.

Root rot This fungal disease affects beans and peas; stem bases discolor and rot, usually leading to plant death. Purchase fungicide-treated seeds; don't grow legumes on the same site for several years.

Slugs and snails These pests eat large holes in foliage and may devour young plants completely. Slime tracks are present. They are most troublesome in spring and fall during moist weather. Scatter slug bait around affected plants, or sink beer traps at intervals along the rows.

Tipburn Lettuces develop brown, scorched leaf edges during sudden hot spells in spring or summer due to water loss. Try to maintain a constant soil moisture level.

White blister This fungal disease causes blisters on leaves and stems of brassicas. These blisters are filled with white powdery spores. Remove and destroy diseased leaves and stems.

Wire stem This disease affects many young plants, especially cauliflowers and other brassicas. Stem bases turn brown and shrink, causing death or stunting. Make sure that seedlings are raised in sterilized soil. Destroy diseased plants.

ROOT CROP PESTS

Unseen at first, pests and diseases in the soil can seriously damage vegetable roots and tubers.

Root vegetable crops, including carrots, onions, parsnips, rutabagas, turnips, asparagus, Jerusalem artichokes, and especially potatoes, are susceptible to a number of pests and diseases, some quite serious. A couple of other problems — forking, or "fanging," of carrots and parsnips, for instance — are related to cultural defects such as poor soil preparation.

The edible portion of all root crops lies hidden under the ground throughout the crop's life, so it is much more difficult to catch a pest or disease problem in its early stages than with leaf or pod vegetables. Keep a constant eye on the health of the foliage and stems of root crops, because they reflect the health of the roots.

Discoloration, wilting, and general stunting or lack of vigor in the top growth, with no visible signs of a pest or disease, generally indicate a soil- or root-borne problem. You should take immediate remedial action.

Ideally, however, routine preventive treatment should be carried out in advance of any such signs of attack. Soils that are known to harbor pests should be cultivated regularly with a fork or hoe to bring the pests to the surface and expose them to predators such as birds.

Plant debris left lying in the vegetable plot harbors pests and diseases, so put it on the compost pile or dispose of it off-site. (Be sure to destroy any obviously diseased growth.) Also, eliminate all weeds in and around the vegetable plot, as many of these are secondary hosts for pests.

Maintain a 3-year crop rotation program to minimize the buildup of persistent soil-borne pests and diseases. Promote strong, quick growth by feeding and watering regularly — plants that are growing weakly tend to be more susceptible to pests and diseases.

Never allow waterlogging problems to persist in the vegetable garden, since these conditions encourage the fungal diseases that cause various root rots. Improve the overall drainage of the bed, and incorporate plenty of organic matter — if appropriate to your crops — when preparing the soil.

Follow the manufacturer's instructions when applying pesticides and fungicides, especially with regard to the safe interval between spraying and harvesting the crop. Spray crops on a calm, overcast day when no rain is forecast, or in the evening, to prevent chemicals from scorching foliage or drifting onto adjacent plants.

The chemical names cited on the following pages refer to the active ingredients, rather than the brand names. Check the label on the bottle or container before you buy, to ensure that your selection is correct.

▲ **Carrot rust fly** This pest can destroy a whole crop of parsnips and both early and main-crop varieties of carrots. The fat maggots tunnel into the roots and often cause them to rot.

▼ **Potato common scab** Unsightly rather than destructive, this disease affects the skin tissues of main-crop potatoes. Where the disease persists in the soil, grow cultivars known to be resistant.

CARROT RUST FLIES

Crops affected Carrots and parsnips (also parsley and celery).
Symptoms Fly maggots tunnel into the roots.
Danger period Throughout the growing season.
Treatment Where common, plant in late spring to avoid insect's first hatch. Cover seedbed with a row cover to prevent egg laying by adults. Destroy infested plants.

CRACKING

Crops affected All types of root vegetables, especially carrots and parsnips.
Symptoms This physiological problem causes the edible root to split lengthwise. No symptoms above ground.
Danger period Throughout the growing season.
Treatment Avoid erratic growth of the plants by watering before the soil dries out completely.

MILLIPEDES

Crops affected All types of root vegetables.
Symptoms Millipedes feed inside roots and extend damage caused by other pests. They differ from beneficial centipedes by having more legs, gray-black coloring, and slower movement.
Danger period Late summer to fall.
Treatment Maintain good garden hygiene. Cultivate deeply.

ONION MAGGOTS

Crops affected Leeks, onions, and shallots.
Symptoms Mushy bulbs. Small white maggots in rotting tissues.
Danger period Late spring to late summer.
Treatment Where common, rotate crops. Apply beneficial nematodes in late spring; treat soil with diazinon at planting time.

BOTRYTIS NECK ROT

Crops affected Onions.
Symptoms A gray velvety mold develops near the neck of stored onions, which rot rapidly.
Danger period Symptoms appear only in storage.
Treatment Buy treated seed, or dust with diazinon. Store only well-ripened, hard onions, and put them in a dry, airy place. Destroy diseased onions.

ONION WHITE ROT

Crops affected Onions; occasionally garlic, leeks, and shallots.
Symptoms The bulb base and roots are covered with a white fungus, and they rot.
Danger period Throughout the growing season.
Treatment Grow in a new site each year — the disease contaminates soil for 8 years or more.

PARSNIP CANKER

Crops affected Parsnips.
Symptoms Brown, orange-brown, or black cankers on the roots, causing rot to different degrees. (Parsnip canker refers to several fungal diseases affecting parsnips.)
Danger period Throughout the growing season.
Treatment Sow seeds early in deep, lime-enriched loamy soil, adding a balanced fertilizer. Parsnips with small roots may be less susceptible, so close spacing in the rows may be beneficial. Rotate crops regularly; grow resistant cultivars, such as 'Andover' and 'Cobham Improved Marrow.' Destroy diseased plants. There is no satisfactory chemical control method. Do not store any parsnips that show signs of canker.

POTATO BLACKLEG

Crops affected Potatoes.
Symptoms A black rot develops at the base of a main stem. Leaves turn yellow, and stems soften and die. This is a common problem for potatoes.
Danger period Early summer to midsummer.
Treatment Plant only certified seed potatoes or whole tubers. Destroy all affected plants; harvest and store only completely healthy tubers.

POTATO LATE BLIGHT

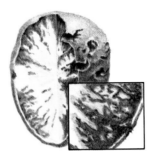

Crops affected Potatoes.
Symptoms Water-soaked spots appear on leaves after blossoming. Spots' centers shrivel and turn dark brown or black. Whitish mold spreads over undersides of leaves; blighted tops stink. Red-brown dry rot spreads through tubers.
Danger period Midsummer on.
Treatment Plant certified seed potatoes of resistant cultivars. Spray with mancozeb, chlorothalonil, or fixed copper.

POTATO COMMON SCAB

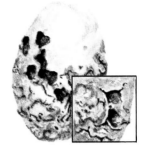

Crops affected Potatoes.
Symptoms Ragged-edged scabs on tubers.
Danger period Growing season.
Treatment Use certified seed potatoes, or treat with mancozeb. Plant resistant strains such as 'Chieftain,' 'Norland,' 'Russet Burbank,' or 'Superior.' Rotate crops; lower soil pH to 5.2 with sulfur.

POTATO INTERNAL BROWN SPOT AND HOLLOW HEART

Crops affected Potatoes.
Symptoms Scattered brown marks appear within the flesh of the edible tuber (internal brown spot), or tubers develop brown hollowed-out hearts (hollow heart). Affected tubers may rot in storage.
Danger period Throughout the growing season. Hollow heart may occur after a prolonged wet spell following a dry spell at any time in summer.
Treatment Dig in plenty of compost, and try to keep the growth even by watering before the soil dries out completely. There is no satisfactory chemical treatment for either of these disorders.

POTATO POWDERY SCAB

Crops affected Potatoes.
Symptoms Uniform round scabs, at first raised but later bursting open to release powdery spores. Affected tubers may be deformed in shape and have an earthy taste.
Danger period Throughout the growing season.
Treatment Avoid low, soggy sites. Don't plant potatoes in the same site for several years.

POTATO SPRAING

Crops affected Potatoes.
Symptoms Curving brown stains in the potato tuber's flesh. The outer skin remains unblemished.
Danger period Throughout the growing season, but symptoms evident only when potatoes are prepared for cooking.
Treatment Destroy infected tubers. Don't plant potatoes in the same site for several years.

SLUGS

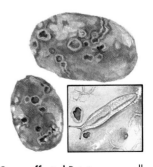

Crops affected Potatoes, as well as many other garden plants and crops.
Symptoms Irregular holes and tunnels eaten into tubers.
Danger period Throughout the growing season.
Treatment Apply slug baits or surround plants with bands of diatomaceous earth in spring. Harvest main-crop potatoes early.

CARROT WEEVILS

Crops affected Carrots and parsnips.
Symptoms Off-white soil-living caterpillars with distinctive brown heads feed on the edible roots, hollowing out the inner tissues. Caterpillars may be seen in the soil during cultivation.
Danger period Throughout the growing season; rarely serious.
Treatment Handpick any caterpillars found during soil cultivation. Maintain good garden hygiene, and eliminate weeds, especially docks and stinging nettles, which frequently harbor these pests. Protect ornamental and crop plants by applying beneficial nematodes in spring; spray with pyrethrin + rotenone to control adults.

VIOLET ROOT ROT

Crops affected Asparagus, carrots, and parsnips.
Symptoms Roots covered with violet fungal threads, which eventually kill the plants.
Danger period Throughout the growing season.
Treatment Destroy affected plants; do not store diseased tubers. Don't plant susceptible crops in the same spot for several years.

WILLOW-CARROT APHIDS

Crops affected Carrots, parsley, and parsnips.
Symptoms Foliage stunted and sticky. Aphids also transmit motley dwarf virus, causing yellow leaf mottling and a reduced yield. Eggs overwinter on willows.
Danger period Late spring and early summer.
Treatment Spray with pyrethrin or rotenone.

WIREWORMS

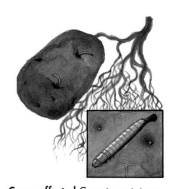

Crops affected Carrots, potatoes, and certain other vegetables.
Symptoms Roots tunneled by yellow-brown wormlike larvae.
Danger period Early spring to early fall.
Treatment Cultivate soil thoroughly before planting. Put potato pieces on sticks and bury 2-4 in (5-10 cm), leaving stick end exposed; dig up and destroy a week later.

OTHER PROBLEMS

Bacterial soft rot can occur in the garden or in storage, and may be serious, especially after a wet season. It affects onions, parsnips, potatoes, rutabagas, and turnips, and often follows damage to tissues by another pest or disease. Small water-soaked lesions break out around a wound. These spread, and the tubers, stems, or leaves rot, becoming a smelly, slimy mass. Improve soil drainage, control other wound-forming pests and diseases, maintain a good crop rotation, and don't use too much manure. Keep only healthy harvested tubers and bulbs in a dry place.

Clubroot is a serious infection of rutabagas and turnips that strikes during the growing season. Roots swell and become distorted, and leaves turn yellow and sickly. Improve drainage, especially in acid soils; rotate crops. Apply a liberal dressing of hydrated lime to raise soil pH to 7.2.

Cutworms may attack the stems of young carrots, potatoes, rutabagas, and turnips, especially in light soils during dry spells. Fat caterpillars eat through shoots at ground level. Control weeds, which encourage cutworms, and protect susceptible plants by working a little diazinon + chlorpyrifos into the soil at planting time, or dust seedlings and transplants at soil level with Bt.

Fanging is a disorder of carrots and parsnips in which the edible root divides into two or more forks. It is caused by too much compost in the soil, or by a stony or poorly prepared site. Use soil that has been fertilized for a previous season's crop. Take care not to compress the seedbed too much.

Nematodes can be serious pests of onions and potatoes, as well as many other plants. The leaves, stems, and bulbs of onions become bloated and distorted as a result of attacks by these minute wormlike creatures. The potato cyst nematode causes pinhead-size yellow or brown cysts to grow on roots, resulting in wilting and death of plants. Where infestations are severe, do not plant the same crop on that site for several years. Dig up and destroy badly affected plants. Chemical control of nematodes is difficult, and no safe and effective compounds are available for use by home gardeners. Some potato cultivars are resistant to or tolerant of cyst nematode attacks.

Sclerotinia is a fungal disease that overwinters in the soil. It attacks many root crops in storage, especially carrots and parsnips, and is frequently restricted to the topmost part of the root. It consists of a white fluffy mass containing hard black structures of resting fungal growth. The roots soften and decay. Store sound roots only. Check stored roots regularly, and destroy all affected material.

BERRY PESTS

Succulent berries can be ruined by birds, pests, and diseases unless they are properly protected.

The softest of all fruit crops, strawberries are particularly susceptible to attack from birds and other pests. Once injured, their tissues soon succumb to further infection by fungal diseases. Other bush and vine fruits — including blackberries, raspberries, loganberries, blueberries, cranberries, black currants, red currants, white currants, gooseberries, and grapes — are also troubled by a fairly wide range of pests and diseases.

Rhubarb, though not a fruit (it is a leafstalk), is usually included in this group of crops. It is prone to a number of pest and disease problems characteristic of plants with soft edible tissues.

Larger animals, especially birds and squirrels, can devastate berry or grape crops. By far the most effective way of avoiding trouble is to construct some type of cage over the entire plant or group of plants. Small-mesh plastic netting is readily available to prevent access by birds. You can drape it over rows of strawberries, anchoring it in the soil with galvanized wire pegs, or throw it over fruit bushes. You will have to undrape the netting whenever you need to attend to the plants, but this inconvenience is rewarded by increased fruit yields.

You can also stretch the netting tautly on a support framework of stakes so that it covers the whole area. Alternatively, you can build walk-in fruit cages from wooden posts, with plastic-coated wire netting attached to battens. Such fruit cages allow easy access to the bushes for soil cultivation, pruning, spraying, and harvesting. It is advisable to take the netting down every winter to prevent damage from wind, weathering, and heavy snowfalls.

Smaller pests, including many insects, are not deterred by a fruit cage. Unless you are a dedicated organic gardener, you will need to prevent undue damage by operating a routine chemical spray program. With all pesticides and fungicides, however, it is best to

avoid using the same chemicals year after year, since certain pests and diseases can develop resistance to them. Never use chemicals indiscriminately: remember that not all insects are pests — some pollinate the flowers, and others are predators of the truly troublesome garden pests.

Good garden hygiene is important in the fruit garden, especially around low-growing crops such as strawberries. Decaying debris must be cleared from the ground — it harbors fungal spores as well as insects and other pests.

Follow the manufacturer's instructions when using chemicals in the fruit garden, paying special attention to the recommended safe period before harvesting and eating the crops.

▲ **Currant aphids** These tiny pests cause characteristic red blistering on the leaves of red and white currants or yellowish blistering on black currants. Young leaves are most affected, and the pests can easily deplete the fruit bush's energy, reducing the yield.

▼ **Botrytis** Also known as gray mold, this troublesome disease affects strawberries and raspberries in wet summers. The fungus spreads rapidly and persists on plant debris all year. Good hygiene is essential.

CURRANT APHIDS

Crops affected Black currants, flowering currants, gooseberries, red currants, and white currants.
Symptoms Irregular, raised red blisters on leaves.
Danger period Late spring and early summer.
Treatment Spray with horticultural oil in late winter to kill eggs. Apply insecticidal soap or rotenone according to manufacturer's instructions on product label.

ANTHRACNOSE

Crops affected Loganberries and raspberries.
Symptoms Purple spots on canes become white and split down the cane. Leaves and fruit are distorted.
Danger period Spring to fall.
Treatment Set bushes where rain or dew will dry quickly. Destroy badly affected canes. Apply lime sulfur according to manufacturer's instructions.

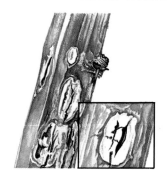

CHLOROSIS (pH-induced)

Crops affected Raspberries.
Symptoms Yellowing leaves.
Danger period Growing season.
Treatment Make the soil more acid with a dressing of acidifying chemicals, or apply 2-3 lb (0.9-1.4 kg) of sulfur per 100 sq ft (9 sq m) of growing area.

CORAL SPOT

Crops affected Figs, gooseberries, and red currants.
Symptoms Red cushionlike masses of fungal spores (pustules) on dead branches and stems. Dieback of shoots or large branches may result. Severe coral spot attacks may kill entire plants.
Danger period All year.

Treatment Cut out and destroy all dead wood. Cut diseased but living shoots back to at least 6 in (15 cm) below the infected area; sterilize pruning knife or shears between cuts. Feed, mulch, water, and improve drainage of the soil as necessary to encourage vigor — healthy fruit bushes are less likely to be attacked by this parasitic fungus.

CROWN ROT

Crops affected Rhubarb.
Symptoms Rotting of the main bud, then of the whole crown, in which a cavity may develop. Spindly and discolored leaves die down early or don't develop at all.
Danger period Growing season.
Treatment Dig up and destroy the entire plant. Don't plant rhubarb again in the same spot.

GALL MITES

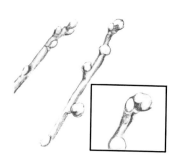

Crops affected Black currants.
Symptoms Infested buds swell up and fail to develop, forming characteristic "big buds."
Danger period Late winter and early spring.
Treatment Remove and destroy affected buds, and spray with lime sulfur in early spring when new shoots are 1 in (2.5 cm) long, and again when canes have made 1 ft (30 cm) of new growth.

NEMATODES

Crops affected Strawberries.
Symptoms Young growth and buds stunted, distorted, and scarred by microscopic leaf-boring eellike worms.
Danger period Growing season.
Treatment No effective chemicals are available. Destroy infested plants. Purchase healthy stock from reputable nurseries.

IMPORTED CURRANTWORMS

Crops affected Currants and gooseberries.
Symptoms Leaf tissues eaten away, with many or all of the leaves reduced to a skeleton of veins.
Danger period Midspring to late summer.
Treatment Control minor infestations with handpicking; for severe ones, spray with pyrethrin + rotenone.

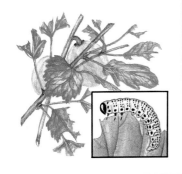

BOTRYTIS (GRAY MOLD)

Crops affected Mainly raspberries and strawberries.
Symptoms Fruit rots and becomes covered with a gray velvety mold.
Danger period Flowering time; symptoms appear on fruits.
Treatment Set plants at proper intervals to promote good air circulation. Destroy diseased berries; harvest fruit regularly. In wet seasons captan may be applied.

BLACK ROT

Crops affected Grapes.
Symptoms Reddish-brown spots appear on leaves; pale spots appear on immature grapes, which turn brown, then shrivel and blacken.
Danger period Midspring to summer.
Treatment Destroy affected fruits and plant parts. Spray with captan, fixed copper, or mancozeb just after bloom and one to three additional times at 10- to 14-day intervals.

MEALYBUGS

Crops affected Greenhouse grapes.
Symptoms Foliage and stems covered with patches of mealy wax threads, hiding colonies of bugs or eggs.
Danger period All year.
Treatment See page 86 for biological control. Apply horticultural oil to dormant vines.

POWDERY MILDEW

Crops affected Gooseberries, grapes, and strawberries.
Symptoms A white powder that turns brown on gooseberries but may show as loss of color on strawberries. Grapes may split.
Danger period Growing season.
Treatment Plant resistant cultivars. Apply sulfur spray or dust except on sulfur-sensitive cultivars such as 'Chancellor,' 'Concord,' or 'Foch.'

RASPBERRY FRUITWORMS

Crops affected All cane fruit.
Symptoms Beetle grubs feed on ripening fruit.
Danger period Summer.
Treatment Collect and destroy all infected fruit. Spray with malathion or rotenone according to instructions on product label.

REVERSION

Crops affected Black currants.
Symptoms Leaves are smaller than normal and have fewer lobes. Flower buds lack their normal hairs and are magenta in color. Affected bushes fail to produce a good crop. Be careful not to confuse the symptoms with those of frost damage or potassium deficiency (where the leaves and yields are small, but the flower buds are not affected in the same way).

Danger period Only obvious on long basal shoots in early summer or midsummer.
Treatment Dig up and destroy the entire plant in winter — there is no cure for this serious disease. In the following spring, replant only bushes certified to be free of virus. As a routine precaution, control the gall mite *(opposite)*, which is primarily responsible for spreading this disease.

SPUR BLIGHT

Crops affected Raspberries.
Symptoms Canes bear purple to silver blotches, spotted with black. Spurs on these die back.
Danger period Spring and summer.
Treatment Thin canes in early spring to enhance air circulation. Eliminate weeds; apply lime sulfur according to label instructions.

STRAWBERRY SAP BEETLES

Crops affected Strawberries.
Symptoms Shiny black ground beetles eat chunks out of ripening fruits (birds cause similar damage). The beetles may be found scuttling under the fruit and the mulch.
Danger period Early summer.
Treatment Maintain good garden hygiene, removing all debris and leaf litter. Keep all weeds down. Slug pellets provide some control.

STRAWBERRY MITES

Crops affected Strawberries.
Symptoms Tiny, barely visible mites (tarsonemid mites) attack plants, causing brittle leaves with curled-down edges. Terminal buds killed.
Danger period Spring and summer.
Treatment There is no effective chemical control. Maintain good garden hygiene. Destroy infested plants, and obtain new stock from a reputable supplier.

VIRUSES

Crops affected Many soft fruits.
Symptoms Variable. Yellow-blotched, often distorted, leaves on raspberry, blackberry, and strawberry bushes *(mosaic virus, shown)*; gooseberry leaves discolored along veins (mosaic virus); strawberry leaves develop yellow mottling (mottle virus), are puckered with red-purple spotting (crinkle virus), or have yellow edges and dwarfed leaves (yellow edge virus). Harmless yellow blotches on raspberry leaves may be caused by mites.
Danger period Growing season.
Treatment Dig up and destroy affected plants. Replant virus-free stocks. Maintain hygiene. Eliminate pests that transmit viruses.

OTHER TROUBLES

American gooseberry mildew is a fungal disease that attacks gooseberry leaves, shoots, and fruits during the growing season, giving them a white powdery coating; it also attacks black currants late in the season. Tips of diseased shoots are distorted. Prune bushes to improve air circulation. Cut off and destroy diseased shoots in late summer. Plant resistant cultivars. Spray with sulfur or lime sulfur (only on sulfur-tolerant varieties) during cool, damp weather according to directions.

Aphids of many kinds attack berries, mainly causing distortion and stunting of young growth, weakening the plant. They may also spread virus diseases. There are aphids specific to gooseberries, raspberries, and strawberries; others are more general in their attack. Spray affected garden plants with a hard stream of water, insecticidal soap, or malathion.

Cane blight disease afflicts raspberries. Leaves wilt and wither in summer; canes discolor and snap off at ground level. Prune out fruiting canes after harvest and all heavily infected canes, working in dry weather only. Apply lime sulfur according to label instructions.

Leaf spot affects blackberries, gooseberries, raspberries, and strawberries, causing brown spots from late spring onward on the leaves, which then fall prematurely; worse in wet seasons. Destroy diseased leaves. Spray with lime sulfur or Bordeaux mixture as instructed on label.

Slugs and snails eat holes in ripening strawberry fruits, leaving characteristic slime trails. Sprinkle slug baits around plants as recommended on label.

Spider mites attack cane fruits, currants, and strawberries during the growing season, especially in the greenhouse. Leaves show a fine, light mottling on their upper surfaces, followed by general yellow discoloration. Predatory mites and soldier beetles provide control. Spray severe infestations with insecticidal soap, acephate, or malathion, coating undersides as well as tops of leaves.

Strawberry leaf rollers in the caterpillar stage spin silken webs over strawberry leaves, pulling the leaf edges together like a tent. Remove and destroy affected leaves by hand. Or spray with pyrethrin before flowering; repeat again after harvesting the fruit.

Tarnished plant bugs *(see also page 134)* attack berries and other soft fruits, causing distortion of shoots and fruits, bud drop, wilting, stunted growth, and dieback. Spray with malathion as soon as insects are observed on plants.

ORCHARD PROBLEMS

**Apples, pears, and all stone fruit grown
as trees or espaliers and on trellis systems
are subject to damage.**

Apples, pears, cherries, plums, damsons, apricots, peaches, and other tree fruits are prone to a number of pests, diseases, and disorders that can ruin the edible fruits or damage the foliage. Severe leaf damage reduces the yield of fruit.

Birds often damage buds and fruits. The best protection is to cover trees with nylon or plastic netting with a 1-in (2.5-cm) mesh. Espaliers are the easiest to protect by means of temporary cages. You can also slip muslin, paper, or plastic bags and sleeves over each fruit. Less effective are bird scarers, bird-repellent sprays, or cotton threads tied among the branches.

Fungal diseases and insect pests, which can seriously damage or kill trees, are the other main problems in growing fruit.

There are many fungicides and insecticides that can be sprayed on fruit, but they should not be used indiscriminately. Regular spraying is not advisable — it kills beneficial insects, such as pollinating ones, as well as enemies. Also, the pest or fungus concerned can develop a resistance to the chemical used. Some red spider mites, for instance, are resistant to all or most of the sprays that have been traditionally used to combat them.

Researchers now advocate the use of predators and parasitic wasps to control pests where possible. However, these are not always suitable for outdoor use, so some chemical control is inevitably necessary.

Keep a keen watch for pests and diseases, and use chemical treatment only when their appearance is obvious or, in some cases, if the plant was attacked the previous year. Confine treatment to the affected plant and those nearby.

When using chemicals, always follow the manufacturer's instructions regarding the dilution and application rate and for the safety period before fruit can be harvested and eaten. Wear all safety gear recommended on the pesticide label. Never spray on a windy day, and spray in the morning or late afternoon to early evening, when pollinating insects are less likely to be active.

Good garden hygiene also helps to keep pests and diseases under control. Never leave old prunings lying about, and in fall and winter remove and destroy any old, rotting, and mummified fruit — these can harbor diseases. Also, prune out and destroy all dead spurs and cankered branches. Rake up fallen leaves, and apply a horticultural oil spray in late winter as a regular routine.

▲ **Peach leaf curl** This common disease affects peaches and nectarines. It reduces the vigor of trees and impairs fruit yield if repeated attacks are not checked.

▼ **Bird damage** Birds help the fruit grower by devouring a wide variety of pests — but may become a nuisance at harvest time by pecking fruit and thus leaving an opening for molds and rots that make the crop inedible.

APPLE BLOSSOM WEEVILS

Crops affected Apples.
Symptoms Flower buds almost reach maturity but fail to open; petals then die. A small weevil larva, pupa, or brown-to-black beetle can be found inside each bud on close inspection. (Similar symptoms, but with no insects visible, may be frost damage.)
Danger period Midspring to late spring.

Treatment Ignore minor attacks: by thinning fruit, the weevils reduce the numbers of apples but increase the size of those remaining. Spray serious infestations with pyrethrin before the flower buds start to open in order to kill the female weevils before they can lay their eggs. Never spray when bees are active.

APPLE CANKER

Crops affected Apples.
Symptoms Oval cankers on the trunk or branches; bark shrinks in rings until inner tissues exposed.
Danger period All year.
Treatment Cut out and destroy infected spurs. On larger branches and trunks, pare away diseased wood and bark, cutting beyond the greenish discoloration. Disinfect pruning tools between cuts. Remove and destroy all infected prunings.

PLUM CURCULIO

Crops affected Apples, pears, plums, and quinces.
Symptoms Crescent-shaped punctures on fruit; grayish-white grubs burrow inside fruit.
Danger period Spring to midsummer.
Treatment Hang 8×10 in (20×25 cm) sticky white cards in trees to trap adults; destroy dropped fruit. Spray with malathion + methoxychlor or rotenone at petal drop; again in 2 weeks.

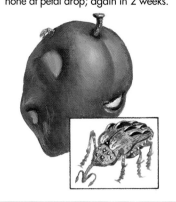

EUROPEAN APPLE SAWFLIES

Crops affected Apples.
Symptoms Caterpillar eats into the core of young fruitlet, which then drops prematurely. This pest also causes superficial scarring of mature fruit.
Danger period Late spring to early summer.
Treatment Pick up and destroy all dropped fruit in June. Spray with pyrethrin or rotenone 1 week after petal fall.

BACTERIAL CANKER

Crops affected Cherries and plums.
Symptoms Elongated, flattened canker-bearing exudations of gum on dying shoots.
Danger period Fall and winter; symptoms don't appear until next spring or summer.
Treatment Cut out infected branches, disinfecting tools between cuts. Spray with Bordeaux mixture or copper fungicide in late summer, early fall, and midfall.

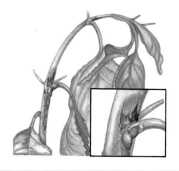

BROWN ROT

Crops affected All tree fruits.
Symptoms Fruit turns brownish white, often covered with concentrically ringed fungus spores; it then withers and shrinks.
Danger period Summer; also during storage.
Treatment Destroy all rotten and withered fruits; apply sulfur spray or dust (as needed) 3 weeks after petal fall and 3 weeks before harvest.

BIRDS

Crops affected Apples, cherries, citrus fruits, peaches, and plums.
Symptoms Blackbirds, crows, grackles, sparrows, and others, often in flocks, eat fruit as it ripens.
Danger period During ripening.
Treatment Cover susceptible plants with netting with 1-in (2.5-cm) mesh. Plant borders of chokecherries, mulberries, mountain ash, or other aromatic fruits to deter birds.

CHERRY APHIDS

Crops affected Cherries.
Symptoms Leaves at the tips of young shoots are curled and twisted by black aphids. Foliage below is sticky with honeydew, which encourages sooty mold.
Danger period Late spring to midsummer.
Treatment Spray with a hard jet of water in the morning, two to three times, every other day. For severe infestations, spray with insecticidal soap. Spray with horticultural oil during late winter.

CODLING MOTHS

Crops affected Apples.
Symptoms Caterpillars eat into the cores of ripening fruit.
Danger period Summer.
Treatment Pheromone traps capture male moths and reduce mating success of females; the catch also warns that insect is active — spray with phosmet if infestation is severe. Pick up and destroy all dropped fruits in August and September as they fall. Kill eggs by spraying with horticultural oil 2 to 6 weeks before blossoming.

CRACKING

Crops affected Apples, pears, and plums.
Symptoms This physiological disorder causes the fruit's skin to split open, exposing the inner flesh. Fruit looks unpleasant, and secondary infection by molds and rots may result.
Danger period Throughout the growing season.
Treatment Try to avoid irregular growth by mulching to conserve moisture and by never allowing the soil to dry out.

GUMOSIS

Crops affected Cherries.
Symptoms Gum exudes on branches and trunks and gradually hardens.
Danger period All year, but worst in summer.
Treatment With good feeding, mulching, and watering, gumming should stop, but gum may have to be removed so that the dead wood beneath can be cut out.

LEAF-CURLING APHIDS

Crops affected Apples, damsons, peaches, pears, and plums.
Symptoms Young leaves puckered and curled.
Danger period Midspring to midsummer.
Treatment Spray with a hard stream of water or with insecticidal soap. Apply horticultural oil in the dormant season to kill eggs. Spray serious infestations with rotenone — but not during blossoming.

PEACH LEAF CURL

Crops affected Nectarines and peaches (also almonds).
Symptoms Leaves with large red blisters become white, then brown, and fall prematurely.
Danger period Before bud burst.
Treatment Spray with lime sulfur or a dormant spray mix containing copper in fall after leaf drop or in early spring before bud swell. Remove and destroy infected leaves and fallen leaves in autumn.

PEAR LEAF BLISTER MITES

Crops affected Pears and occasionally apples (cotoneasters and mountain ashes may also be hosts).
Symptoms Tiny mites feed in leaves, causing numerous pink or yellow blisters (pustules) to appear on both sides of the young leaves in spring. As the leaves age, these blisters turn brown. Badly infested leaves may fall.

Vigor and fruiting ability are generally not affected.
Danger period Midspring to late summer.
Treatment Pick off and destroy infested leaves. Spray with horticultural oil in late winter to kill eggs.

SCAB

Crops affected Apples and pears (also ornamental pyracanthas).
Symptoms Brown or black scabs on the fruit, which may, in severe cases, crack when the scabs have merged and become corky. Olive-green blotches of fungal growth also appear on leaves, which fall prematurely. Small blisterlike pimples may develop on young shoots, later burst the bark, and then show as ringlike cracks or scabs.
Danger period Growing season.
Treatment Plant resistant cultivars; prune trees to ensure good air circulation around foliage. Eliminate weeds; rake up and destroy fallen leaves. Apply captan, benomyl, copper, lime, or lime sulfur — consult local experts for regional spray schedule.

SHOT HOLE

Crops affected Cherries, peaches, and plums.
Symptoms Brown patches on leaves, then irregular holes caused by a fungus.
Danger period Throughout the growing season.
Treatment Feed trees yearly; mulch to prevent soil from drying out. Give small trees foliar feed. If trouble recurs, spray with Bordeaux mixture in summer.

STONY PIT VIRUS

Crops affected Old pear trees.
Symptoms Fruit pitted and deformed in shape, with patches of dead, stony cells in the flesh, making it inedible. Symptoms first appear on one branch and over the years gradually spread until all the fruit on the tree is affected.
Danger period All year.
Treatment Cut down and destroy diseased trees.

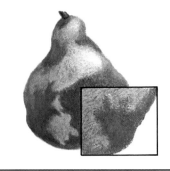

WOOLLY APPLE APHIDS

Crops affected Apples.
Symptoms Woody swellings and tufts of white wool on trunks and branches. Swellings may crack and cankers appear.
Danger period Midspring to early fall.
Treatment Spray with horticultural oil during the dormant season, or with malathion when infestation observed.

OTHER TROUBLES

Bitter pit affects apple fruits, causing slightly sunken brown spots beneath the skin and throughout the flesh. It occurs throughout the growing season, but is not apparent until harvesting or in storage. Feed and mulch trees, and never allow the soil to dry out.

Dieback is a disorder of fruit trees that starts at branch tips and works back, causing foliage to turn yellow or brown, wilt, then die. Prune branches to healthy wood. Feed and mulch to keep other branches healthy. Spray with a foliar feed.

Fruit tree spider mites infest apples, pears, and plums. Older leaves turn bronze-yellow, dry out, and die. If spider mites were troublesome the previous year, spray with winter-rate horticultural oil during the dormant season or with summer oil when flowers are at tight cluster.

Pear aphids feed on the sap of pear shoots, leaving sticky excretions on young growth in spring, which becomes distorted. Spray with a hard jet of water or insecticidal soap as needed.

Plum sawfly caterpillars tunnel into plums, causing reduction in yields. Holes eaten in the fruits exude a sticky black ooze. Infested fruits drop prematurely. Control as for European apple sawfly.

Scale insects are tiny creatures, each covered with a flat or rounded yellow or brown scale. They occur in colonies on older shoots of apples and peaches, mostly in late spring or summer. Spray with winter-rate horticultural oil in dormant season; when crawlers are active in summer, spray with insecticidal soap or horticultural oil at the summer rate.

Split stone is a disorder of nectarines and peaches, causing the stone to split and the fruit skin to crack open at the stalk end during the growing season. Feed and mulch the tree. Water regularly, and add lime if the soil is acid. Pollinate blooms by hand.

Tarnished plant bugs are light brown insects about ¼ in (½ cm) long (see page 134); targets include apple, peach, pear, and occasionally citrus. Bugs inject poison, which causes flowers to droop, and suck sap from leaves, leaving irregular bronze spotting. Spray with malathion or carbaryl.

Tortrix moth caterpillars (leaf rollers) eat holes in young leaves of apples and pears, and draw together the edges of the leaves by silk threads. Fruits may be nibbled. Caterpillars wriggle backward when they are disturbed. Handpick or apply Bt to minor infestations; for severe infestations, spray with pyrethrin or carbaryl.

INDEX

ACKNOWLEDGMENTS

Photo Credits
A-Z Botanical Collection 116(tl,bl); Bernard Alfieri 139; Biofotos/Heather Angel 53, 69; Brian Carter 133; Bruce Coleman Ltd. 120(bl); Collections/Patrick Johns 125(t); Derek Fell 109; Eric Crichton 14, 18, 25, 40, 51, 57, 72, 85, 95, 169(b), 114(tr), 116(tr,br), 117(bl), 118(tr), 119(tl,tr,bl); Philippe Ferret 41; Garden Picture Library (Brian Carter) 28, (Bob Challinor) 6, 56, (David Russell) 7,19, 36, (Ron Sutherland) front cover, 4-5, 67, (Brigitte Thomas) 112, (Dider Willery) 45, (C. Woodyard) 70; Grant Heilman (Jim Strawser) 118(bl); John Glover 54, 128; Hall's Homes and Gardens Ltd. 105(b) Samuel Dobie and Son Ltd. 105(tr); Holt Studios 117(tr); Jacqui

Hurst 114(tl), 115(tl,tr); Photos Lamontagne 129; Andrew Lawson 49; S. and O. Mathews 152; Tania Midgley 33; Mise au Point (Jean-Pierre Soulier) back cover; Natural Image/R. Fletcher 24; Natural Selection/Paul Morrison 114(bl); Nature Photographers (D. Hawes) 115(br), (Paul Sterry) 113, (D. Washington) 120(tl); Clive Nichols, 2-3; Simon Page-Ritchie/Eaglemoss 125(b); Perdereau/Thomas 21; Photo/Nats, Inc. (Gay Bumgarner) 108 Photos Horticultural 11, 13, 15, 44, 52, 59, 73, 77, 89, 103, 114(br), 115(br), 117(br), 118(tl), 119(br), 121, 143, 147, 161, 165(t); Positive Images (Jerry Howard) 63; Annette Schreiner 121; Harry Smith Collection 9, 21, 27, 29, 32, 37, 47, 48, 50, 117(tl), 118(br), 120(tr,br), 137, 157, 169(t); Sue Stickland 153, 155; Elizabeth Whiting and Associates 81, 165(b), (Michael

Dunne) 99; Steve Wooster 102.

Illustrations
David Ashby 58, 71, 104-6; Sylvia Bokor 130(tr), 134(ml), 140(mr), 141(tl), 144(tr), 167(tr) 170(mc,br); Elisabeth Dowle 11-13, 20-23, 31, 34-35, 38-39, 42, 46, 90-94 124(b); Christine Hart-Davies 8, 26-27, 60-62, 74-76, 78-80, 82-84, 96-98, 100-101, 122-123, 124(t), 148-150, 154-156; John Hutchinson 64(tl), 65(r), 66(tl,b); Marianne Markey 65(tl); Stan North 86-88; Reader's Digest 130(tl,tm,cl,cr,b), 131-132, 134(t,mc,mr,bl,bc,br), 135-136,170(t,ml,mr, bl,bm),172; Ray Skibinski 10, 30, 43, 64, 66(tr,c, ml),110-112, 118(bl); Ann Winterbotham 1, 16, 17, 138, 144(tl,tc,ml,mc,mr,b), 145-146, 158-160, 166- 167(all except tr),168; Clare Wright 140(all except mr), 141(all except tl),142.